Conqueror

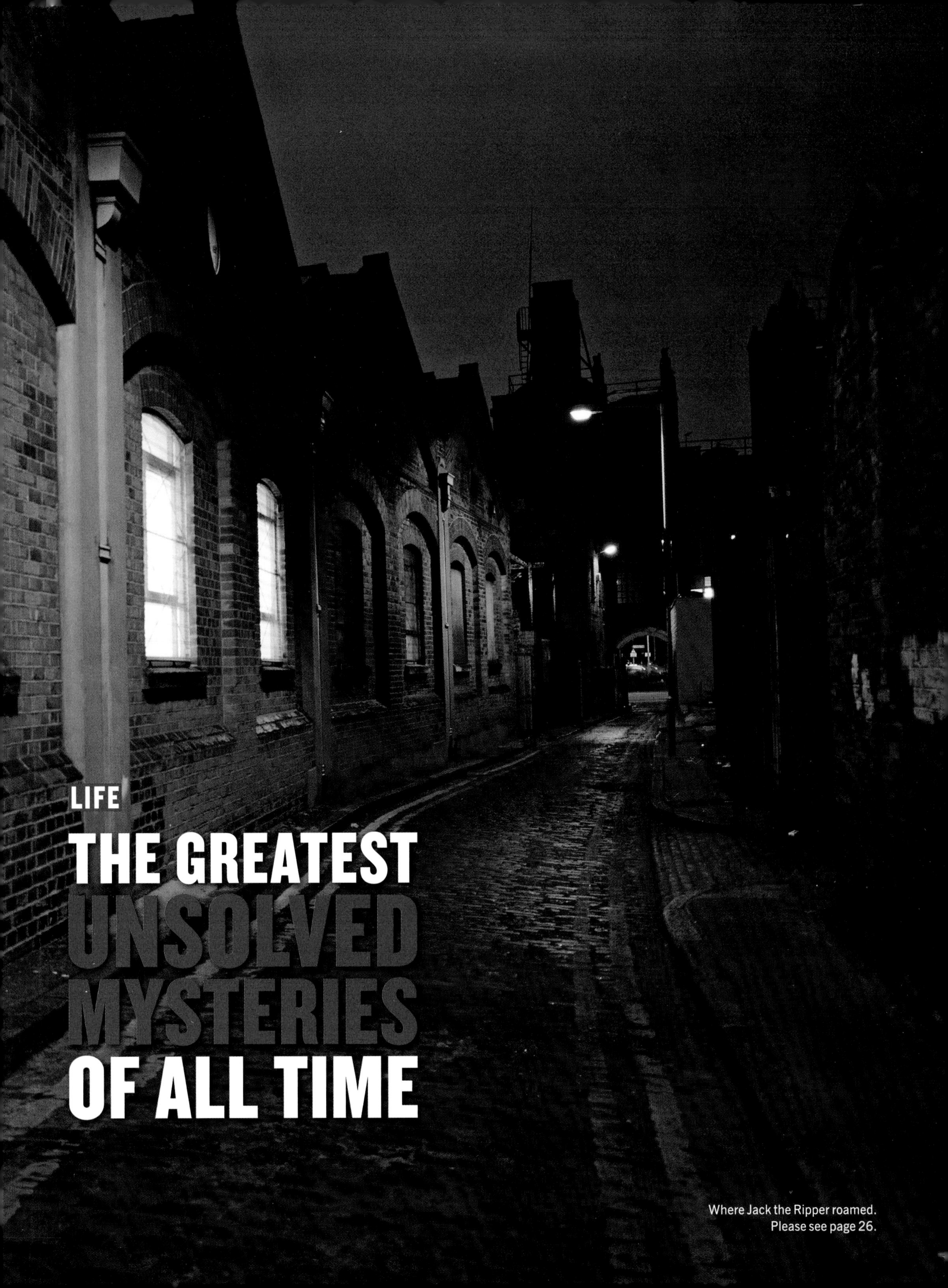

LIFE

THE GREATEST UNSOLVED MYSTERIES OF ALL TIME

Where Jack the Ripper roamed.
Please see page 26.

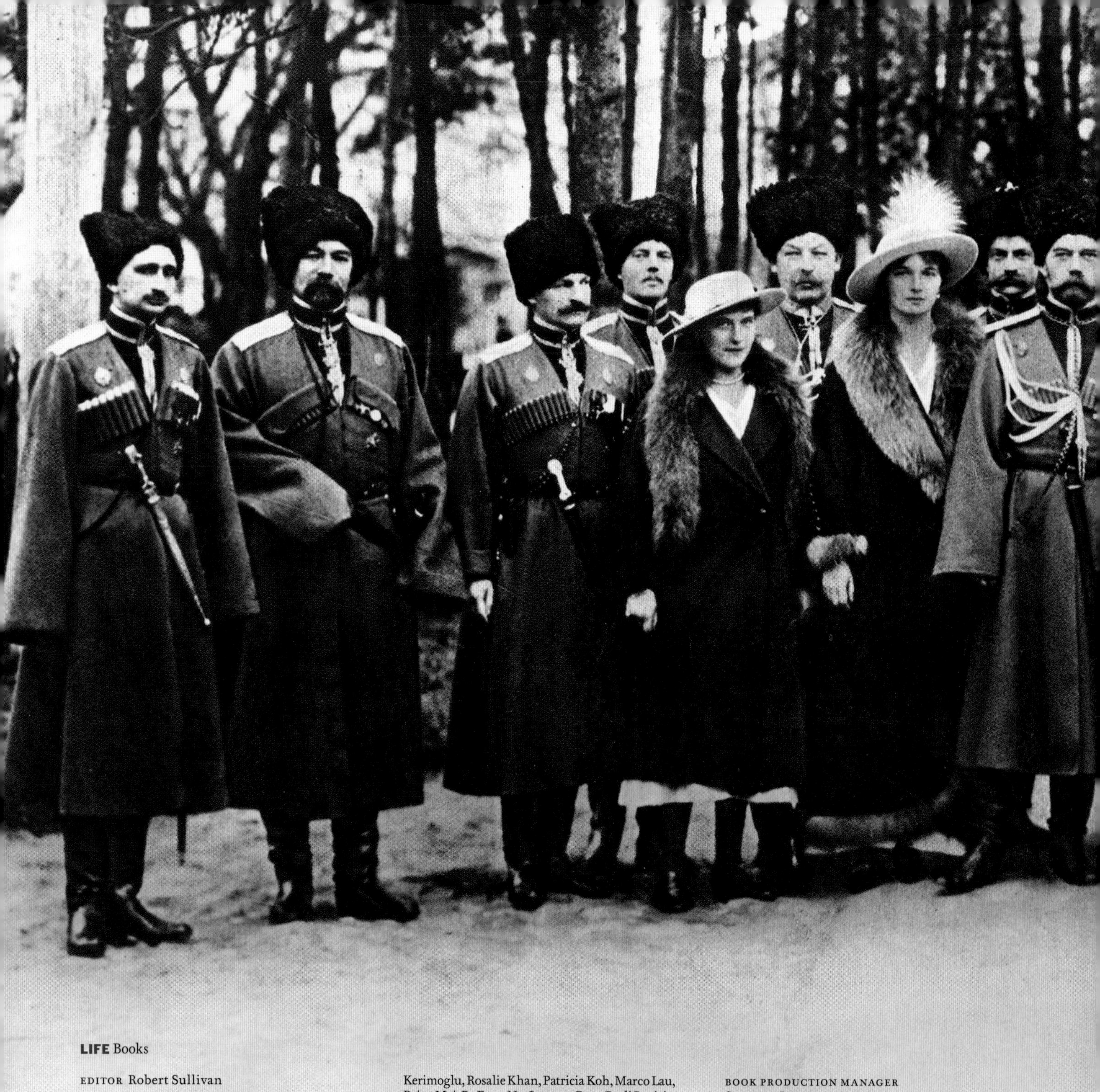

LIFE Books

EDITOR Robert Sullivan
DIRECTOR OF PHOTOGRAPHY
Barbara Baker Burrows
CREATIVE DIRECTOR Anke Stohlmann
DEPUTY PICTURE EDITOR Christina Lieberman
WRITER-REPORTERS Hildegard Anderson, Danielle Dowling
COPY EDITORS Barbara Gogan (Chief), Parlan McGaw
CONSULTING PICTURE EDITORS
Mimi Murphy (Rome), Tala Skari (Paris)

SPECIAL THANKS TO Arnold Horton

PRESIDENT Andrew Blau
BUSINESS MANAGER Roger Adler
BUSINESS DEVELOPMENT MANAGER Jeff Burak
EDITORIAL OPERATIONS Richard K. Prue (Director), Brian Fellows (Manager), Keith Aurelio, Charlotte Coco, John Goodman, Kevin Hart, Norma Jones, Mert Kerimoglu, Rosalie Khan, Patricia Koh, Marco Lau, Brian Mai, Po Fung Ng, Lorenzo Pace, Rudi Papiri, Robert Pizaro, Barry Pribula, Clara Renauro, Donald Schaedtler, Hia Tan, Vaune Trachtman, David Weiner

TIME INC. HOME ENTERTAINMENT

PUBLISHER Richard Fraiman
GENERAL MANAGER Steven Sandonato
EXECUTIVE DIRECTOR, MARKETING SERVICES
Carol Pittard
DIRECTOR, RETAIL & SPECIAL SALES Tom Mifsud
DIRECTOR, NEW PRODUCT DEVELOPMENT
Peter Harper
ASSISTANT DIRECTOR, BOOKAZINE MARKETING
Laura Adam
ASSISTANT PUBLISHING DIRECTOR, BRAND MARKETING Joy Butts
ASSOCIATE COUNSEL Helen Wan

BOOK PRODUCTION MANAGER
Suzanne Janso
DESIGN & PREPRESS MANAGER
Anne-Michelle Gallero
BRAND MANAGER Roshni Patel

SPECIAL THANKS TO Christine Austin, Glenn Buonocore, Jim Childs, Susan Chodakiewicz, Rose Cirrincione, Jacqueline Fitzgerald, Lauren Hall, Jennifer Jacobs, Brynn Joyce, Mona Li, Robert Marasco, Amy Migliaccio, Brooke Reger, Dave Rozzelle, Ilene Schreider, Adriana Tierno, Alex Voznesenskiy, Sydney Webber, Jonathan White

PUBLISHED BY **LIFE** Books

Time Inc.
1271 Avenue of the Americas
New York, NY 10020

ISBN 13: 978-1-60320-081-3
ISBN 10: 1-60320-081-9
Library of Congress Control Number: 2009928250

"LIFE" is a trademark of Time Inc.

We welcome your comments and suggestions about
LIFE Books. Please write to us at:
LIFE Books
Attention: Book Editors
PO Box 11016
Des Moines, IA 50336-1016

If you would like to order any of our hardcover
Collector's Edition books, please call us
at 1-800-327-6388 (Monday through Friday,
7:00 a.m.–8:00 p.m., or Saturday, 7:00 a.m.–6:00 p.m.,
Central Time).

Classic images from the pages and covers of LIFE
are now available. Posters can be ordered at
www.LIFEposters.com.

Fine art prints from the LIFE Picture Collection and
the LIFE Gallery of Photography can be viewed at
www.LIFEphotographs.com.

The family Romanov: Here we see the extended
clan and support crew of Czar Nicholas II
of Russia (center) and Czarina Alexandra,
immediately at the czar's right hand. The story
behind the mysterious death of the Romanovs'
great confidant, Rasputin, is told in our book
(please see page 38), as is that of the lovely
Anastasia, standing here beside her mother.
Did she perhaps survive her family's harsh
fate? Please see page 42.

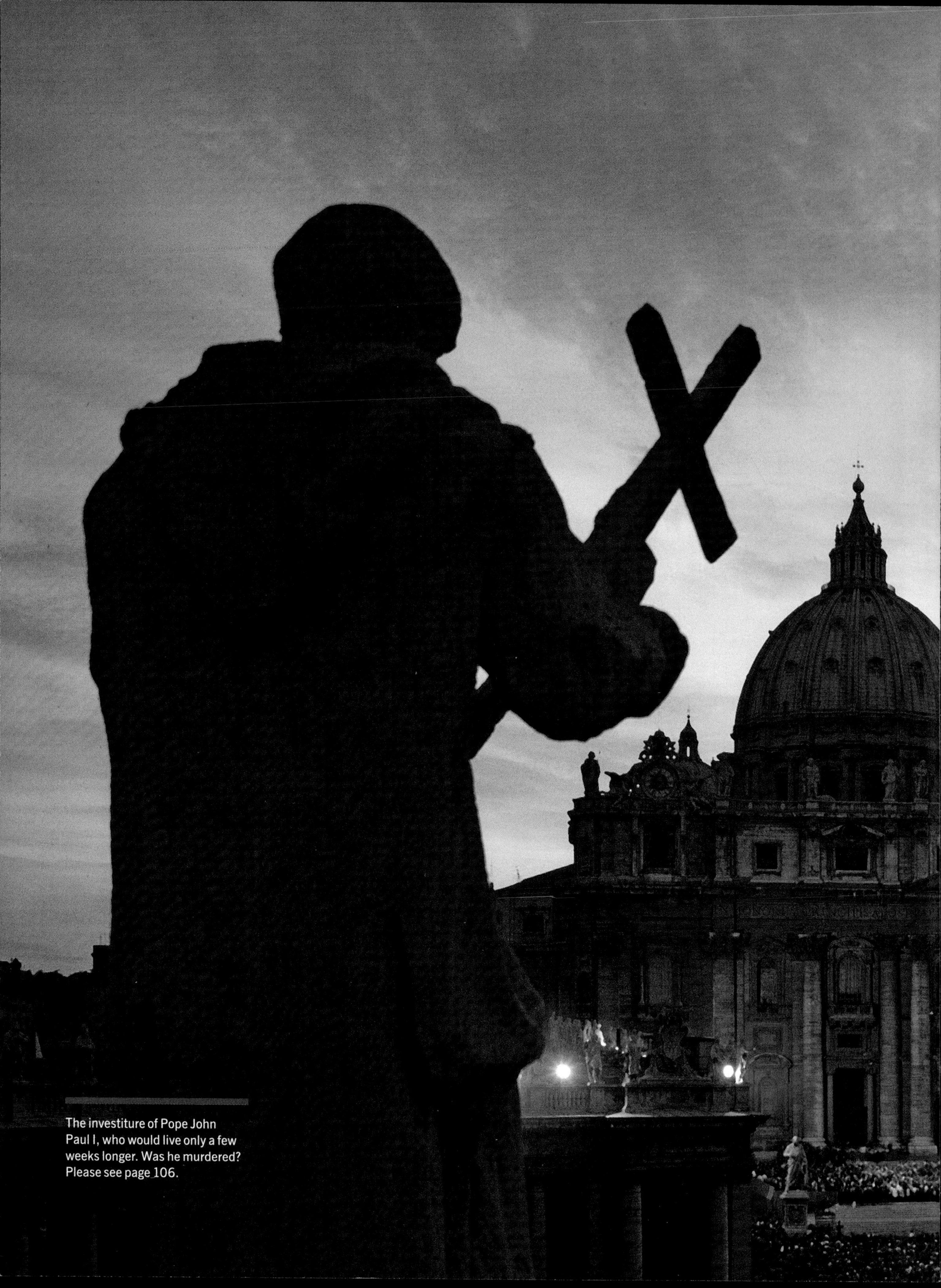

The investiture of Pope John Paul I, who would live only a few weeks longer. Was he murdered? Please see page 106.

LIFE
THE GREATEST UNSOLVED MYSTERIES OF ALL TIME

The Romance of Mystery

There is something in human nature that draws us to the mysterious. We seek conclusions—but not really. We want answers but are entertained when they prove elusive. A mystery fascinates us, intrigues us, beguiles us. In its uncertainty, it has a softness and a sense of wonder that a solved, buttoned-down case lacks. An unsolved mystery can be romantic.

This assertion is by no means applicable to all of the mysteries in our book. There's nothing romantic about a child abduction case or a murder spree. But many of the tales in this volume are real-world examples that inspired the fanciful fictions of such as Agatha Christie, and they enthrall us in the same way. (The chapter involving Dame Agatha's own disappearance, which begins on page 56, certainly does this in spades.) What happened to the philandering Judge Crater, and did Lucky Lord Lucan get away with murder? Forgive us, but we smile when we consider the possibilities.

We claim in the title of our volume that these are the Greatest Unsolved Mysteries of All Time, and we should fess up here at the outset: This, too, is not applicable to all the stories that will follow. To take two famous examples, let us consider the Lost Dauphin and Anastasia. In the former narrative, a young boy, the uncrowned king of France, escapes his captors during the French Revolution and lives out his life anonymously—probably in America. In the second legend, the teenage grand duchess of Russia, daughter of the last czar, flees the murderous Bolsheviks and also establishes an alias—perhaps in Europe. These are two of world history's most enduring myths. We say "myths" with confidence because we are now living in the 21st century, during the first decade of which the remarkable science that is DNA testing has finally laid these fables to rest. But what is a book of Great Unsolved Mysteries

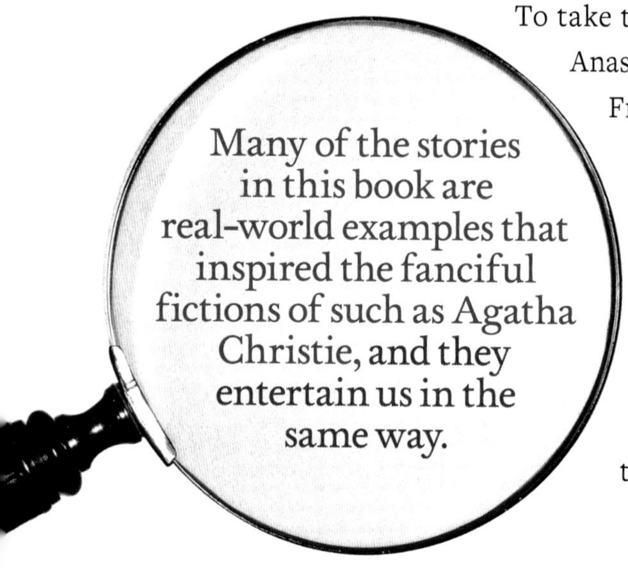
Many of the stories in this book are real-world examples that inspired the fanciful fictions of such as Agatha Christie, and they entertain us in the same way.

without the tales of the Lost Dauphin and Anastasia? If these chapters finally have denouements in the modern day, they only wrap up what have been, for many decades, two enormously enigmatic tales. It is fascinating to revisit these stories and see why they proved impossibly intoxicating to so many.

That our narratives are true and not inventions allows this book the signature feature of any LIFE volume: sterling photography. We have combed our archives and those of others, both in our own country and abroad, to find the best pictures to illustrate each story. Furthermore, some of these events occurred while our famous weekly magazine was in operation. LIFE covered Judge Crater's vanishing act, Commander Crabb's possible murder, the disappearance of the West Point cadet and other titillating tales. That photography, unseen for many years, resurfaces here—as do the riveting stories themselves.

This book is, in a small way, a sequel to one we published a few years ago that was well received by the public: *The Most Notorious Crimes in American History*. In tone and approach it is similar; and in fact a couple of the crimes have returned here as mysteries, since any comprehensive look at the latter topic needs to recount once more the Lizzie Borden case and the much more recent and still unsolved Gardner Museum art heist. But in the precious few instances when we have repeated ourselves, we have made certain to take a new photographic approach. Maybe we can't change the facts, but we can offer you a new perspective.

So here they are: 50 cases from the annals of true-life mystery—accidents, abscondings, crimes of passion and of profit, disappearances galore. As the balladeer once asked: Isn't it romantic?

What Is the Voynich Manuscript?

There resides in the Beinecke Rare Book and Manuscript Library at Yale University in New Haven, Connecticut, a strange and beguiling illustrated book that dates to at least the 17th century, probably to the 15th or 16th, maybe to as long ago as the 13th. Lovely to behold, it is a torment to ponder. No one has ever been able to figure out quite what it is.

And so many have tried! Some of the most talented and successful code breakers of World War II, men who had outsmarted the Third Reich, were beaten by the Voynich manuscript. Academics of the highest stripe and hundreds of professional and avocational cryptographers have been similarly foiled, as have computer programs designed to solve the mystery. While the pictures in the manuscript are easily understood—there are botanical drawings, mystical and probably mythical landscapes, astronomical and cosmological diagrams, naked women—the script used in the writing, which was applied with a quill pen, is unknown, and the text has never been deciphered. It seems there are about 30 common "letters" in whatever alphabet is being employed, and approximately 35,000 "words" in the 240 vellum pages of the manuscript that survive. But what all this writing signifies is a mystery and was long before the American rare-book collector Wilfrid M. Voynich acquired the volume in 1912 after it had passed through many hands.

One of those pairs of hands may have belonged to Rudolf II,

the Holy Roman Emperor and King of Bohemia at the turn of the 17th century, who was known to have a strong collection of manuscripts and was said to have paid 600 ducats—the equivalent of more than $30,000 today—for this one. According to one account, Rudolf believed that the author of the volume was Roger Bacon, the British philosopher and Franciscan friar who lived from 1214 to 1294 and was, in his philosophizing and scientific inquiry, a rare and brilliant source of intellectual light during the Middle Ages. Today, most Bacon scholars who have looked at the Voynich manuscript say that he had nothing to do with its writing, and there is speculation that the manuscript is in actuality an elaborate hoax, originally designed to relieve Rudolf (who unwittingly bought other counterfeit volumes) or some other ardent collector of a vast sum.

Will we ever know what the Voynich manuscript is trying to say? That's impossible to tell. But unless and until it is deciphered, it remains one thing and one thing only: an enigma unlike any other.

> Some of the most talented and successful code breakers of World War II, **men who had outsmarted the Third Reich,** were beaten by the Voynich manuscript.

MARY EVANS PICTURE LIBRARY/THE IMAGE WORKS

Above: Wilfrid Voynich ponders. Opposite: If you can decipher this representative page, you're smarter than us—and a whole lot of others, Voynich among them.

BEINECKE LIBRARY

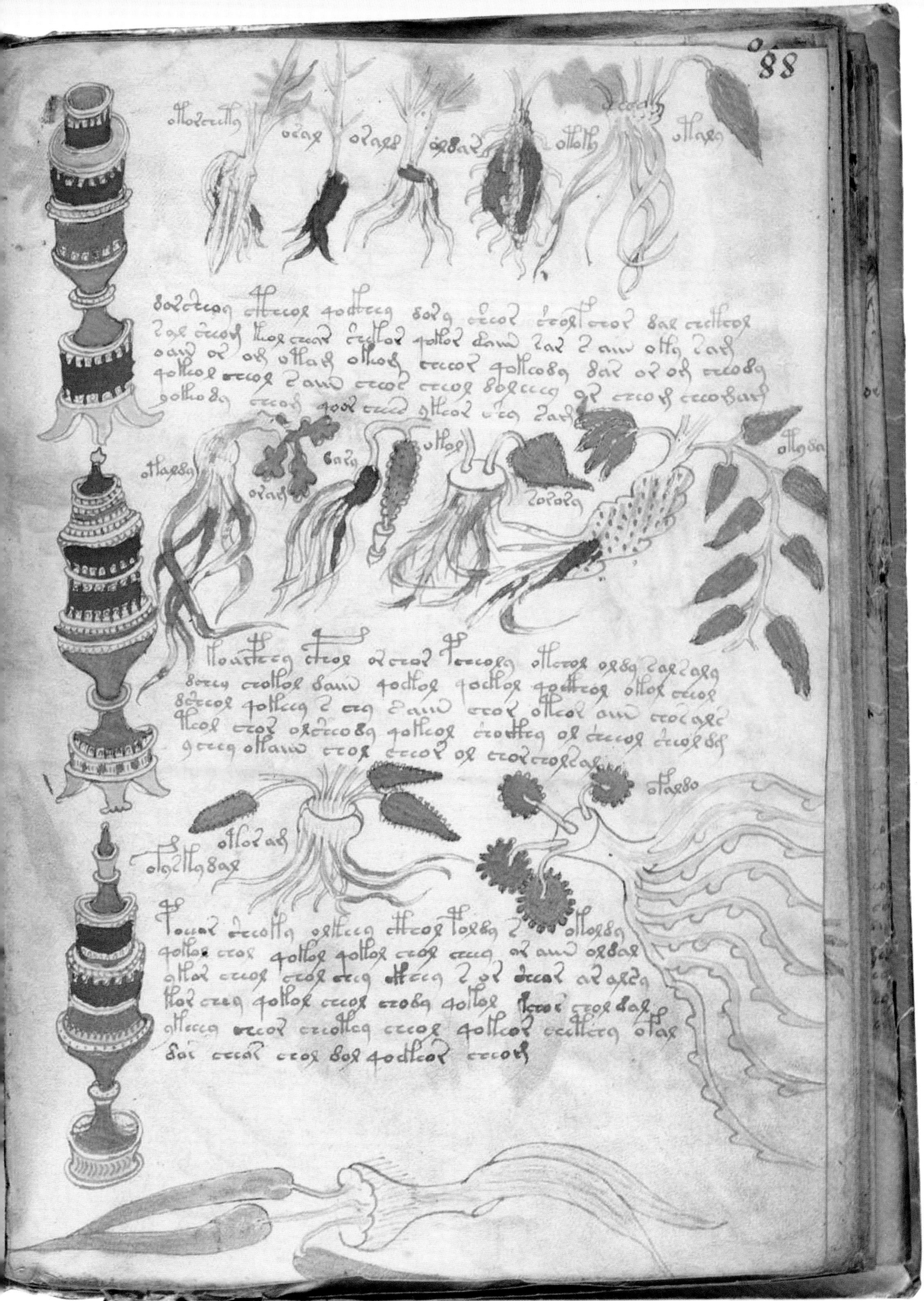
88

Who Killed Lord Darnley?

This story begins with the infancy of a far more famous historical personage, Mary Stuart, who at the age of six days in 1542 became Mary Queen of Scots upon the untimely death of her father—the first of several untimely deaths that would mark her operatic life. Three years after Mary's birth, Henry Stuart, the first Duke of Albany—better known as Lord Darnley—was born. He was Mary's first cousin and would eventually become her second husband. The queen's first marriage, to the dauphin of France, who became that country's King Francis II, ended when he died at age 16 of an ear infection. Mary was yet only 18 years old when she returned from Paris to her homeland in 1561, reassuming rule of Scotland. One year earlier, the Scottish parliament had declared the nation Protestant, and as Mary was Catholic, the crown sat precariously upon her head—with thrusts made against her on regular occasion by rebellious noblemen.

Back in Edinburgh, Mary fell hard for Darnley, a boisterous "long lad" (in the words of England's Queen Elizabeth). In the 18th century, Sir Walter Scott was more descriptive in his account: "Young Darnley was remarkably tall and handsome, perfect in all external and showy accomplishments, but unhappily destitute of sagacity, prudence, steadiness of character, and exhibiting only doubtful courage, though extremely violent in his passions." Mary, heedless of any of Darnley's negative traits and of Elizabeth's disapproval (since both he and Mary were in the line of succession for the English throne, Elizabeth saw theirs as a dangerous union), wed a second time in July 1565. She was quickly pregnant (with a boy who would one day become King James I of England), but the marriage was just as quickly on the rocks, owing to Darnley's philandering and dissolute ways. Mary came to rely more and more on her personal assistant, David Rizzio. A band of Protestant lords who opposed Mary inflamed Darnley's jealousy and recruited him in a murderous plot. On March 9, 1566, Rizzio was seized as he supped beside Mary, then stabbed 56 times by the assassins. Darnley was pardoned, which is the way things went back then.

Was Mary an accomplice in her husband's murder? No one knows for sure, but certainly his death did her little good.

Seeing an opening, the brutally ambitious James Hepburn, a Protestant who was the fourth Earl of Bothwell, quickly arrived at Mary's side and helped her quash any further rebellion. Her husband, meantime, grew ever more debauched and then became ill, possibly with syphilis. He was convalescing at Kirk o' Fields, a few hundred yards from Mary's Holyrood Palace, when, at two a.m. on February 10, 1567, that house, which had been packed with explosives, blew sky-high. The bodies of Darnley and his servant were found in the gardens, but perhaps they had been in flight, because they had been killed not by the blast but by strangulation.

All these centuries later, Hepburn remains the most attractive suspect. Was Mary an accomplice? No one knows for sure. Whether she was or not, the murder did her little good in the long run—or even the short. Hepburn raped her and made her marry him. Then the Protestant insurgents forced her to flee to England, where Elizabeth promptly had her arrested and imprisoned for 18 years before ordering her execution at Fotheringhay Castle in 1587. As Sir Walter Scott wrote many years later: "Thus died Queen Mary, aged 44 years. She was eminent for beauty, for talents, and accomplishments, nor is there reason to doubt her natural goodness of heart, and courageous manliness of disposition. Yet she was in every sense one of the most unhappy Princesses that ever lived..."

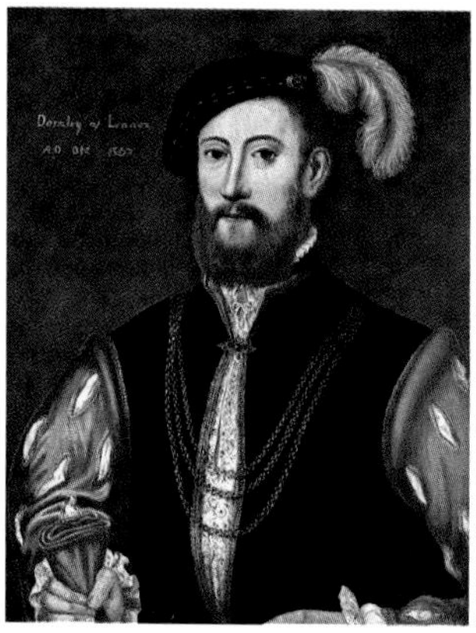

PRINT COLLECTOR/HERITAGE/THE IMAGE WORKS

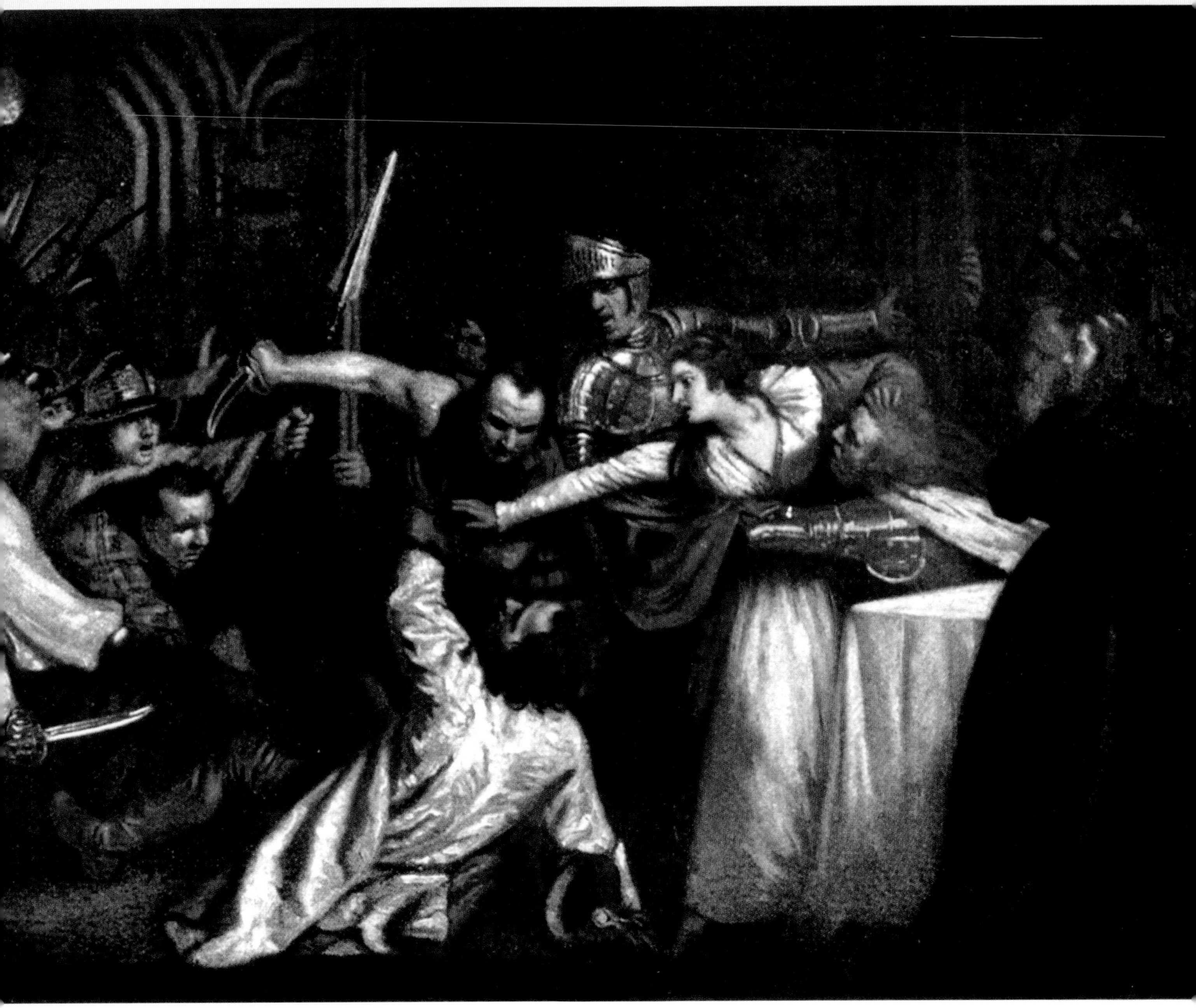

MARY EVANS PICTURE LIBRARY/DOUGLAS MCCARTHY/THE IMAGE WORKS

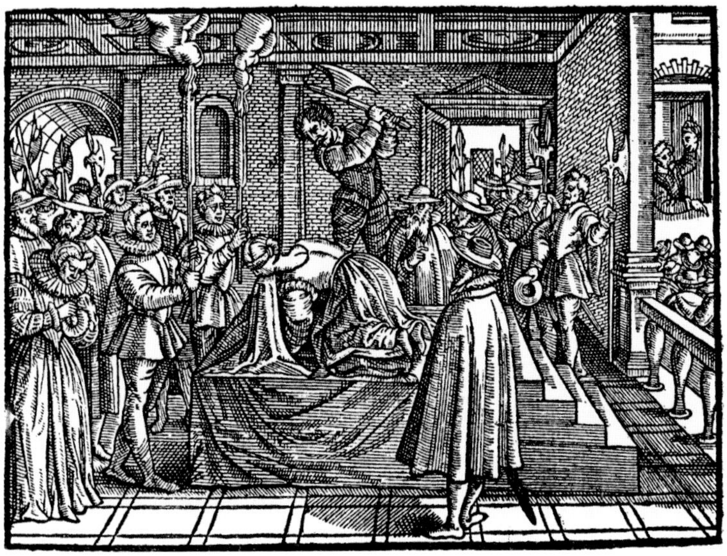

GRANGER

On the opposite page, the hot-wired Darnley is seen in a rare calm moment, while above he dispatches Rizzio. Left: His widow, Mary, loses her head at Fotheringhay Castle.

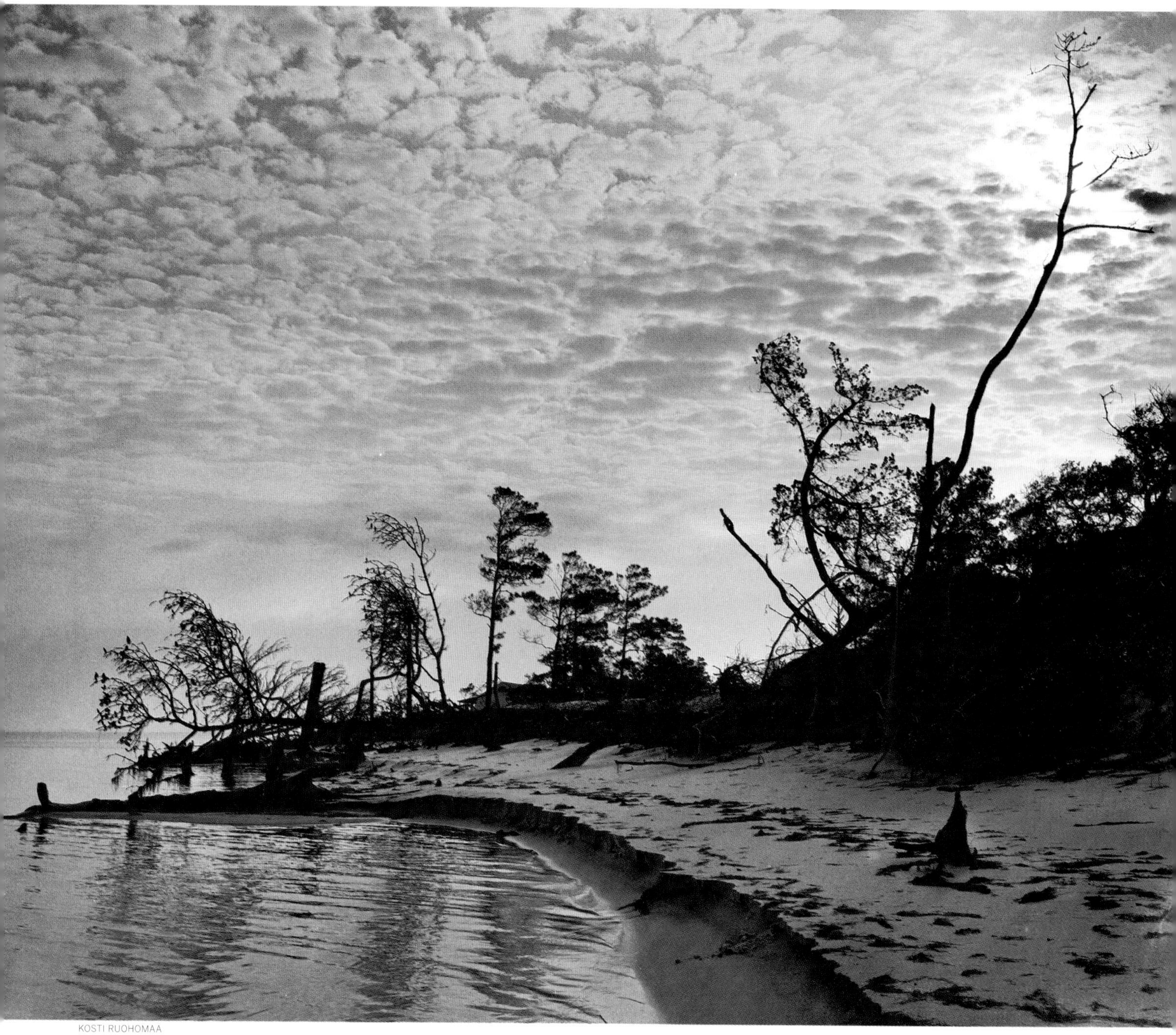

KOSTI RUOHOMAA

What Became of the Lost Colony?

As we all know, the Native Americans were here first, from coast to coast, in what we now call the United States. Then the Europeans arrived, and even in the prelude to nationhood, America was becoming quite a melting pot, as the Spanish were followed in their efforts at colonization by the British, French and Dutch, opening the way for waves of Irish, German, Finnish and Swedish immigrants. Many came in search of wealth; others for individual or religious freedom. Their aspirations informed what would become known as the "American character."

But in the beginning of this endless tide of immigration, there was no thought of joining or becoming part of an American anything. Rather, these fretful refugees and adventurers were embarking upon a wholly new life in a strange, largely unsettled place, peopled by natives who lived in ways completely foreign to the European experience. Danger and the prospect of premature death were constant for the earliest settlers from Europe.

The beleaguered colonists implored White to go back to England and inform the crown of their plight and the need for reinforcements. He did so and then returned—but never saw his friends alive again.

Sir Walter Raleigh's attempt in 1585 to establish a British settlement on Roanoke Island, off the coast of what is now North Carolina, failed, with the colonists, all of whom were men, many of them veterans of the military, returning to England the next year. Raleigh tried again in 1587, sending 91 men, 17 women and nine children; their leader was John White, an artist friend of Raleigh's. The fate of these people, collectively known for four centuries as the Lost Colony, remains one of America's eeriest mysteries.

A few things are known: They landed on Roanoke on July 22, and within a month White's daughter, Eleanor, gave birth to the first English child born on New World soil. She was named Virginia Dare. Although some local Native Americans who had mixed it up with earlier colonists refused to powwow with White, the Croatans did reestablish relations with the English. Before the year was out, however, a colonist named George Howe was attacked and killed while hunting crabs in the sound. The colonists implored White to return to England and inform the crown of their plight and the need for reinforcements. He did so, leaving for the homeland aboard a vessel piloted by Simon Fernandez.

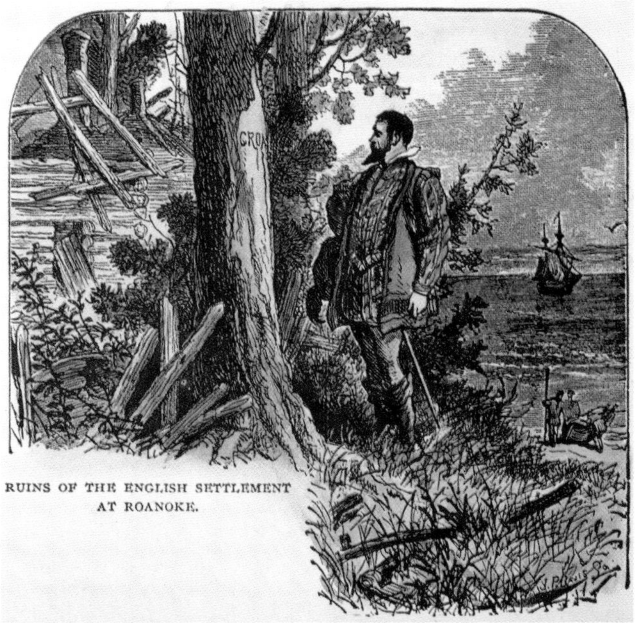
CRO
RUINS OF THE ENGLISH SETTLEMENT AT ROANOKE.

GRANGER

This is what John White returned to: Where once there had been a colony, there was now a deserted landscape (opposite). In the 19th century illustration above, he comes upon the cryptic carving.

Winter weather and battles with the Spanish Armada prevented the British navy from giving White the men and matériel that he needed to return to Roanoke in due haste. Finally, he was able to hop a ride on a privateering expedition and arrived there on his granddaughter's third birthday: August 18, 1590. He and the other sailors found no trace of the colony, only the letters CRO carved into one tree, the word CROATOAN into another. The colonists' intentions, White knew, had been to travel north to Chesapeake Bay and establish a new community. Perhaps they had done so, and perhaps they had run afoul of the Indians there. Or maybe they were taken in by the friendly Croatans to the south of the original settlement (still today, the Lumbee Indians of southeastern North Carolina maintain that they have Lost Colonists in their family tree). The truth remains unknown and probably ever will.

What Happened to the Lost Dauphin?

Perhaps this is a mystery no longer, depending on your confidence in modern science and one 21st century test in particular—as we shall see.

But first: Let's remain *mysterious*. In 1785, Louis XVI, king of France, and his wife, Marie-Antoinette, had a son named Louis-Charles. Not long thereafter, the French Revolution grievously upset their world; the parents were first unseated by the rebels, then beheaded. The son, who in the eyes of those who supported the monarchy was now the uncrowned King Louis XVII, was imprisoned for two years. And then he died in a small cell on June 8, 1795, at 10 years of age, of tuberculosis, or some other disease, or at the hands of a murderer, or simply of neglect.

End of story? Hardly.

The prevailing opinion immediately after the lad's death became known was that he had been assassinated by the Committee of Public Safety, the Revolution's controlling administration. But quite quickly the belief that the dauphin had escaped gained currency, and after the monarchy was restored, the official palace historian announced, in 1814, that indeed Louis-Charles was still alive—somewhere. The story that emerged as the most popular—among many—was that loyalists to the crown had substituted another child for the dauphin and then covertly taken Louis-Charles to the safety of distant America.

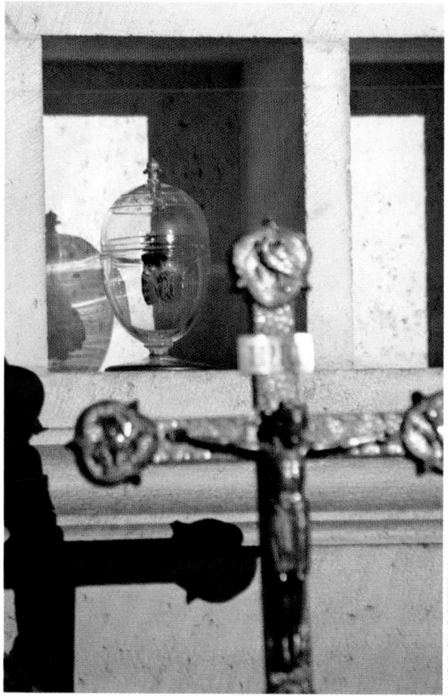

ISABELLE SIMON/SIPA

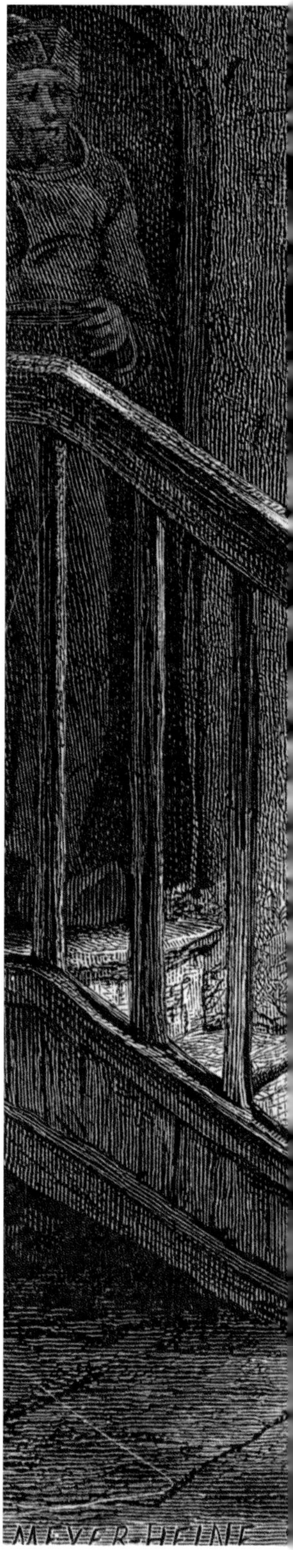
MEYER-HEINE

BETTMAN CORBIS

The illustration captures the poignancy of the boy as he sits in the Temple prison, awaiting his fate; his heart, preserved in a crystal vase (above), is more poignant still. DNA collected from it in 2000 convinced many the dauphin had died in jail. In 2004, days after this photograph was taken, the heart was placed in the basilica of Saint-Denis's royal crypt.

The floodgates were now open for claimants. John James Audubon was rumored to be the dauphin, and the eccentric (if brilliant) naturalist and painter did not discourage speculation, writing to his wife from France in 1828 that he was "patient, silent, bashful, and yet powerful of physique and of mind, dressed as a common man, I walk the streets! I bow! I ask permission to do this or that! I . . . who should command all!" In point of fact, Audubon was the illegitimate offspring of a Haitian native and a French sea captain.

Then there was Eleazer Williams, an Episcopal minister who was instrumental in the founding of Green Bay, Wisconsin. He swore he was Louis-Charles, although he was actually the biracial son of a white woman who had been kidnapped by Mohawk Indians.

And then there was Karl Wilhelm Naundorff, a German clockmaker who, when questioned by the dauphin's former nurse, was convincing enough in his answers to be recognized as king by many, including the government of the Netherlands, where he settled.

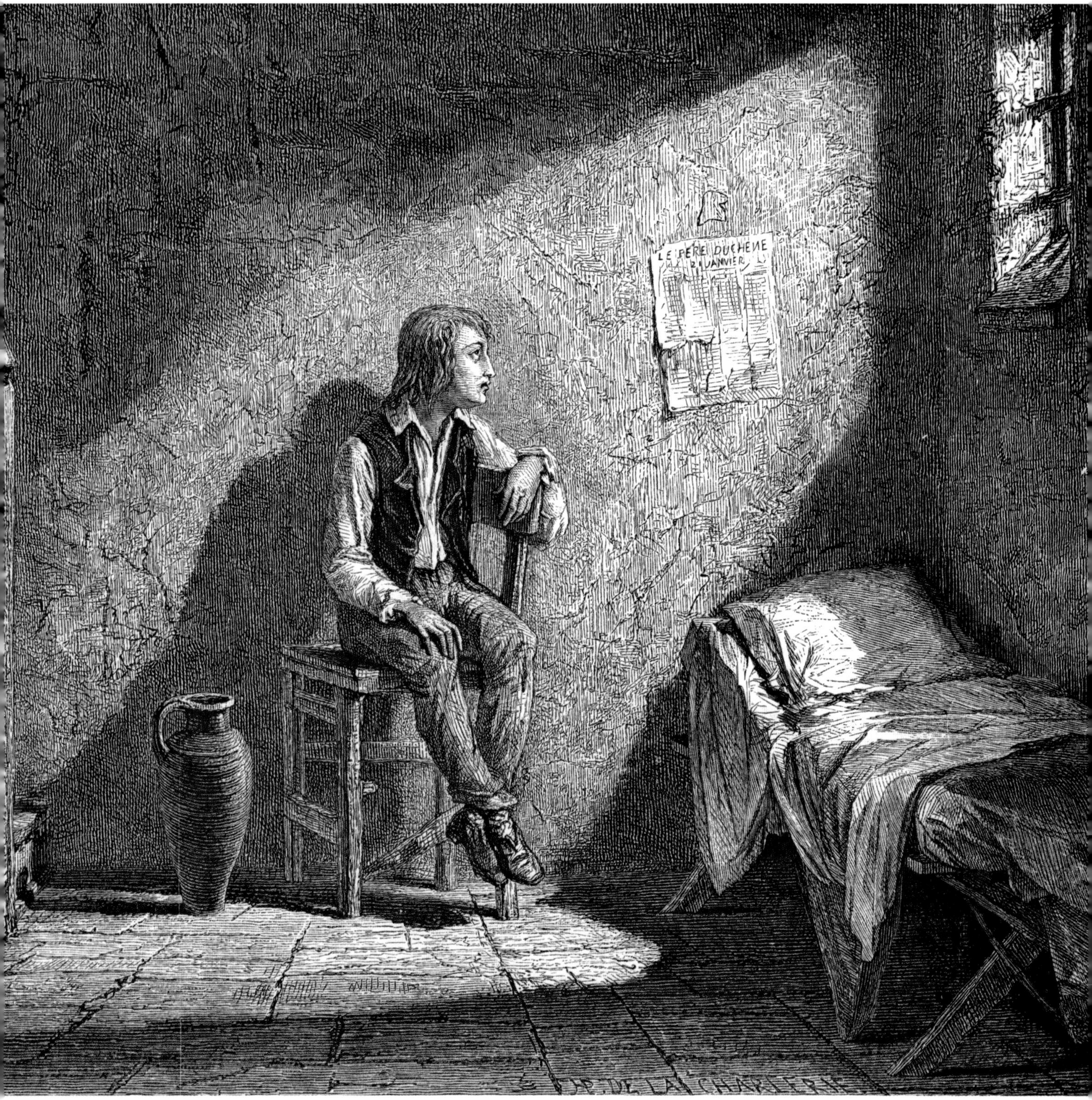
LE PERE DUCHENE

Ah, but: The heart of the boy who had died in prison back in 1795 had been removed from the body at the time of his death, as was customary among royalty. It had traveled through the decades preserved in alcohol. In 2000, DNA from this organ was compared with that of a lock of hair belonging to a member of Marie-Antoinette's family. The results indicated a maternal relationship.

Was this really the heart of the boy who had died? Were the results conclusive beyond doubt?

With a story as romantic as this, those questions will never be answered to the satisfaction of all. And so the fate of the Lost Dauphin remains, for many, lost.

For others, it has been found.

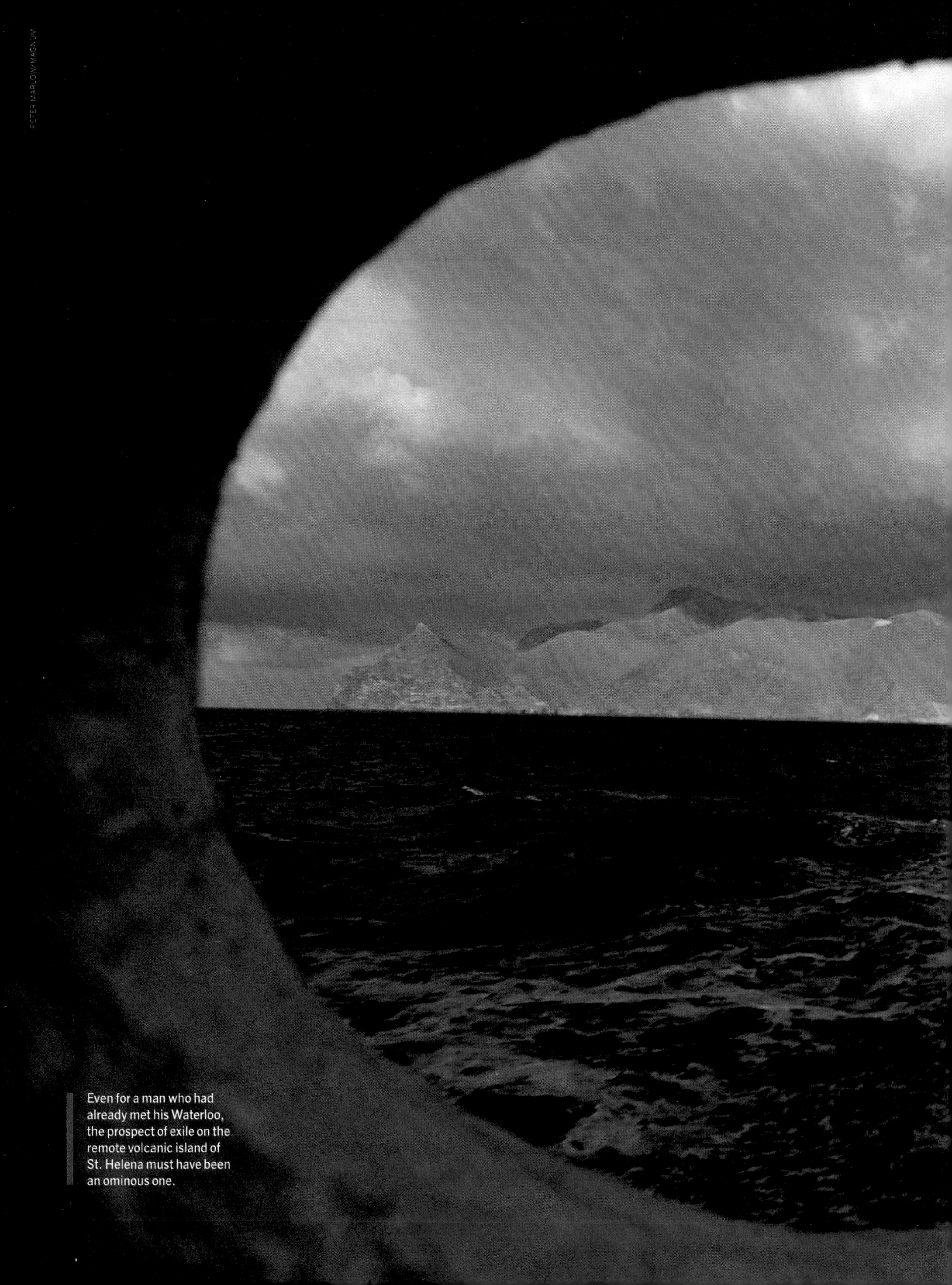

PETER MARLOW/MAGNUM

Even for a man who had already met his Waterloo, the prospect of exile on the remote volcanic island of St. Helena must have been an ominous one.

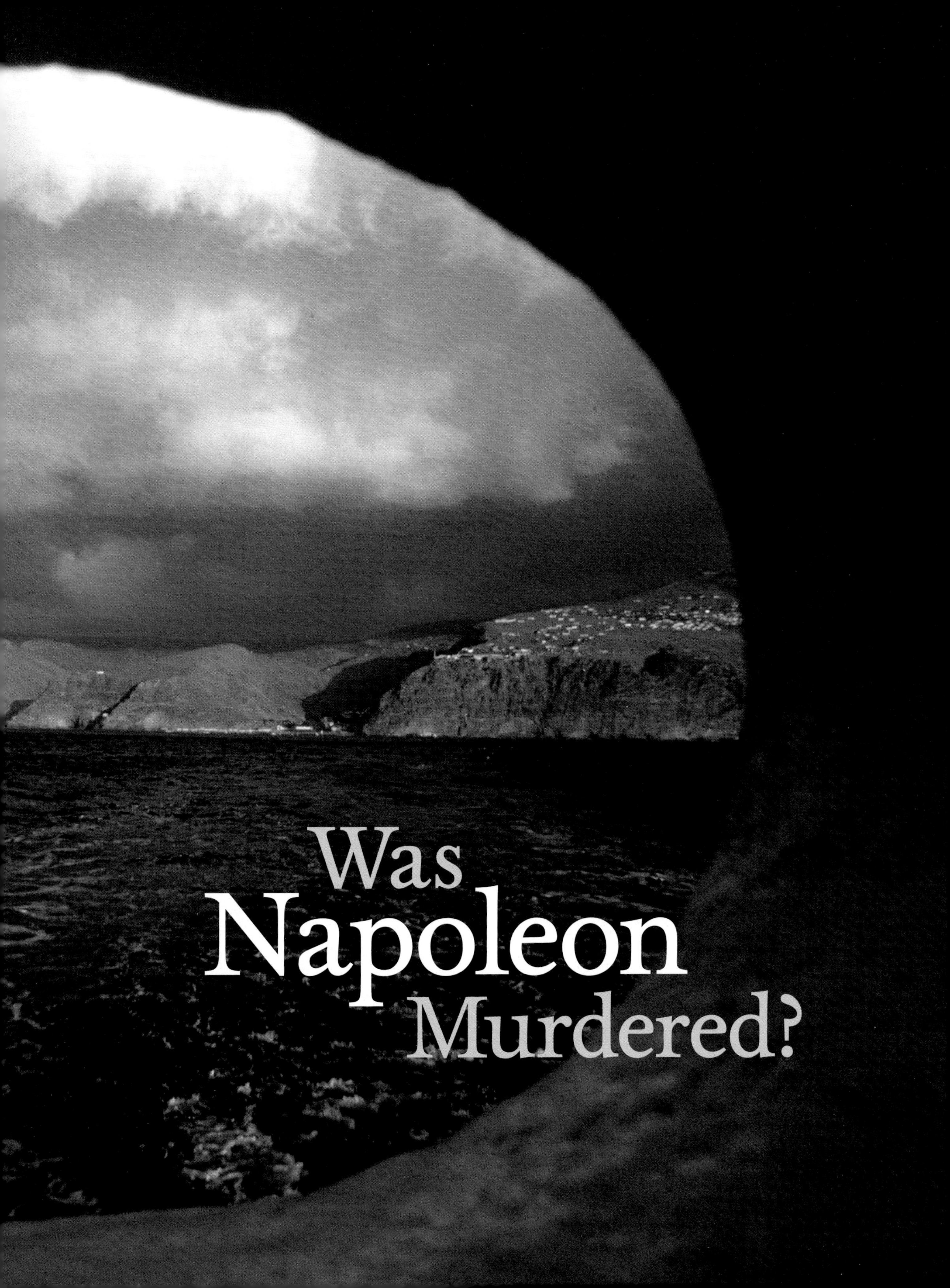

Was Napoleon Murdered?

We know for a certainty where and when the famous French emperor Napoleon Bonaparte died: in exile on the island of St. Helena on May 5, 1821. And we know that he had been suffering a bladder infection for years and was prone to fainting caused by either this condition or some other ailment. And we know that the official cause of death was listed as a cancerous stomach ulcer.

Yet nearly two centuries later, with more than 200,000 books having been written about one of history's most famous figures, opinion remains wildly split on what killed Napoleon. Of the more than 30 different possibilities forwarded—theories ranging from gonorrhea to syphilis to scurvy to hepatitis—the two most often nominated are the original diagnosis of cancer and . . . the possibility that he was poisoned. *Murdered.*

About a month before he died, Napoleon began violently vomiting. This certainly could have been related to any illness he was suffering, but conspiracy theorists have long said that it would be consistent with his being systemically poisoned. Certainly there were reasons some would want Napoleon either sick or dead, and these reasons as put forth by various historians are also all over the map. One hypothesis is that a supporter of Napoleon purposely made the erstwhile emperor ill so that public opinion back in France, which was already pro-Napoleon, would swell with sympathy, and pressure to bring the hero back to Paris would be irresistible. At the other end of the spectrum, we have Hudson Lowe, the English governor of St. Helena, colluding with Count de Montholon of France to kill Napoleon once and for all. Both men would have been well aware of several facts: that after an earlier exile on Elba, Napoleon had escaped and returned to France and war between their two nations had been re-engaged; that Napoleon still had the support of the French army and if he escaped from St. Helena a similar consequence might ensue; and that nothing would be stable or certain until Napoleon was no longer part of the equation.

Conflicting modern studies seem to support either the cancer or poison hypothesis. In 2007, an American-Swiss-Canadian team of researchers, using current medical knowledge, as well as the memoirs of physicians who treated Napoleon during his last days at Longwood House, concluded that he died of advanced gastric cancer; a new, central piece of evidence was information regarding Napoleon's shrinking trouser size in the last six months of his life, which indicated he lost perhaps 20 pounds in that period. But back in 2001, the Strasbourg Forensic Institute, having examined strands of Napoleon's hair, determined the man had been exposed to "major" doses of arsenic. Could these have come from the paint on the walls of Longwood House, as some think, or did St. Helena's governor tamper with Napoleon's supply of vin de Constance?

Was this most famous man assassinated?

Will we ever know?

> In 2001, the Strasbourg Forensic Institute, having examined strands of Napoleon's hair, determined the man had been exposed to "major" doses of arsenic. And what did that prove?

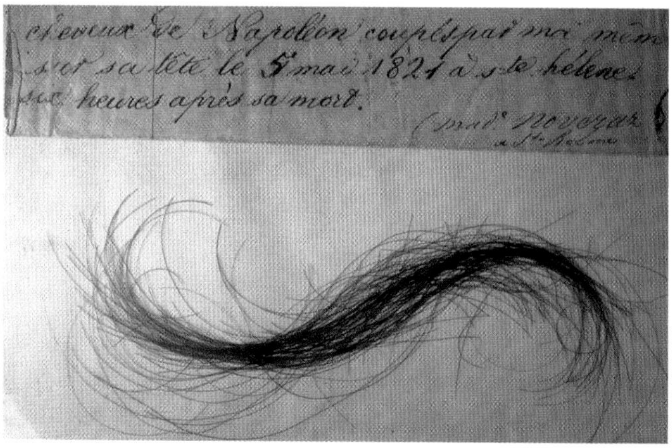
cheveux de Napoléon coupés par moi même
sur sa tête le 5 mai 1821 à ste helene.
six heures après sa mort.

STEPHEN ELLISON

The handwriting immediately above this lock of Napoleon's hair (right) is testimony by a linen maid who snipped it before the emperor's body (opposite) was buried. Nearly two centuries later, the hair would provide a clue.

ROGER-VIOLLET/THE IMAGE WORKS

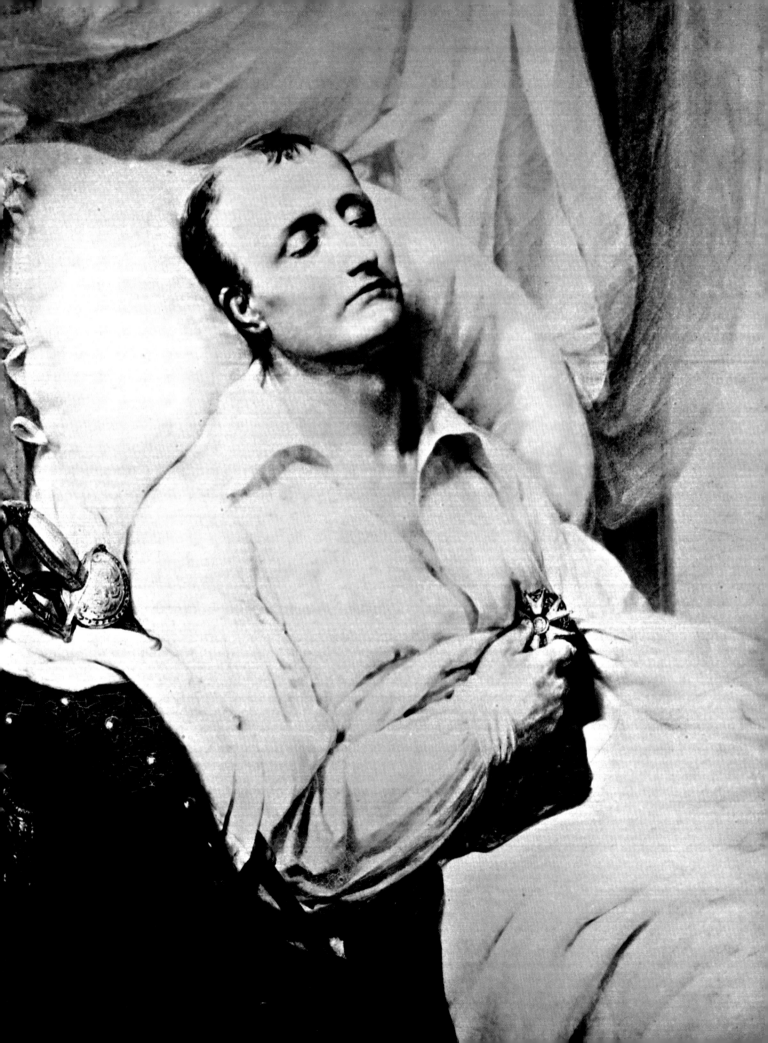

How Did Edgar Allan Poe Die?

Please pardon us for tell-tale heartlessness if we say it seems fitting that a writer who gave us some of our most mysterious and terrifying tales died in a mysterious and terrible way, having lived a dark, twisting and often horrendous life. We are certainly sympathetic, but ironic facts cannot be ignored.

Poe, a Boston native raised by a foster father who later disowned him, was something other than a nice man, though when sober he could be hardworking and courteous. Certain of his genius, he was inarguably imperious and arrogant, often feeling that he deserved greater rewards than he received for his service as a magazine editor and as a writer of tales and poems. He may well have been right, but as the country was plunged into a prolonged and pronounced economic depression by the Panic of 1837, the career of many a literary man was fraught with financial peril. Publishers weren't paying much when they were paying at all, and Poe was constantly poor and sometimes destitute. Plus, he was personally unstable and married—therefore, he had responsibilities. And he was an alcoholic. And he was probably—most probably—mad. He certainly seemed destined for no good end; indeed, he would fulfill his destiny.

Personally unstable and an alcoholic, he seemed destined for no good end, and indeed he would fulfill his destiny.

The death of his wife, Virginia, after a prolonged illness, in January of 1847, when Poe was 37, triggered a final period of decline that would, two years later, result in his own demise. He had already, during Virginia's convalescence, suffered a breakdown and, as he admitted, "drank, God only knows how often or how much." Now his mental and emotional state collapsed altogether. He continued to live with his mother-in-law in Fordham, New York, but he essentially withdrew from the world. He suffered further collapses when he indulged, as he would do when depressed, which was a routine state. Some biographers assert that he tried suicide with an overdose of laudanum at one point. He said months before his death, "I was never *really* insane, except on occasions where my heart was touched. I have been taken to prison once since I came here for getting drunk; but then I was not. It was about Virginia."

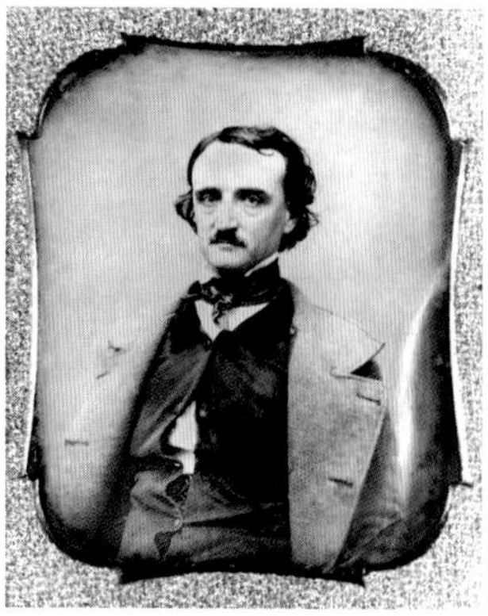

TOPHAM/THE IMAGE WORKS

Poe is austere in this portrait (above), but his life was chaotic, as symbolized in the picture opposite, which was created for LIFE in 1959 by our storied photographer Nina Leen, whose assignment was to depict Poe's world.

The night in prison was spent in Philadelphia during his final, mysterious journey in 1849. From there it's known he went to Richmond, Virginia, where a series of lectures went off well enough. Then he boarded a steamer for Baltimore, where he arrived on September 29. Either in Richmond or on the boat or in Baltimore he took the first of his last, fatal drinks. What happened between then and October 3 is unknown, but on that day he was found thoroughly dissolute in a bar, wearing clothes that were not his own. He was taken to a hospital, where, four days later, he died in a delirium.

The lost days? One theory is particularly intriguing. Baltimore's politics at the time were notoriously corrupt, and one element of the game was for operatives to shanghai or kidnap the downtrodden, ply them with drink and then have these "floaters" vote over and over at the polling stations. It is suspected that Poe may have been thus "cooped" in that year's October 3 election.

Such a sad and sorry end, if so, for one of America's greatest writers—whose voice was heard nevermore.

NINA LEEN

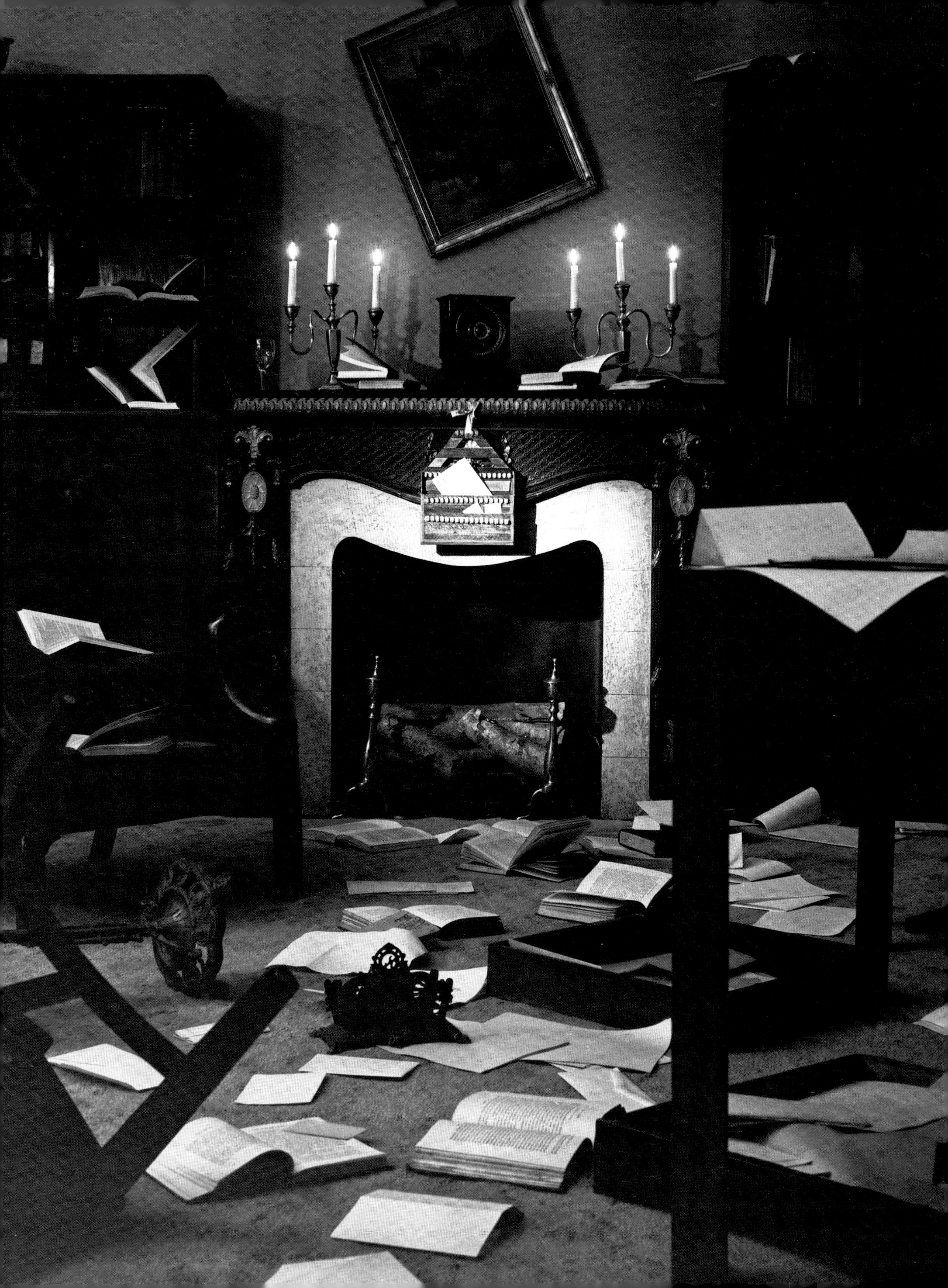

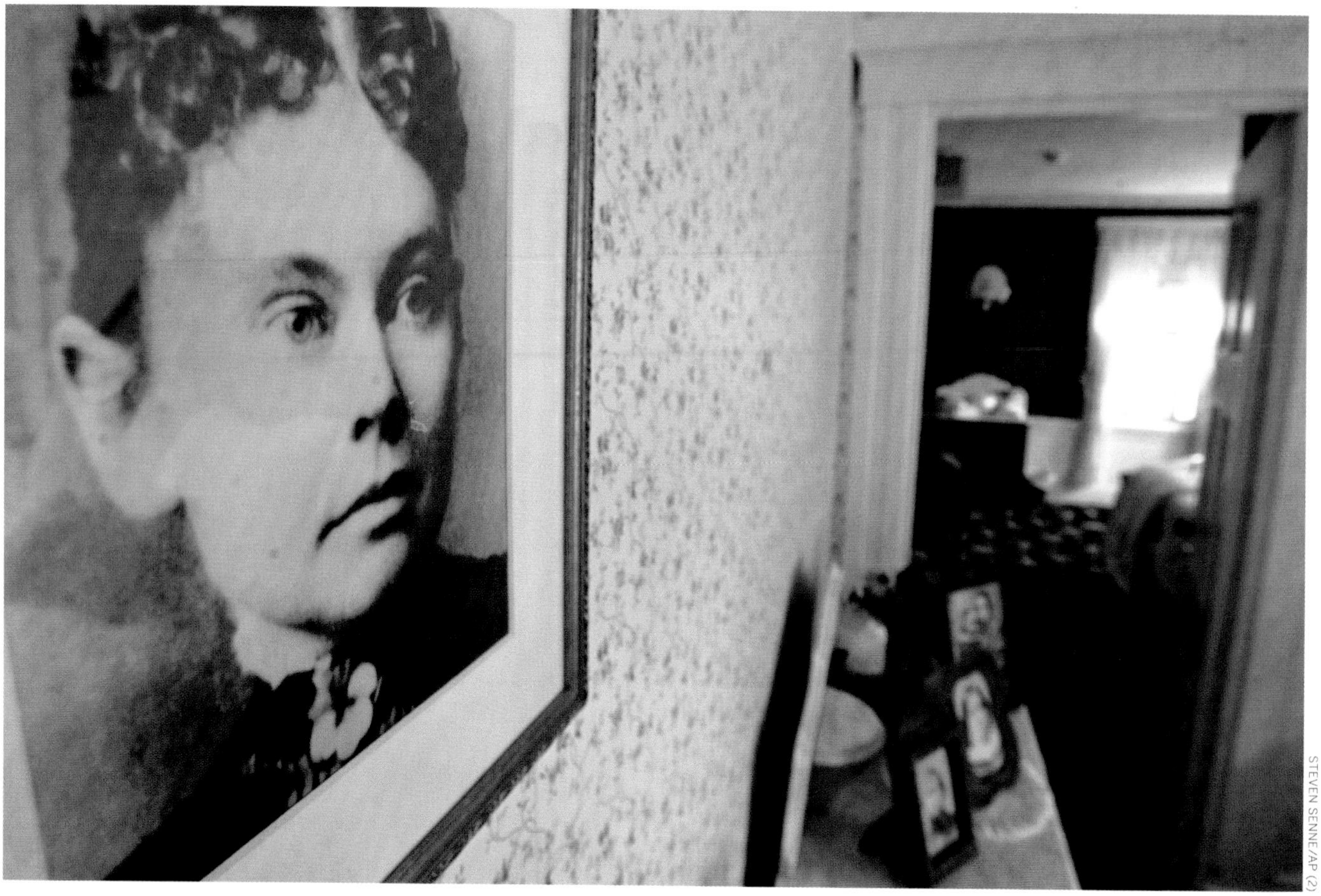

STEVEN SENNE/AP (2)

Did Lizzie Borden Whack Her Parents?

The prosecution obviously felt theatrics would help and opened the case by dramatically tossing the shattered skulls of the victims onto a table.

The ubiquitous playground rhyme purports to answer the question posed immediately above, asserting that Lizzie "took an ax/And gave her mother 40 whacks/And when she saw what she had done/She gave her father 41." A Massachusetts jury in 1893 begged to differ, acquitting Lizzie of the brutal murder the previous year of Andrew Borden, a wealthy, parsimonious and rather unpleasant 70-year-old bank president, and Andrew's second wife, Abby.

A hot and uncomfortable day dawned in Fall River on Thursday, August 4, 1892. Andrew went out that morning, conducted some business in town, then returned to his home at 92 Second Street at around 10:45 a.m. A half hour later, Bridget Sullivan, the family's housekeeper, was upstairs when she heard Lizzie, the older of Andrew's two daughters, shout, "Come down! Come down quick! Father's dead! Somebody's come in and killed him!" The horror of discovering Andrew's body in the sitting room escalated to pandemonium after Abby's corpse was found in a second-floor room shortly thereafter. Both had been bludgeoned about the head, apparently with an ax.

SHOCKING CRIME, shouted the headline of *The Fall River Herald*, A VENERABLE CITIZEN AND HIS AGED WIFE HACKED TO PIECES IN THEIR HOME. The paper reported that "the bodies of the victims are . . . almost beyond recognition." According to the autopsy, Abby was butchered first, struck at least 18 times. The killer then rained 11 blows on Andrew's head. (And so, the famous poetry represents an exaggeration.)

As these photographs indicate, the bed-and-breakfast in Fall River is not the least bit shy about its notorious past; in fact, it shouts the news at every turn, with a wild-eyed Lizzie watching the hall and a very dead dad adorning a tabletop.

national frenzy. The prosecution obviously felt theatrics would help and opened the case by dramatically tossing the shattered skulls of the victims onto a table. But from there on, the prosecutor was armed with mostly circumstantial evidence. An ax that had been found in the basement of the Borden home couldn't be clearly identified as the murder weapon, and in a crucial decision, the judge ruled out Lizzie's pretrial testimony, which was said to be full of contradictions, as having been coerced. The jury acquitted after deliberating only an hour.

The court of public opinion disagreed, and Lizzie was ostra-

Initially, police suspected a laborer whom Andrew had refused to pay that morning, but soon the focus turned to Lizzie. An inquest uncovered her attempt to buy a deadly poison just before the murders, and rumors of trouble between her and her stepmother surfaced.

Lizzie's trial commenced in nearby New Bedford on June 5, 1893, and news from the proceedings traveled to every corner of the country; this murder trial was one of the first to generate a

cized in Fall River the rest of her days—which ended on June 1, 1927, when she was 66 years old. Lizzie died, but the case lived on—in books, plays, musicals, folk songs, rock songs, operas, ballets (Morton Gould's *Fall River Legend* is a modern classic), films and around-the-campfire ghost stories. The house on Second Street has endured as well. It's now a bed-and-breakfast. Spend a night there—if you dare. As might be imagined, it is said to be well and truly haunted.

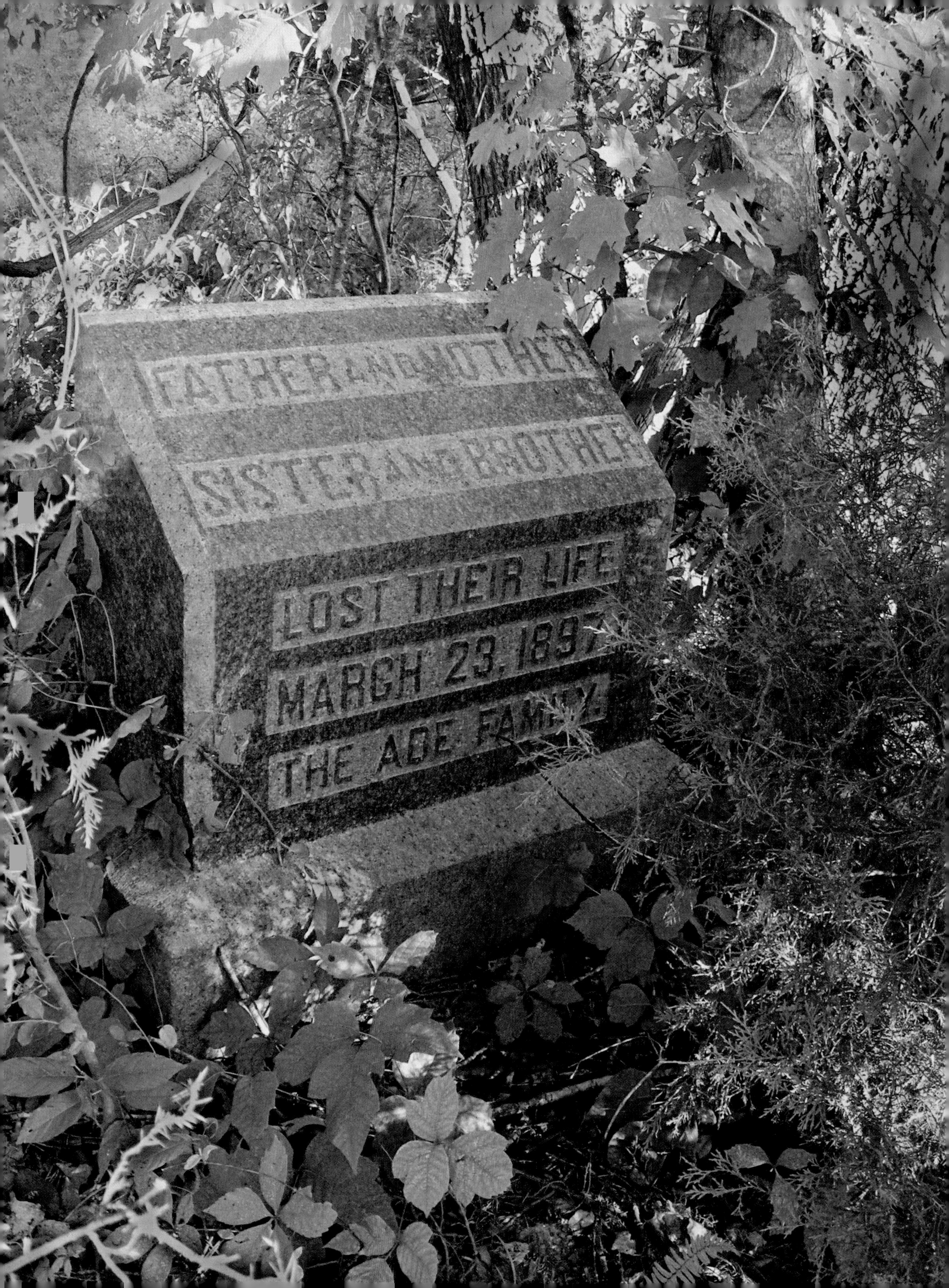
FATHER AND MOTHER
SISTER AND BROTHER
LOST THEIR LIFE
MARCH 23, 1897
THE ADE FAMILY

Who Wiped Out the Ade Family?

In 1897, a crime was committed in Nashville that seems now a template for the one that would be made famous in the 1960s by Truman Capote's celebrated book *In Cold Blood*: A prosperous, well-liked family was summarily dispatched by a brutal killer or killers for no immediately apparent reason. The principal difference in the two cases is that no suspect was ever prosecuted for the Ade family murders.

It remains poignant from the distance of more than a century to note that the part of town where the horror ensued was called Paradise Ridge. There, in the Ade house on the evening of March 23, were gathered the patriarch, Jacob, age 60; his wife, Pauline, 50; their daughter, Lizze, 20; their son, Henry, 13; and Rosa Moirer, the 10-year-old daughter of a neighbor. They were all in the parlor at around eight p.m. when an intruder bashed Mr. Ade as he was sitting placidly in front of the fireplace. The others tried to escape through a window and were either met there by an accomplice or caught from behind by the first assailant and felled, one after another, by a blunt object. The house was then set afire.

At 10 o'clock that night, Justice Simpson was getting a drink of water in his house a half mile away. He noticed the conflagration at the Ade place

Opposite: Where the Ade spread once stood on Paradise Ridge, today only a commemorative stone hides in the brush—the softest whisper of what went on there.

and hastened there. The house was quickly collapsing, and the smokehouse was aflame. Simpson started throwing meat from this outbuilding and, having assumed the Ades had escaped the inferno and were somewhere on the grounds, yelled for assistance. When no response came, he worked his way to the fiery house, and there he discovered the bodies. He then ran for help.

There was an overnight rain, which may have erased any traces left by the killler or killers by the time Sheriff John D. Sharp began his investigation the next day. A few hundred dollars were found in an oyster can that had been stashed in a bedroom closet, and so it was difficult to establish robbery as a motive. Perhaps someone was stealing meat, because it seemed some was missing from storage. But why would anyone murder five people over a provisions heist?

Ed Anderson had quarreled with the well-respected Jacob Ade: a question of whether Anderson had stolen some hogs. Anderson knew this would be a problem, of course, and recognized that he would be a suspect, so he went forthrightly to Sheriff Sharp with his alibi, which cleared him. The subsequent investigation ultimately proved fruitless, and no one was ever charged with the crime, a senseless *In Cold Blood*–type murder that had no Truman Capote to immortalize it.

At 10 o'clock that night, Justice Simpson, getting a drink of water in his house a half mile away, noticed the fire at the Ade place and hastened there. He came upon a gruesome scene.

Who Was Jack the Ripper?

In a book dedicated to history's Greatest Unsolved Mysteries, some mysteries are perforce greater than others, and this one maybe the topper, the paragon, the ne plus ultra—the most famous and infamous cold case of all time. Who was the serial killer active in the down-and-dirty Whitechapel district of London in the latter half of 1888? He gruesomely murdered prostitutes—maybe five of them, maybe more—and thereby gained a lasting if anonymous fame usually reserved for conquerors or kings. It would be impossible to estimate the number of trees that have been felled to supply paper for the treatises and tomes that have been written about Jack the Ripper in the past century and a quarter.

The writing began early, in London's then blossoming and already florid tabloid industry, and established Jack's eternal notoriety from the first. Reporters—and their rapt readers—were particularly interested in the savagery of the killings: Throats were being slit, bodies mutilated, organs removed. Responding to the public fascination and indeed furor, Scotland Yard was frantic in its pursuit of the perp. Frantic but unsuccessful.

A spicy aspect of this story has always been that many suspects were of the upper crust. The notion that an aristocrat was, in the city's dankest precinct, preying upon prostitutes made for an intoxicating narrative.

In a precursor of the behavior that would be exhibited by 20th century American criminals like the Zodiac killer and the Son of Sam, the Ripper—or someone—began sending letters to the press and even the authorities concerning the crimes. One shipment, to George Lusk of the Whitechapel Vigilance Committee, included half of a human kidney, along with the claim that the sender had "fried and ate" the other half. A post received on September 27, 1888, by the Central News Agency was the first that bore the name Jack the Ripper, and in it the correspondent said he would "clip the ladys [sic] ear off." Three days later, the body of Catherine Eddowes was found in Mitre Square in the City of London. The removal of a portion of one of her ears was the least of the mutilations visited upon her tragic corpse.

Since evisceration was a hallmark of the murders, the constabulatory wondered if the murderer was a medical man or someone else with sufficient sophistication to execute such surgery; a spicy aspect of the Ripper story has always been that many of the suspects in the case were of the upper rather than the lower crust. This was Victorian England, and the notion that an aristocrat was, in the

3
police officers just for jolly wouldnt you. Keep this letter back till I do a bit more work then give it out straight. My knifes so nice and sharp I want to get to work right away if I get a chance. Good luck.
Yours truly
Jack the Ripper
Dont mind me giving the trade name

AKIRA SUEMORI/AP

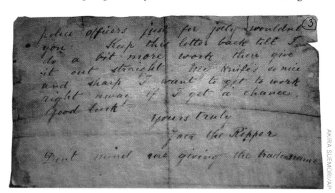

Jack was nothing if not theatrical, using blood-red ink in this missive to the press (above). Opposite: An alleyway in London's Whitechapel district where the Ripper stalked prostitutes.

PETER KINDERSLEY/LOOP IMAGES/CORBIS

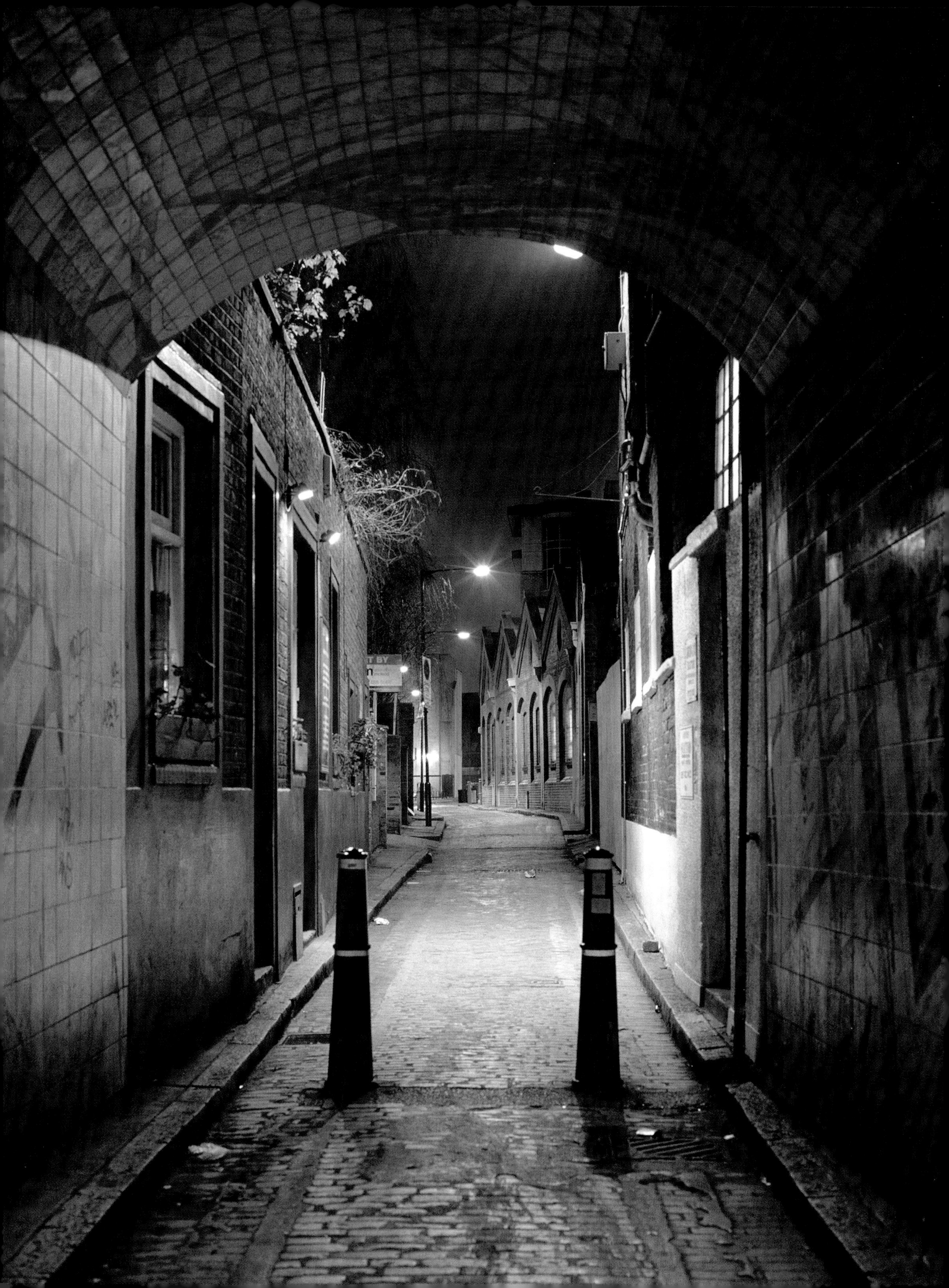

No. 1423.—Vol. 55

SEPTEMBER 8, 1888

THE PENNY ILLUSTRATED PAPER AND ILLUSTRATED TIMES

REGISTERED AT THE GENERAL POST-OFFICE AS A NEWSPAPER.

London: Printed and Published at the Office, 10, Milford-lane, Strand, in the Parish of St. Clement Danes, in the County of Middlesex, by THOMAS FOX, 10, Milford-lane, Strand, aforesaid.

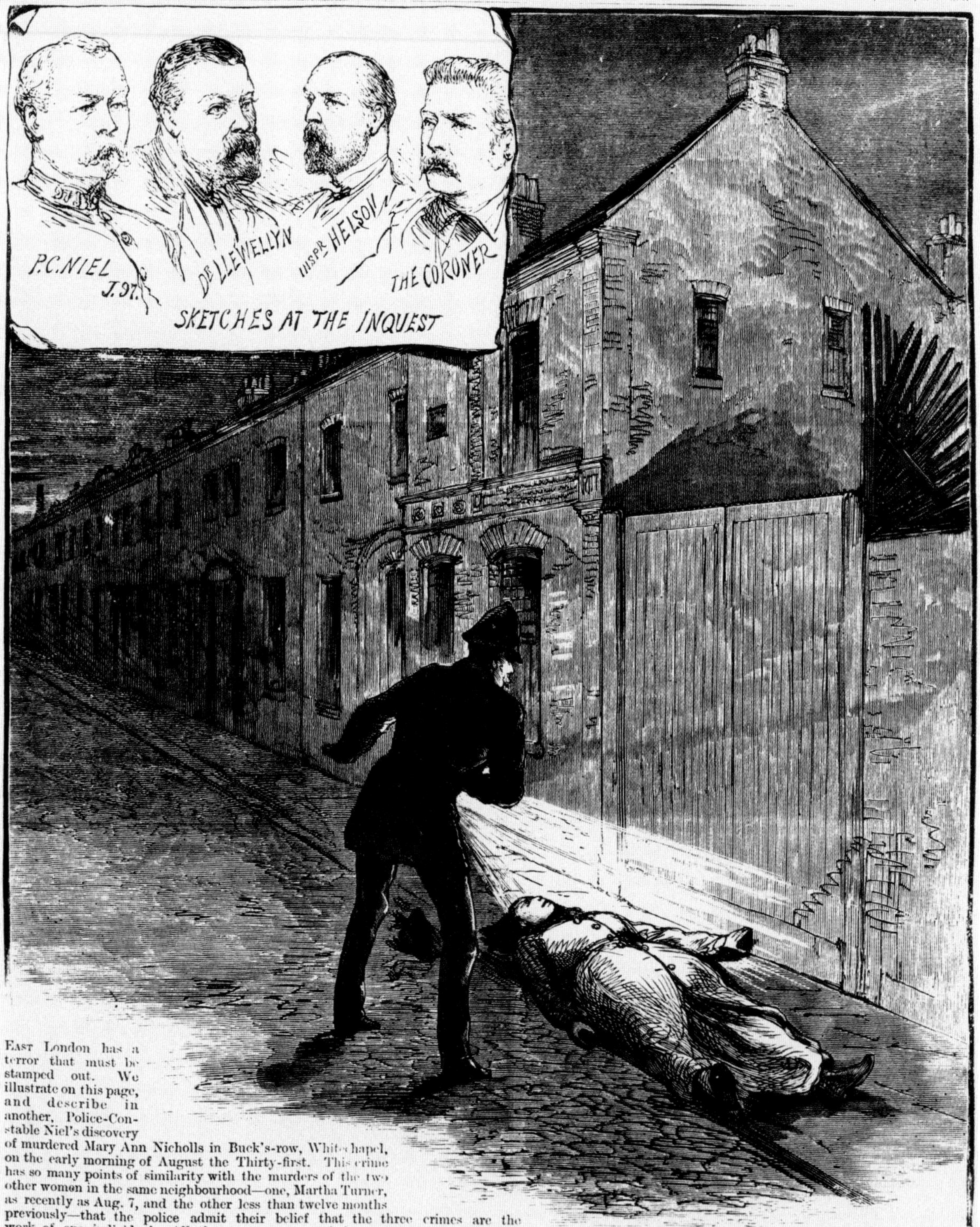
P.C. NIEL J. 97.
DR. LLEWELLYN
INSPR. HELSON
THE CORONER
SKETCHES AT THE INQUEST

EAST LONDON has a terror that must be stamped out. We illustrate on this page, and describe in another, Police-Constable Niel's discovery of murdered Mary Ann Nicholls in Buck's-row, Whitechapel, on the early morning of August the Thirty-first. This crime has so many points of similarity with the murders of the two other women in the same neighbourhood—one, Martha Turner, as recently as Aug. 7, and the other less than twelve months previously—that the police admit their belief that the three crimes are the work of one individual All three women were of the same class, and each of them was so poor that robbery could have formed no motive for the crime. **The three murders were committed within a distance of 200 yards of each other**

THE WHITECHAPEL MYSTERY.

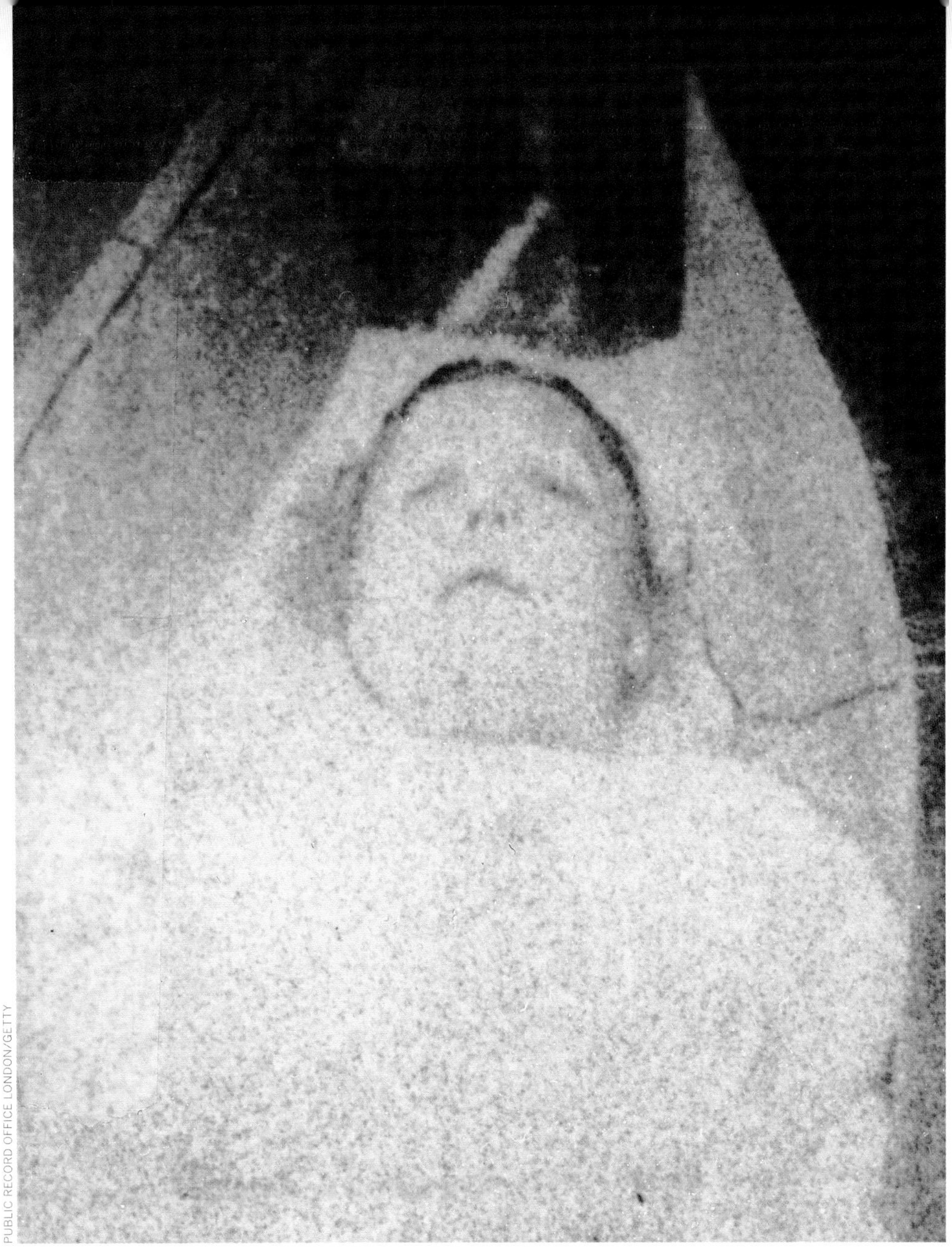

PUBLIC RECORD OFFICE LONDON/GETTY

The writing began early in London's then blossoming, already florid tabloid industry and established Jack's eternal notoriety from the first. Reporters—and their rapt readers—were interested in the savagery of the killings.

darkest part of night and in the city's dankest precinct, preying upon prostitutes . . . Well, that was an impossibly intoxicating narrative, better than the best of Dickens or Austen.

There were patterns to the killings—certain dates, certain days of the week—and this only made the puzzle more intriguing. Eventually, there were more than a hundred cited suspects. A Russian physician and convicted thief named Michael Ostrog . . . another doctor named Montague John Druitt . . . an unstable individual named Aaron Kosminski—they were only the first three mentioned in the initial report of police commissioner Sir Neville Macnaughten. Scores of candidates were put forth later, and their names are still mentioned today. A book to be published in early 2010, *Jack the Ripper's Secret Confession,* pins the killings on textile millionaire Henry Spencer Ashbee, who also allegedly penned, under the pseudonym Walter, the ferociously debauched *My Secret Life*—a stunningly vivid, even microscopic, sexual memoir of a Victorian *(ahem)* gentleman.

The parade of names extends, and Jack lurks in the shadows.

The tabloids went to town (opposite) while the poor victims went to their graves. Above: Mary Ann Nicholas, who is believed to be the second of five women killed by the Ripper in 1888. Right: One of his knives and a framed drawing of one of his victims.

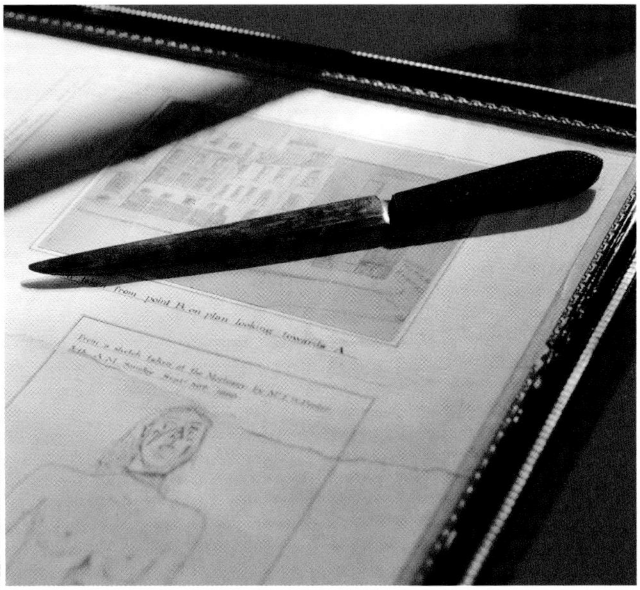
from point B on plan looking towards A

ALEN MACWEENEY/CORBIS

Was Émile Zola Murdered?

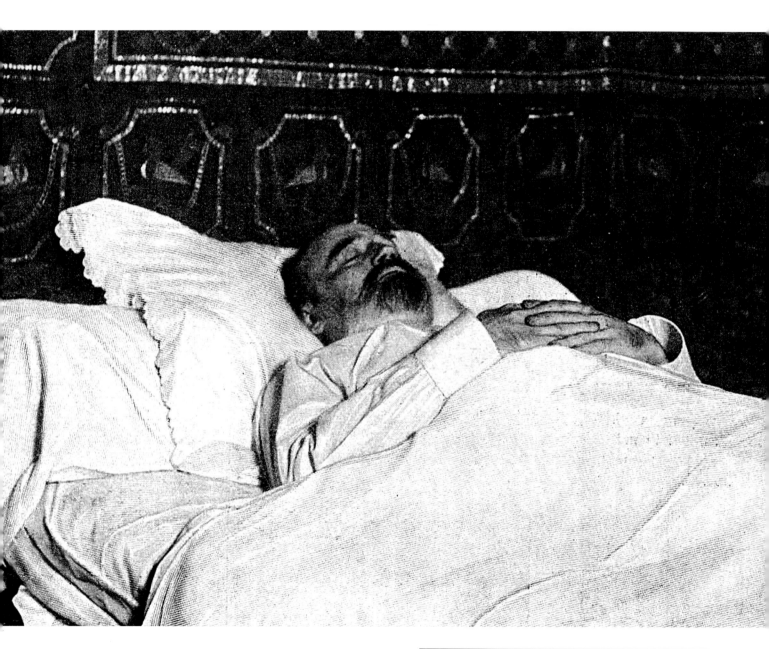

Zola was on the floor when killed by the fumes; later he was transferred to a sofa in the study (above). His wife, Alexandrine, recovered in time to attend his funeral (opposite), where she was joined by hundreds of Parisians in mourning the great man.

On September 29, 1902, the most celebrated French writer of his generation, a deeply philosophical and political man with many friends and some fierce enemies, died at age 62 in his house in the rue de Bruxelles in Paris. He and his wife, Alexandrine, had

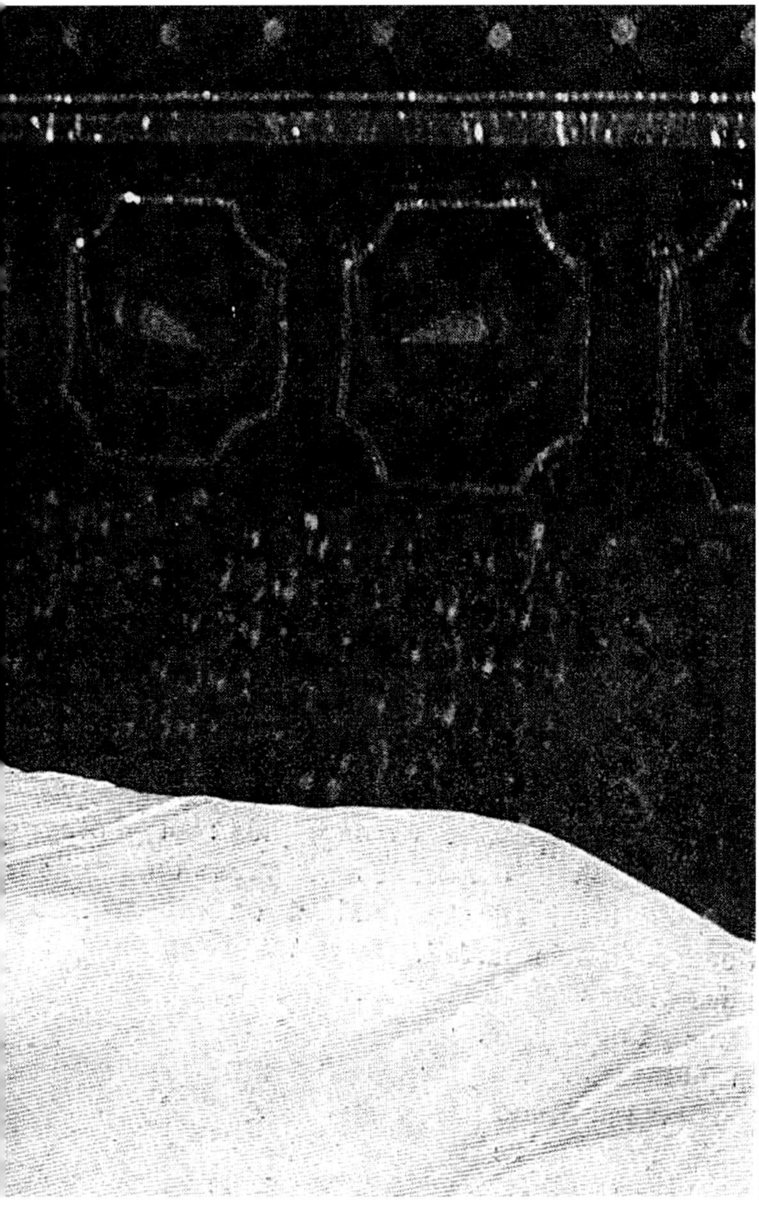

PHOTO 12/THE IMAGE WORKS

returned from a stay in the country and, as it was a chill evening, had built a fire in the stove in their bedroom before retiring. Zola locked the bedroom door, as was his nightly habit since death threats had been made against him. The fireplace was faulty; perhaps a stopped-up chimney was to blame. At three o' clock in the morning, both Émile and his wife were feeling ill. Some time later, he rose to open a window. He fell and passed out on the floor, where the carbon monoxide concentration was greatest. If Alexandrine tried to raise him, she was unable to and fell back in the bed. When the door to the bedroom was broken open at 9:30 that morning, she was unconscious and he was beyond being revived; their two dogs had survived only because they had slept on the bed and on a chair, respectively—thus raised above the worst of the poisonous fumes.

Zola locked the bedroom door, as was his nightly habit since death threats had been made against him.

Alexandrine would recover quickly enough, and among the first people she would inform of her husband's death was Jeanne Rozerot, Zola's mistress of 14 years standing, and the two children Jeanne had borne via her affair, Denise, 13, and Jacques, 11. (Alexandrine was relatively okay with this situation; remember, we're talking about France.) Jeanne, 27 years younger than the late writer, was the first to cry "Murder!"

She had ample reason for suspicion. Her lover had been detested by many in the French government's hierarchy since 1898, when he published in *L'Aurore* newspaper his letter-cum-essay "J'accuse," a defense of Captain Alfred Dreyfus, who was being held on Devil's Island for divulging military secrets to Germany. In the ensuing

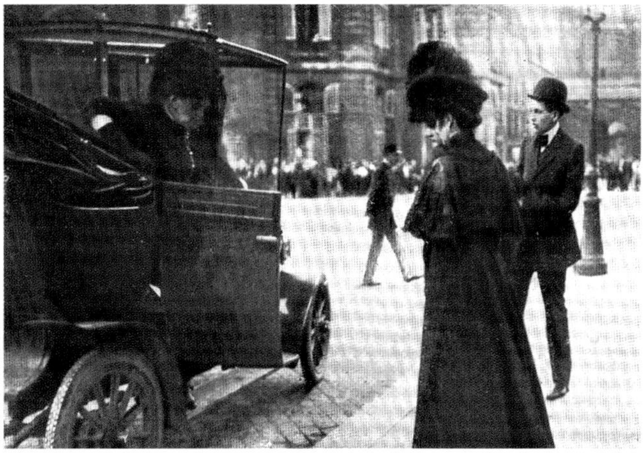

YLI COLLECTION/SIPA

controversy, Dreyfus would be justly exonerated and released—but Zola would be forevermore hated by some.

It is probable, at the end of the day, that this dramatic man's dramatic life closed with an accidental asphyxiation. But the idea that he was done in by his enemies—that they plugged the chimney or jimmied the stove—lingers in the minds of conspiracy theorists. There are few cases of authors who might have been dispatched for their writings, and so we cling to this one.

The Daily Picayune.

UNION · JUSTICE · CONFIDENCE

VOL. LXXVII — NEW ORLEANS, LA., WEDNESDAY, APRIL 23, 1913. — NO. 89

MRS. DUNBAR SAYS COLUMBIA BOY IS LONG-LOST CHILD

Opelousas Mother, After Second Inspection, Makes Identity Complete.

"YOU ARE MY MAMMA," CRIES LITTLE TOT

Joy of the Woman So Great Over Recovery of Lad That She Falls in Dead Faint.

DEMONSTRATION IS HELD

Automobile Parade Preceded by Brass Band, and Prominent Citizens Make Speeches.

COLUMBIA, MISS., April 22.—(Special.)—This morning at 8 o'clock Mrs. C. P. Dunbar positively identified the boy who was found in the possession of William Walters last Sunday as her own. "Bobbie," as the child is popularly called now, was brought here this morning from West Columbia, where he had been left in the care of

ROBERT DUNBAR,
From a Picture Taken at the Time of the Child's Disappearance in August, 1912.

Jeff Wallace for the night, for his mother to make a final examination of him.

The child was taken out to the summer home of W. E. Lampton, two miles east of here, where Mr. and Mrs. Dunbar had repaired for a brief rest before facing the trying ordeal. Here, in the quiet and peace of the country home, away from the curious throngs, the mother took the child, which fought her at first, and talked to it as only a mother can, and won its confidence.

Suddenly, while Mrs. Dunbar was still fondling and talking with "Bobbie," he threw his arms about Mrs. Dunbar's neck, kissing her, and cried:

"YOU ARE MY MAMMA!"

"You are my mamma," and "I have been lost."

Then a scene was enacted that will long remain in the memory of those who were present. The joy of the mother was so great that she fell in a dead faint. Friends soon revived her, and soon "Bobbie" was telling her of his former life, calling the names of his brothers.

He told of the "big white house" in which he used to live at Opelousas, La., and of the "big town with lots

Continued on Third Page.

WOODLAWN BREAK 1,000 FEET WIDE; TRAINS ANNULLED

Mississippi Flood Waters Rapidly Spread Throughout Three Counties.

CREVASSE IS STILL CAVING AT TWO ENDS

Towns of Mayersville and Rolling Fork and Other Places Are Partially Inundated.

RELIEF WORK IS PROMPT

Hundred Thousand Rations Issued by Government—Refugee Camp Established at Vicksburg.

VICKSBURG, MISS., April 22.—Having widened beyond a thousand feet, the Woodlawn crevasse continues caving slowly on either end and the rushing waters, which have rapidly spread throughout the Counties of Issaquena, Sharkey and part of Washington, have also invaded the towns of Mayersville and Rolling Fork and various other smaller places in the path of the flood will soon be under water.

Official announcement was made today that the Yazoo and Mississippi Valley Railroad train service north of here was annulled, following the 8 o'clock train, which was the last to leave for Greenville.

Captain W. B. Baker, U.S.A., has issued 100,000 rations to various points north of here to provide for approximately 10,000 persons whom it is believed will be affected, in addition to which the issuing of rations from the steamer Nokomis, at the scene of the Woodlawn crevasse, will be added to the prompt relief work.

VICKSBURG RELIEF CAMP.

Captain Baker announced that after a conference with Governor Brewer and Mayor Hayes, a relief and refugee camp is to be established at Vicksburg. Mayor Hayes is appointed to take charge of the local relief work. Rations and food for stock have been sent to the following points in anticipation of the needs which will occur: Rolling Fork, Mayersville, Blanton, Fitlers, Valley Park, Browns Point, Flowerree, Rodney, Ashland, Urcina, Smedes and several other points.

Captain Shaw, of the steamer Ben-Hur, said there is no panic at the scene of the break, and there are still some "dry spots" in and around Mayersville. He does not believe there will be any hasty exodus from that locality, and says that most of the negroes have been taken out and are on the levees and other high points waiting to see what the "water will do."

Captain Shaw had a conference with Mayor Hayes and Captain Baker, to whom he said:

MAYERSVILLE HOLDS OUT.

"We turned aside freight and passenger going north, hurrying to the scene of the break, and I was glad to find upon arrival that things did not seem to be as bad as first reported. The water is not spreading so rapidly as far as I could see at Mayersville, and there are lots of dry spots there yet.

"The steamer Nokomis is back in the bend near the break, and from there is doing relief and rescue work, and a number of negroes have been brought out to the levees from the overflowed section. There were reports of several being drowned, but these reports were

Continued on Second Page.

FREE MILK
HAVE YOU CHILDREN OF YOUR OWN?

MILK OF HUMAN KINDNESS.

CONFEDERATE VET LOSES HIS BRIDE

Romance That Began at Macon Reunion Cruelly Shattered at Magnolia.

BISBEE IS STRANDED

"Colonel" Turns Out to Be Inmate of Texas Soldiers' Home—Mrs. Scott Disgusted.

MAGNOLIA, MISS., April 22.—(Special.)—"Colonel" Chester M. Bisbee, of Texas, who came here to be married to Mrs. Myra Scott last Wednesday—and was married to her Thursday, at McComb—is stranded here, and a popular subscription is being made up to get him to New Orleans, where he claims to have friends.

Mrs. Bisbee, a lady of refinement and culture, mother of four grown sons and a daughter, of Auburn, Ind., met "Colonel" Bisbee at Macon, Ga., during the Confederate Reunion there last May. He impressed himself upon her as a man of wealth and standing, and recently when, after persistent correspondence, he proposed marriage by letter, she accepted, although her children vigorously opposed the match.

Still passing himself off as a man of distinction and wealth, "Colonel" Bisbee came here last Wednesday, purchased a license from the circuit clerk on credit, went to McComb, met his bride there by prearrangement, and was married.

INMATE OF TEXAS HOME.

The couple returned here the next day, and on Sunday "Colonel" Bisbee astonished the community by openly appealing to prominent citizens here for financial aid, saying that he was "temporarily embarrassed."

Close questioning of the old gentleman this morning disclosed the fact that Bisbee had no money when he got here. As a matter of fact, he is an inmate of the Old Soldiers' Home at Austin, Tex., and has been for the last nine years.

Mrs. Bisbee discovered that he had deceived her and yesterday separated from him, and the management of the hotel where he was stopping put him out, since it was obvious he could not pay for the service being rendered him. She wired her daughter at Auburn, Ind., of her predicament, and received a reply advising her to go to McComb, where she has relatives, and there await transportation back home, which would be sent her.

CASE OF "BOTH FOOLED."

Humiliated and disgusted, she left last night, declaring that she had seen the last of "Colonel" Bisbee.

"Colonel" Bisbee claimed to be an intimate friend of former United States Senator Bailey and Governor Colquitt, of Texas, and he had in his possession letters recommending him as "a person worthy of consideration" from the city clerk of Austin. A telegram was sent to the latter yesterday afternoon, but up to noon to-day no reply had been received.

"Colonel" Bisbee is 75 years old and his bride is nearly 60. He admitted that he thought she had some property, so it seems to be a case of "both fooled."

He will be sent to New Orleans this afternoon.

Foss to Ferret White Slavers.

BOSTON, April 22.—An investigation of the white slave traffic in this state

BIXBY DECLARES IT'S BLACKMAIL

Los Angeles Millionaire Claims He Was Selected As Victim in White Slave Agitation.

LOS ANGELES, CAL., April 22.—District Attorney McCartney refused today to issue a felony warrant against George H. Bixby, a Long Beach millionaire, in connection with the alleged enslavement of twoscore young girls.

Chief of Police Sebastian demanded the warrant as a result of the story told by Irene Mary Brown Levy, one of the young women who said they were enticed to a lodging-house by Mrs. Josie Rosenburg, the woman now in jail on charges of having acted in behalf of a man known as the "Black Pearl."

Mr. McCartney said he must have evidence corroborating the story of the Brown-Levy girl, and immediately Sebastian brought in two new girls, Jeanette Ellis and Marie Devaughn.

Their narratives resulted in the arrest of Bennie Espey and her alleged associate, W. H. Wood, who were charged with pandering to the "Black Pearl" and his alleged millionaire associates.

Mr. Bixby, who is 49 years old and has a wife and five children, declared he was the victim of an extensive scheme of blackmailing. As head of two banks and director in many corporations, he said, he was selected as an easy victim.

Chief of Police Sebastian said that if the corroborative evidence offered by Jennette Ellis and Marie Devaughn did not cause Mr. McCarthy to issue the felony warrant against Bixby to-day he would take the whole case to the county grand jury.

COLONEL GREEN NO LONGER SEEKS WIFE

ST. LOUIS, MO., April 22.—(Special.) Colonel E. H. G. Green, son of Mrs. Hetty Green, was in St. Louis for forty-five minutes this morning on his way from New York to Texas.

The colonel is still a bachelor. It was two years and a half ago that he told of his desire for a wife—an old-fashioned, modest, stay-at-home, fireside woman, who would not think too much about his money or keep a weather eye on possible alimony.

But the trouble was that the girls all spoke at once. The colonel knew they couldn't all be the kind he wanted, and he became pessimistic as to his chance of finding the right one anywhere in the lot. He therefore to-day declared he was no longer in the matrimonial market.

NEW HAVEN'S $400,000 LOSS.

Dicker With Pullman to Take Over Sleepers Told by Commissioner.

BOSTON, April 22.—An alleged loss to the New York, New Haven and Hartford Railroad of more than $400,000 annually as a result of its recent contract with the Pullman Company, by which the latter took over the parlor and sleeping car service of the Railroad Company, was described by David E. Brown, the examining accountant of the Interstate Commerce Commission to-day. The testimony

LITTLE GIRL DIES IN HEETER STRIKE

Run Down by Car During Demonstration Against Pittsburgh Educator.

THOUSANDS IN MARCH

Committee of Seven Prominent Men Asked to Investigate Alleged Charges of Immorality.

PITTSBURGH, April 22.—The strike of school children against S. L. Heeter as superintendent of the city's public school system spread rapidly to-day and resulted in one death. A little girl was run down by a street car and killed during one of the demonstrations.

Beginning yesterday, when hundreds of children remained away from school as a protest against Heeter, who last Friday was acquitted by a jury of two serious charges preferred by a female domestic employed at his home, the strike gained great proportions to-day. In all parts of the city thousands of school children paraded the streets, tieing up traffic at a number of busy points. Police reserves were called out to maintain order.

Late in the afternoon, when the demonstrations of the children had ceased, the Pittsburgh Board of Education held a meeting, at which a committee of seven prominent men was asked to investigate the various alleged charges of immorality against Superintendent Heeter.

MINISTERS ARE NAMED.

The committee follows: W. H. Stevenson, president of the Chamber of Commerce; Valentine Barle, president of the Iron City Central Trades Council; Bishop Cortlandt Whitehead, of the Pittsburgh Episcopal diocese; A. Leo Weil, president of the Voters' League of Pittsburgh; Bishop J. Regis Canevin, of the Pittsburgh Roman Catholic diocese; Rev. George W. Shelton, pastor of the Second Presbyterian Church and president of the Ministerial Union, and Rev. Dr. J. L. Levy, rabbi of the Rodeph Shalom Synagogue.

The unique strike of the children caused the police considerable inconvenience. A score of the youthful marchers were detained at the various police stations until their parents could be notified.

CHILD KILLED BY CAR.

One little girl was run over and killed by a street car during the excitement occasioned by one of the parades.

Charles McCool, aged 35, was arrested in front of a school building and charged with disorderly conduct. He is alleged to have been attempting to prevent children from entering school.

William Slater, aged 67, was taken into custody charged with inciting a riot. Slater and several women attacked two officers who were breaking up banners carried by children inscribed "Kick Heeter Out."

Banners of all description, some of them inflammatory, are in evidence all over the city. At a number of points during the day Heeter was hanged and burned in effigy.

There were few demonstrations tonight. In all police districts reserves were held for eventualities. Police

BULGARIANS AND GREEKS RAPIDLY NEARING A WAR

Clash Expected Between Rival Allies Over Possession of Saloniki.

HELLENIC SOLDIERS BACKED BY SERVIA

Monenegrins Resume Efforts to Take Scutari and Fall of City Is Thought Imminent.

HEAVY ARTILLERY USED

Belief That Frontier Was Closed and Wire Service Suspended to Prevent Powers' Interference.

LONDON, April 22.—Pending conclusion of a formal armistice covering the operrtions of all the allies, the Montenegrins are renewing their desperate efforts to capture Scutari, the fall of which, according to an official report issued at Cettinje, is imminent.

There is no confirmation of the story from Triest that owing to the exhaustion of food the commander of Scutari is endeavoring to negotiate for its surrender, but a Belgrade dispatch says the Montenegrins still have all the Servian heavy artillery before Scutari and are employing it in their present attack, although the Servian troops have either left or are leaving that district. It is stated that Montenegro is endeavoring to arrange with Servia for the purchase of this artillery.

COMMUNICATION CUT OFF.

It is supposed that the Montenegrin Government has closed the frontier and suspended postal and telegraph service in order to prevent interference on the part of the powers until Scutari falls.

A report published at Bucharest says that under the settlement arranged at St. Petersburg, Rumania will receive Silistria with about two miles of territory around the town and the right to erect fortifications.

Bulgaria and Greece are rapidly drifting towards war over the possession of Saloniki, according to the Chronicle's correspondent at that town.

The Greeks have mobilized every available soldier and concentrated one army in the neighborhood of Saloniki, while another is being landed at Orfani, in the Gulf of Orfani, to watch movements of Bulgarians at Drama and Kavala.

SERBS SUPPORT GREEKS.

The victorious Epirus army from Janina is being distributed along the strategic front of Saloniki to Orfani.

In the meantime, adds the correspondent, the Bulgarians have suspended passenger traffic between Dedeagatch and Saloniki and are utilizing the railway for concentration of troops in the neighborhood of Drama close to the Greek position.

They have already brought one division each from Adrianople, Tchatalja and Bulair, and it is estimated that the Bulgars now have 90,000 soldiers facing the Greeks and a Servian force, supporting the Greeks, which is assembling along the railway north of Saloniki and on the right side of the Vadar River.

FINDS 1861 NICKEL IN YOLK OF EGG

Housewife at Camden, N. J., Also Discovers Buckshot—Grocer Wants Coin Returned.

CAMDEN, N. J., April 22.—(Special.)—Rebate eggs are the latest thing. They were laid in this city, which made the Quakers famous. Even the hens are protesting against the high cost of living and are now trying sabotage to make the poultry farmers, middle men and others realize that they will not stand for the ultimate consumer being held up for their lay.

The first appearance of the rebate egg came when Mrs. George Simpson, of 2725 Concord Street, broke an egg which she had just bought at a grocer's where they are sold by weight. The egg weighed five ounces, and she thought she was getting a bargain, and paid 6 cents for it. She also paid the same amount for eleven other eggs which weighed less.

Mrs. Simpson decided to make a cake with the "strictly new-laid" eggs when she reached home. The first one she broke was the one that weighed five ounces. There was a click as she broke it in a bowl.

Looking to see what had caused the noise she saw a dark circular object in the yolk. It proved to be a 5-cent piece minted in 1861. This does not signify, however, that it was a new coin when the hen swallowed it.

Besides the nickel she found a buck-

BASEBALL 'TRUST' BRANDED AS THE MOST AUTOCRATIC

Gallagher Would Probe Operations of National Commission.

CONTRACT SYSTEM TARGET OF ATTACK

Resolution Directs Attorney General to Seek Out Violations of the Sherman Law.

HORACE FOGEL BEHIND CASE

Conference Planned With Senator Hoke Smith, Who Has Copy of "Ty" Cobb's Contract.

WASHINGTON, April 22.—Characterizing organized baseball as "the most audacious and autocratic trust in the country," Representative Gallagher, of Illinois, to-day introduced a resolution for an exhaustive inquiry into the operations of the National Baseball Commission by a special committee of Congress, and would also direct the attorney general to investigate the baseball contract system with a view to instituting prosecutions for violation of the Sherman antitrust law.

Mr. Gallagher expressed a willingness to co-operate with any other member of Congress interested in any specific case and planned to confer with Senator Hoke Smith, of Georgia, who, upon request, was forwarded a copy of "Ty" Cobb's contract with the Detroit club. Senator Smith wants to examine the terms of Cobb's contract.

ASKS PROBE COMMITTE.

The resolution would direct the speaker to appoint a special committee of seven to investigate "the operation and practices of the baseball trust" to ascertain whether:

"Unjust discriminations have been practiced in favor of or against players; whether players are now or have been prejudiced, coerced or restrained from the exercise of their just rights to enter into contracts of a fair and equitable nature; whether such a combination has been effected among baseball magnates throughout the country as would preclude competition and operate in restraint of trade."

This is sought, the resolution sets forth, "because the most audacious and autocratic trust in the country is the one which presumes to control the game of baseball; its officials announcing daily through the press of the country the dictates of a governing commission.

PLAYERS ARE "ENSLAVED."

How competition is stifled; how territory and games are apportioned; how the prices are fixed which millions must pay to witness the sport; how men are enslaved and forced to accept salaries and terms or forever be barred from playing, and of other acts incident to trafficking in a national pastime for pecuniary gain."

Representative Gallagher has been in correspondence regarding his resolution with Horace Fogel, former owner of the Philadelphia National League team. Fogel, in a recent letter to Congressman Gallagher, said he could put him on the track to "lay the foundation for the investigation and subpoena witnesses necessary to easily make out a clear case to turn over to the Department of Justice for immediate action to bust up this arrogant baseball trust."

FRATERNITY IS NEUTRAL.

NEW YORK, April 22.—The Baseball Players' Fraternity will take no action in the controversy between "Ty" Cobb and the Detroit club unless requested to do so by the parties, and then only as mediator. In so announcing this afternoon David E. Fultz, president of the fraternity, asserted that he regarded the matter as purely a business transaction between Cobb and President Navin, and that it was not only unfair but silly to attack the fraternity for not settling it.

"We have pledged the organization to have every reasonable obligation of the players' contract lived up to by both contracting parties," reads Mr. Fultz's statement, "and we shall do all within our power to see that the contract with the player is not violated.

IS A PRIVATE MATTER.

"But enforcing a contract after made is a very different matter from attempting to dictate to others what the erms of heir contract shall be.

"This whole affair is a private matter between Cobb and Mr. Navin; there are no legal obligations resting on either party. Mr. Cobb has a right to value his services at $15,000 or $150,000, as he chooses, and Mr. Navin has a right to pay it or not, just as he sees fit.

"Should Mr. Navin and Mr. Cobb desire the offices of the fraternity in the settlement of this difference we should be very glad to do what we could, but any attempt to bring pressure to bear upon either party would not only be a violation of our by-laws, but would be contrary to the fundamental purpose of the organization."

SAYS GOOD WILL RESULT.

CINCINNATI, OHIO, April 22.—August Herrmann, chairman of the National Baseball Commission, issued a statement to-day regarding the proposed investigation by Congress, say-

GUIDE TO THE NEWS.

What Happened to Bobby Dunbar?

There would be many claimants for Crime of the Century during the 1900s in the U.S.: the Leopold and Loeb killing, the Lindbergh kidnapping and murder and the O.J. Simpson case being three prominent examples from different time frames. But the disappearance, possible abduction and presumed death of Bobby Dunbar in 1912 was an early candidate.

It was characteristically hot and humid in Opelousas, Louisiana, that August day when Percy and Lessie Dunbar took their family on a group fishing trip to the muddy shores of Swayze Lake. When they and their friends returned to camp for lunch, their four-year-old son, Bobby, apparently wandered off. He was not seen again that day—and perhaps nevermore.

We say "perhaps," for this is a most confusing case, one worthy of any collection of unsolved mysteries. Percy Dunbar was a man of no small means, having succeeded in real estate and insurance sales, and so he hired a detective and printed up flyers that were circulated from Texas to Florida: "Large round blue eyes, hair light, but turning dark, complexion very fair with rosy cheeks, well developed, stout but not very fat, big toe on left foot badly scarred from burn when a baby." Eight months later, in April of 1913, a boy in the keep of a drifter, William Cantwell Walters, in Hub, Mississippi, was found who matched the description. The Dunbars sped to the scene and saw a scar on the boy's left foot and a mole on his neck and said, "Yes." Lessie fainted. The boy, initially reluctant to embrace his presumptive parents, eventually realized he might have a better future with the Dunbars and accepted his role as Bobby. Walters, who was facing a possible death sentence if convicted of kidnapping in Louisiana, wrote to the Dunbars: "I know, by now you have Decided, you are wrong it is vary [sic] likely I will Loose my Life on account of that and if I do the Great God will hold you accountable." He claimed in his defense at trial that the boy was Charles Bruce Anderson, the illegitimate son of a woman who had cared for his parents. The trial was monitored nationally with barely less attention and press coverage than would attend the Lindbergh and Simpson cases.

Margaret Dunbar Cutright is the granddaughter of the person who grew up as Bobby Dunbar. She began her research in 1999, and by 2004, when the photograph below was taken during a family reunion—and when the DNA evidence that she lobbied for revealed the startling truth—she had read more than 1,400 newspaper articles about Bobby, tracked down principal relatives of all families concerned and put together the pieces. It was she who cracked the case.

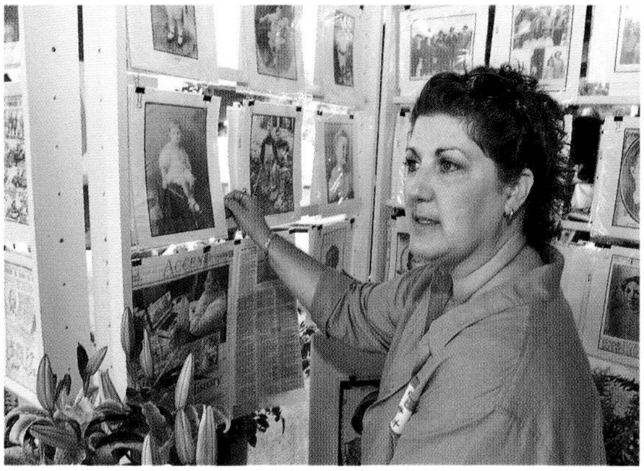

STEVE HUMBERT/THE ROBESONIAN/AP

Walters's imprecations to the Dunbars and the court were unavailing, and he was convicted and sentenced to life in prison. "Bobby Dunbar" grew up, married, fathered children of his own and died in 1966—but never outran the rumors. In 1954 his own son, Bobby Dunbar Jr., asked his dad, "Well, how do you know that you're Bobby Dunbar?"

"I know who I am and I know who you are," the father responded. "And nothing else makes a difference."

Not quite true.

In 2004, Bobby Jr., over the objections of some family members, gave a DNA sample, which was compared with one given by a son of the real Bobby's brother, Alonzo. The results proved that a man had lived his life as a lie and indeed was probably the son of William Walters's brother and a servant who was working for Walters's parents.

Said Bobby Jr., "I have had to do some readjusting of my thinking." And all others who knew of this complex and once famous case were forced to wonder again: What happened to Bobby Dunbar?

THE TIMES-PICAYUNE

Did Rudolf Diesel Commit Suicide?

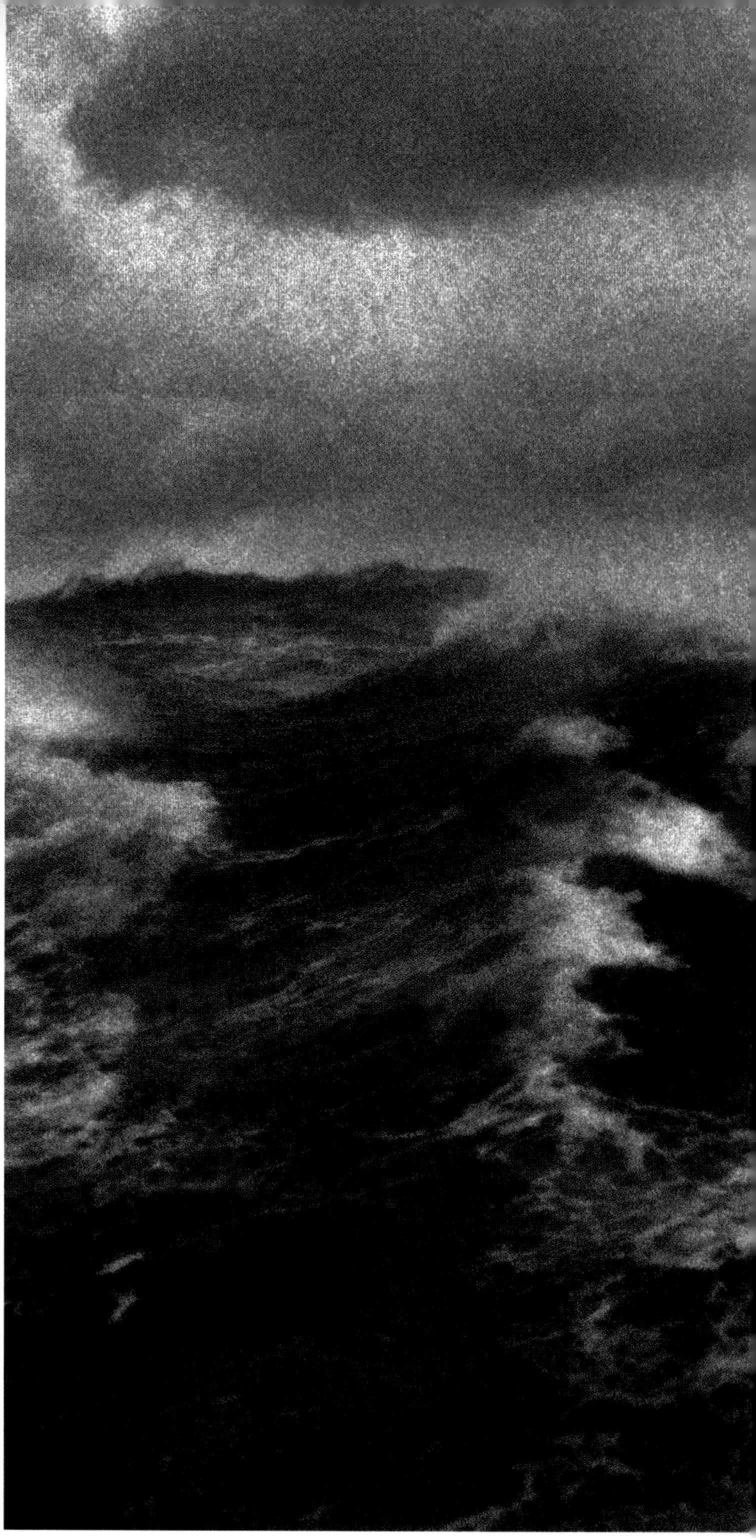
JEAN GAUMY/MAGNUM

It was headline news in 1913: "LONDON, Sept. 30.—Dr. Rudolf Diesel, the famous inventor of the Diesel oil engine, has disappeared in most mysterious circumstances. He left Antwerp yesterday to attend in London the annual meeting of the Consolidated Diesel Engine Manufacturers. He embarked on the steamer *Dresden* . . . On the arrival of the vessel at Harwich at 6 o'clock this morning he was

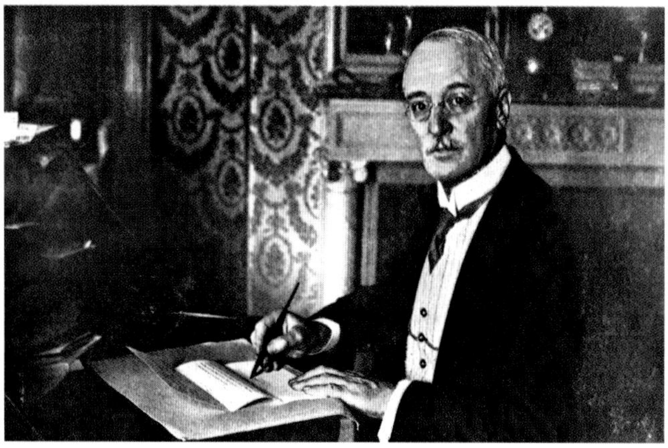
BETTMANN/CORBIS

missing. His bed had not been slept in, though his night attire was laid out on it.

"It is conjectured by his friends that Dr. Diesel fell overboard . . ."

So read the October 1, 1913, dispatch in *The New York Times* under the banner DR. DIESEL VANISHES FROM A STEAMSHIP. There was no need to explain who Dr. Diesel was—he was the inventor and mechanical engineer who was the Edison of the engine, having devised the mechanism that would forever bear his name. He was already world famous, and his death at age 55 reverberated.

He grew up in France, the son of German-born immigrants. With the advent of the Franco-Prussian War of 1870, the family hastened to London. He was sent away to private school in Germany and showed an inclination and precocious brilliance for

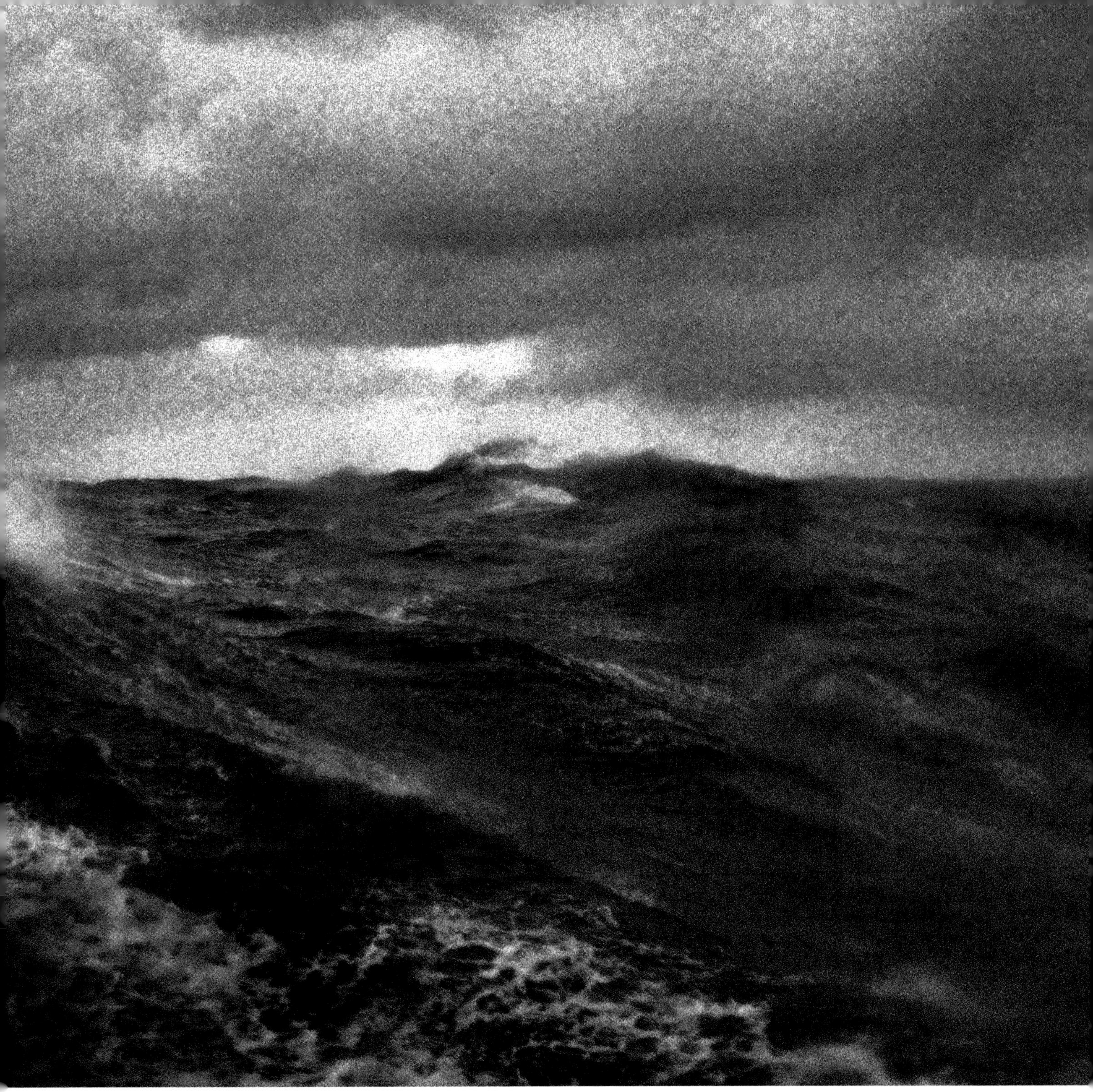

engineering. In the 1890s, working in Berlin, he developed his revolutionary ideas for an internal combustion engine to replace—or at least improve upon—the steam piston engine.

That's the nutshell biography. The death requires as much explication, even if it fails to lead us to a conclusion.

As the *Times* account indicates, he went missing, almost certainly overboard in the English Channel. Although associates said that he had been recently cheerful, the sturdiest suspicion is that the cause of death was suicide; the support for this theory was an earlier mental breakdown. But Diesel's family was emphatic that he had been murdered. As his innovative technology might have threatened the petroleum monopoly, there would be business reasons to push him over the rail. Then, too, the Germans might have wanted to kill Diesel, whose inventions might have profited Great Britain in the looming Great War.

Opposite: The inventor in a portrait made circa 1912. Above: The watery deep of the English Channel where he came to rest.

The intrigues are, all these years later, still intriguing. And the answers remain elusive.

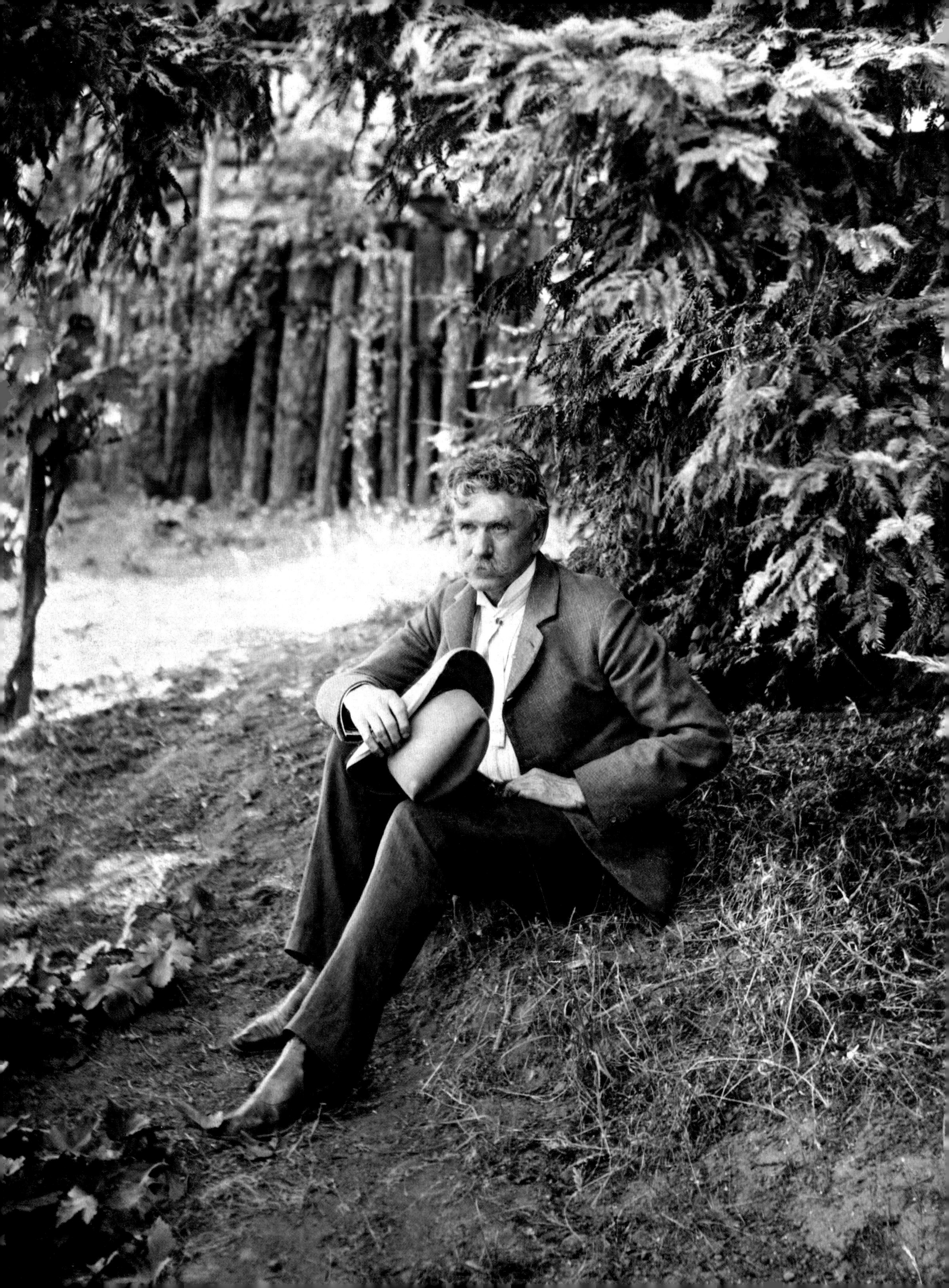

How, When and Where Did Ambrose Bierce Die?

The native Ohioan, born in 1842, grew to become one of the most famous, most popular and most controversial literary figures in the land. After fighting gallantly for the Union in the Civil War, during which time he saw some horrific things and was seriously wounded—experiences that would inform his later writings—Bierce launched his journalism career in San Francisco. Eventually he would become one of the first regular columnists of William Randolph Hearst's *San Francisco Examiner,* and his influence became great. As a critic, he could be caustic, and he found himself with a nationally known nickname: Bitter Bierce.

His personal life probably contributed to his cynical worldview. His two sons both died young, one shot during a fight over a woman and the other from pneumonia exacerbated by his alcoholism. Bierce left his wife after he found letters written to her by a suitor. So he had reason to look at life with a jaundiced eye.

But while his editorials were meant to pierce and wound, he wrote as well several wonderful, realistic and moving short stories, many rooted in his military experience, including "An Occurrence at Owl Creek Bridge," "Killed at Resaca" and "Chickamauga."

War was on his mind when he embarked in the fall of 1913 on a tour of battlefields where he had once fought. He kept traveling all the way to Texas, and at El Paso, he crossed into Mexico. At 71 years old, he found himself drawn by the rebel Pancho Villa's ongoing revolution—he was seeking "the good, kind darkness." It is known that he

In this portrait from the late 1800s (opposite), Bierce is probably pictured in California. On this page are Pancho Villa's men fighting federal troops near Torreon, Mexico, in early 1914, at about the time Bierce was with them.

had hooked up with the rebel troops, and what happened to him thereafter is a mystery. One theory is that he was killed at the siege of Ojinaga in January of 1914, and a letter he wrote to his cousin Lora certainly implied that he knew himself to be in harm's way: "Good-bye—if you hear of my being stood up against a Mexican stone wall and shot to rags please know that I think that a pretty good way to depart this life. It beats old age, disease, or falling down the cellar stairs. To be a Gringo in Mexico—ah, that is euthanasia." Another hypothesis has Bierce crossing back into the States and killing himself at the Grand Canyon. Another letter that he wrote back home near the end of his life said that he was "going away to South

> "Good-bye—if you hear of my being stood up against a Mexican stone wall and shot to rags please know that I think that a pretty good way to depart this life. It beats old age, disease, or falling down the cellar stairs."

America, and have not the faintest notion when I shall return," and this has become part of the version that has Bierce being held captive and maybe killed by a tribe of Brazilian natives.

Carlos Fuentes's novel *The Old Gringo,* later a film, was an account of Bierce's last days. It, at least, is known to be fiction.

GRANGER

BETTMANN CORBIS

How Did Rasputin Die?

In a small Siberian village near the frigid Tura River, Grigori Yefimovich Rasputin was born into a peasant family in the winter of 1869. It is said that his otherness—his charisma, his mystical powers—were evident even in boyhood, but in truth not much is known about Rasputin's earliest years beyond the fact that his sister drowned and his brother also died young, of pneumonia, greatly affecting the surviving sibling. He spent three months in a monastery at age 18, coming into contact with the Khlyst sect, who believed that to be redeemed one must first engage in sin. So the sect's followers practiced ritualistic flagellations and sexual orgies—to fall that they might rise. Shortly after his time in the monastery, two events changed Rasputin's life: He reportedly saw the Mother of God, and he definitely fell under the thrall of a holy man, Makariy, whose hut was not far from the monastery. Makariy cast his spell on the young man, who came out of Siberia in 1901 to travel the world as a *strannik,* or pilgrim. He went to Greece and Jerusalem, and then he returned to Russia. Father Grigori's reputation there as a mystic grew quickly, and in 1905 the royal Romanov family, headed by Czar Nicholas II and Czarina Alexandra, implored Rasputin to help in the treatment of the heir to the throne, Alexei, who was suffering from hemophilia. Rasputin prayed, he perhaps practiced hypnosis, and he offered some pretty simple advice, such as "Let him rest." The boy eventually got better, and Czar Nicholas proclaimed Rasputin a "holy man" and, more consequentially for all concerned, "our friend."

A friend, as it eventuated, of increasing and ultimately vast influence. Rasputin came to control access to the royal family, and this soon caused friction with many people of stature in St. Petersburg. Prime Minister Peter Stolypin was no fan of the Mad Monk and was moving to bring him down through scandal—he was accumulating evidence of Rasputin's illicit sexual behavior—when he himself was assassinated while attending the opera in 1911. Had Nicholas ordered the hit? It was never proved but was suspected.

After his son got better, Czar Nicholas proclaimed the healer Rasputin a "holy man" and, more consequentially for all concerned, "our friend."

The so-called Mad Monk had an eerie gaze like no other (opposite), but Czar Nicholas II and Czarina Alexandra came to trust him implicitly after his ministrations supposedly saved the life of their son, Alexei, heir to the throne. Below: The royal couple is trailed by their boy, who is being carried by a man believed to be Rasputin.

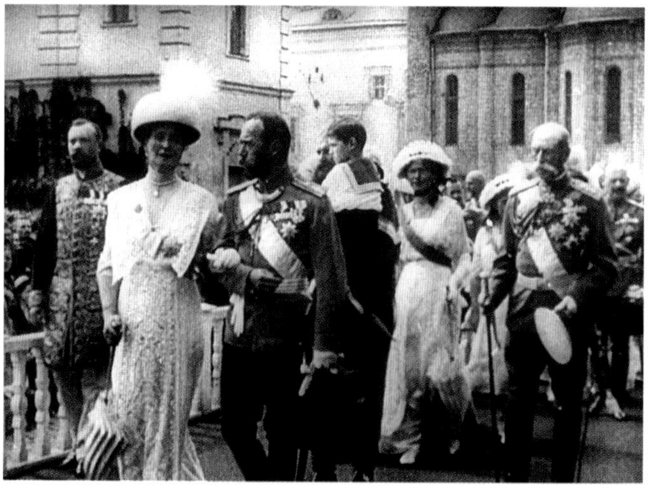

TOPHAM/THE IMAGE WORKS

It was not only Rasputin but all of the Romanovs whose rosters of enemies were growing, as civil unrest became more widespread with Russia's entry into World War I in 1914, consequently draining the economy; the czarina, who was of German descent, was even

TOPICAL PRESS/GETTY

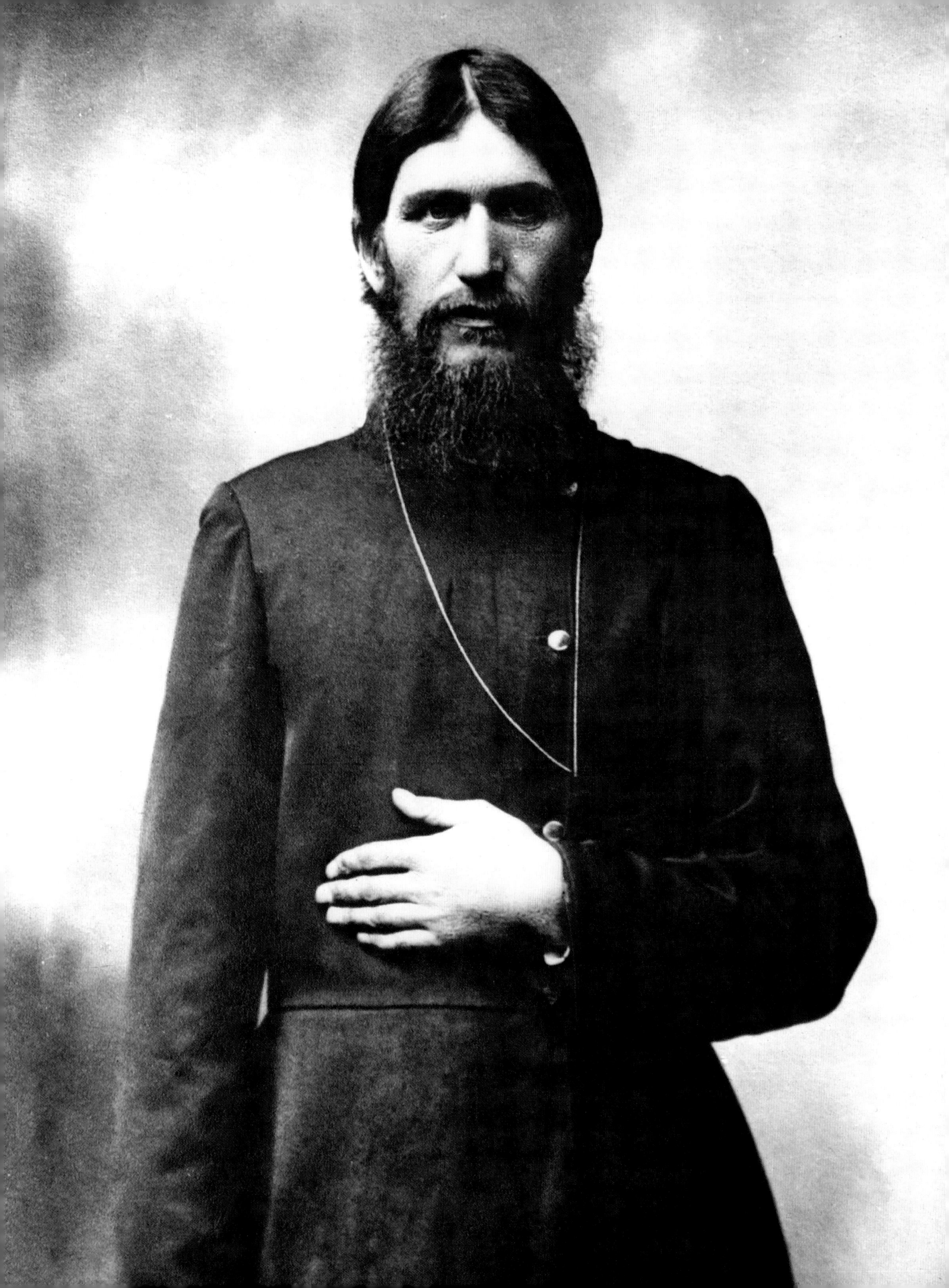

accused in this period of spying for the enemy. Rasputin told the czar that a revelation he had experienced indicated Nicholas himself should go and lead the army, which the czar did. With "Papa" away, Rasputin became Alexandra's top adviser and essentially a coruler, and in this role stacked the government with cronies who either would do his bidding or had paid him bribes. Meantime, he continued to cohabitate with myriad women in the capital, and his notorious and very public behavior, influenced routinely by way too much alcohol, appalled many, including Prince Felix Yusupov.

Yusupov invited Rasputin to come to his palace in the early morning hours of December 17, 1916. Yusupov and his coconspirators and a plateful of cakes and wine laced with enough cyanide to kill several men awaited. When the poison seemed to have no effect on Rasputin (it may have burned off in cooking), Yusupov shot the monk in the back. Rasputin fell. Yusupov and company went to another room to celebrate the deed, then the prince retuned to check on the body and was horrified when Rasputin opened his eyes—"the green eyes of a viper," Yusupov later recalled—and tried to flee. Rasputin was chased into the backyard, shot twice more and beaten with a club. His body was bound and thrown into the Neva River. When the corpse was found three days later, a fourth bullet hole was noticed in Rasputin's forehead, but the arms were in an upright position as if he had died clawing at the ice above him. The official cause of death at the

Below: Courtiers of the Russian czar surround the mystic, who had quite a thing for the ladies. Opposite: Prince Felix Yusupov, the principal plotter against Rasputin, and the icy surface of the Neva River in St. Petersburg, which can be regarded as the lid of Rasputin's casket.

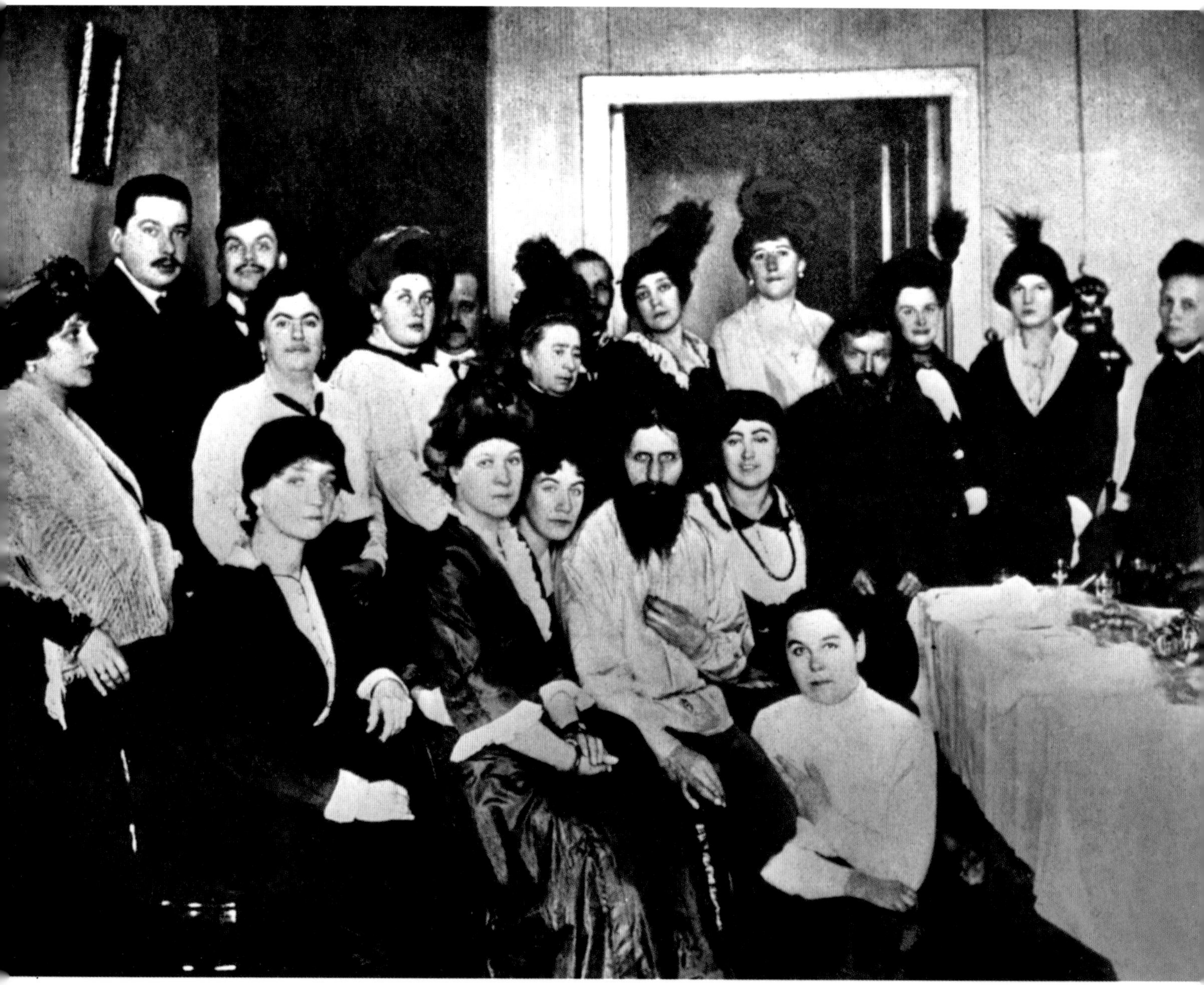

time was listed as hypothermia.

Case closed?

No.

First, the accounts of Yusupov and other eyewitnesses differed in detail and in fact changed over time. And there has arisen at least one other intriguing theory: Rasputin had been arguing for a withdrawal of Russian troops from the Eastern front. This was

When the corpse was found, it was said that the arms were in an aspect that indicated Rasputin had died while clawing at the ice above him.

of concern to the British, who were entangled with Germany on the Western front. There was a British intelligence officer, Oswald Rayner, stationed in St. Petersburg at the time, who'd been acquainted with Yusupov when the two studied together at Oxford. Furthermore, it seems that the shot to the forehead, which could have been lethal, involved a different type of bullet from the other three in Rasputin's corpse—a type used by the British but not the Russians. There are reports that upon returning to England, Rayner said he had been present the night Rasputin died, but we'll probably never know whether London conspired in the killing since Rayner burned all his papers before his death in 1961.

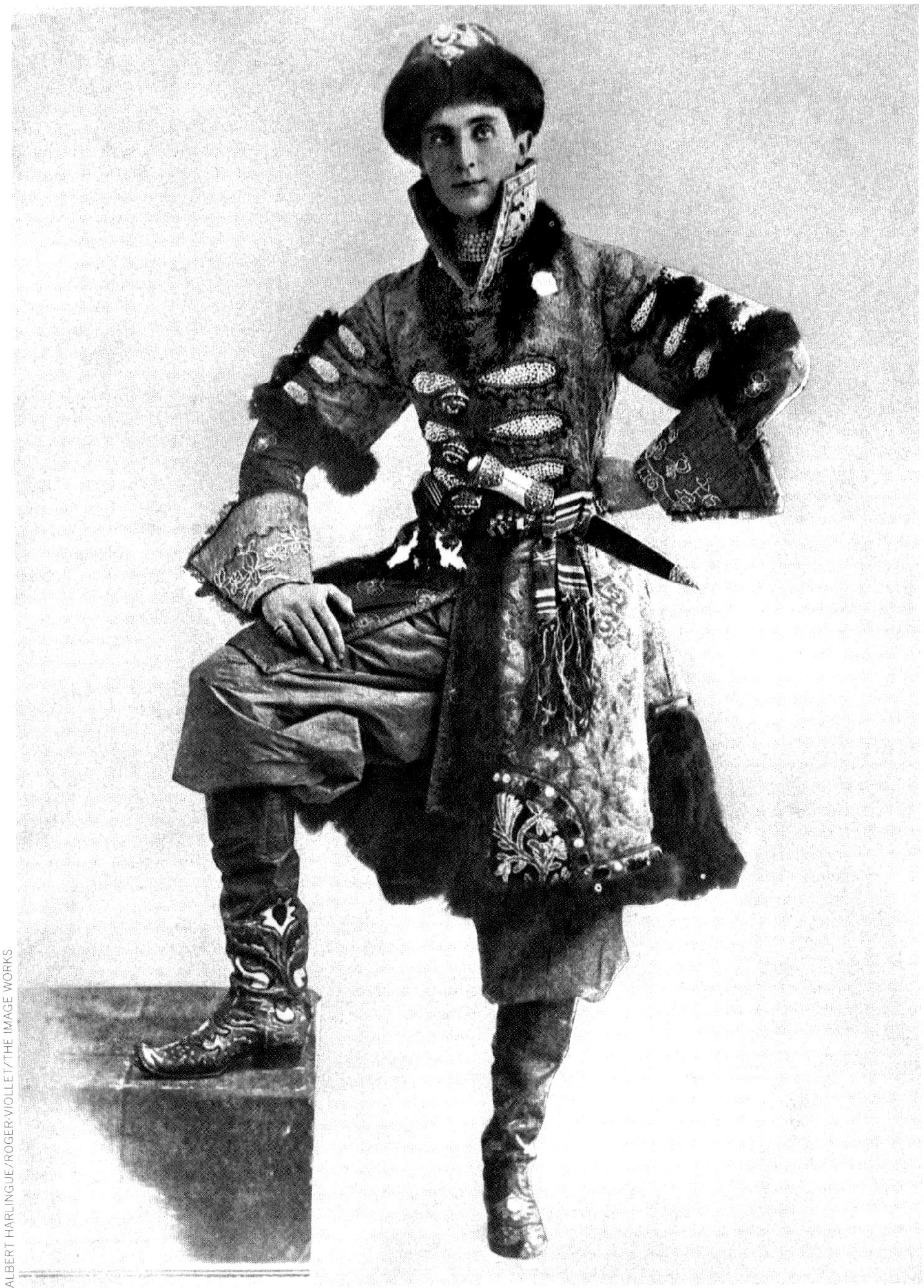

ALBERT HARLINGUE/ROGER-VIOLLET/THE IMAGE WORKS

A letter from Rasputin supposedly written only weeks before he was killed predicted that he would be murdered before the year was out and further prophesied: "Czar of the land of Russia, if you hear the sound of the bell which will tell you that Grigori has been killed, you must know this: If it was your relations who have wrought my death, then no one in the family, that is to say, none of your children or relations, will remain alive for more than two years. They will be killed by the Russian people."

Yusupov was married to a niece of the czar and therefore was a relation. Did the mystic's final vision play out? Turn the page.

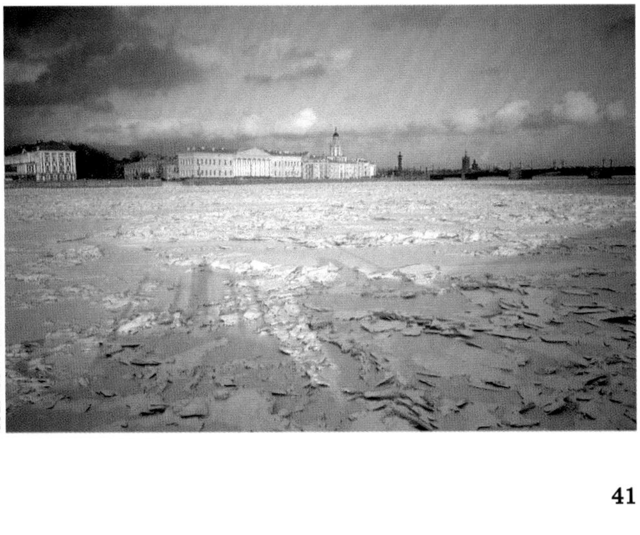

GUEORGUI PINKHASSOV/MAGNUM

HULTON/GETTY

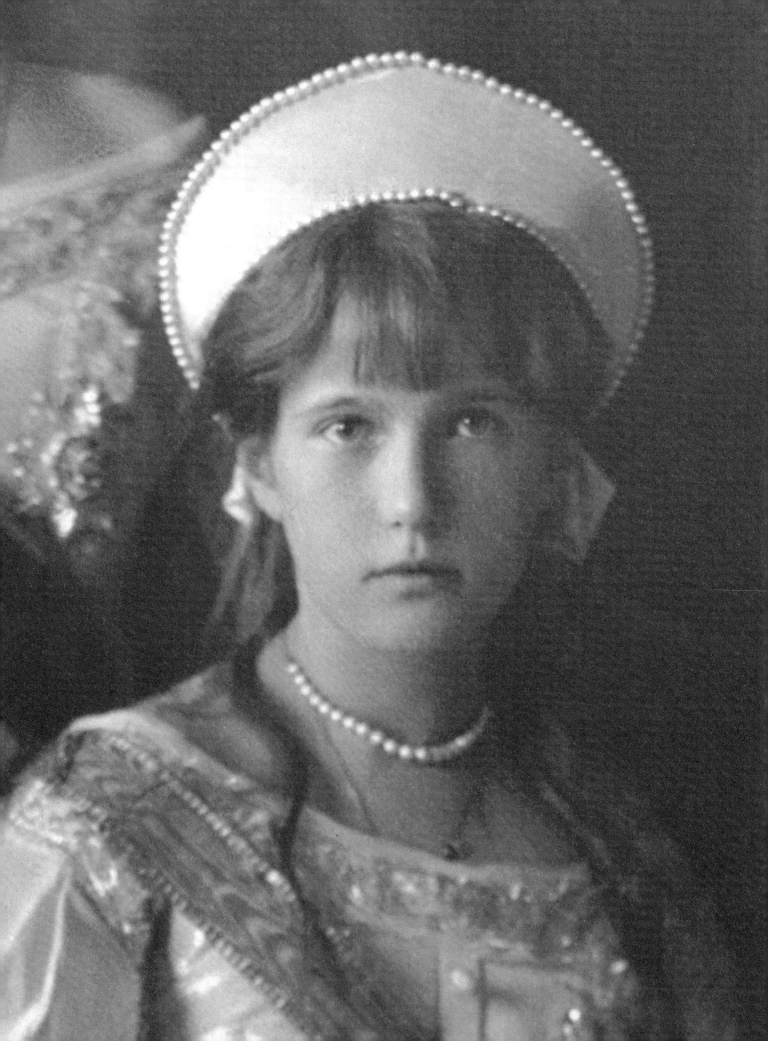

Did Anastasia Survive?

The Romanov family, whom we just met in our account of Rasputin's death, had ruled Russia for more than 300 years—Nicholas II had ruled for 23 years—but now, in 1917, the Romanovs were in deep, deep trouble. World War I had claimed more than a million Russian lives, the country's economy was in tatters, and the Bolsheviks were on the march. The age of the czars was about to end forevermore.

The family of the last czar consisted of Nicholas II and his wife, Alexandra, four daughters—the Grand Duchesses Olga, Tatiana, Maria and Anastasia—and that one son, Alexei, the heir to the throne.

The birth of Anastasia Nikolaevna on June 18, 1901, greatly distressed her father, who had been hoping for a boy to extend the Romanov reign. But the young girl was not shunned or mistreated by her parents, and by all accounts grew into a spirited, engaging, mischievous and endlessly entertaining child. She would play pranks on her siblings and tutors; Gleb Botkin, the son of the court physician and a man who would be executed along with the Romanovs, once observed, "She undoubtedly held the record for punishable deeds in her family, for in naughtiness she was a true genius."

During World War I, she and her sister Maria, not yet old enough to serve as nurses, would visit the wounded in the hospital and try to offer good cheer. One of the wounded was Felix Dassel, who remembered that Anastasia had a "laugh like a squirrel."

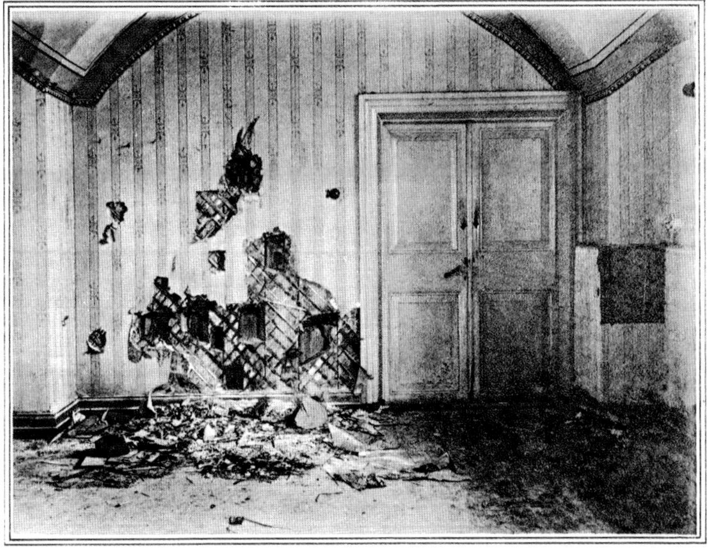

MARY EVANS PICTURE LIBRARY/THE IMAGE WORKS

The portrait of the lovely young grand duchess on the opposite page was taken circa 1910, about eight years before her family was shot to death in the room in Yekaterinburg (above). Bodies were found near there on two separate later occasions, even as would-be Anastasias sought fame and perhaps even fortune.

The czar did not resist when revolutionaries demanded that he abdicate in early 1917. The family was placed under house arrest and moved by their Bolshevik captors to various locations, ostensibly for their protection. With the Bolshevik Revolution of October 1917, Russia was plunged into a chaotic civil war, and the fate of the royals became a crucial issue between the insurgents and forces loyal to the czar. The Romanovs were being held at Yekaterinburg as a loyalist army advanced, and in the very early morning of July 17, 1918, the family was awoken and told they were being taken to a location out of harm's way. They and their associates were led to the basement by the guard, and after several minutes, a squad of executioners entered the room; an order was instantly given and a hail of gunfire rent the room. The bodies were buried nearby, and when the loyalists searched Yekaterinburg, the czar and his family were nowhere to be found.

Interestingly, initial reports that some of the children had survived were issued by their captors to placate the Germans, who demanded "the safety of the princesses of German blood," with an assurance that they were in a safe location. This spurred a slew of claims, as the strongest rumor was that 17-year-old Anastasia had escaped. The most famous and persistent of these claimants was Anna Anderson, who pressed a decades-long case in the German courts to prove she was the grand duchess. She eventually lost the court case and subsequently disappointed her many supporters when DNA testing 10 years after her death in 1984 proved she was not a Romanov. In 1991, a mass grave was discovered outside Yekaterinburg, and when it was found to contain the remains of only five members of the family—the boy and a young sister were missing—speculation flared anew. But in 2007, Russian scientists said that two more sets of bones had been located, and DNA tests published in 2009 indicated these remains, too, belonged to the Romanov family.

Sadly, the mathematics finally indicate that the romantic story of Anastasia's escape was just that—a story.

GRANGER

Who Was the Axman of New Orleans?

While Great Britain could make a claim—if for whatever reason it might want to—that the most famous serial killer of all time was the knife-wielding ripper named Jack, the United States has certainly been plagued by more than its fair share of psychopathic, terror-inducing mavens of murder, ranging from the Boston Strangler to the Son of Sam to the Zodiac killer (the latter of whom will make an appearance later in this book, on page 94). An early and now largely forgotten spree murderer was operative in Louisiana for a year and a half beginning in May of 1918 and earned himself the sobriquet the Axman of New Orleans for brutally attacking a dozen victims, eight of whom died, and turning the Big Easy into the Hugely Uneasy.

Whoever the Axman was, he seemed to be a student of the methodology that had made the Ripper so famous, as he followed his own crimes with dispatches to newspapers that attempted to create in the public's mind a fearsome personality (in his case, "from hell") and gave obscure clues of murders to come. It is perhaps interesting to note, in a historical sense, to what degree Jack the Ripper built a behavioral template that would be followed so very closely by people such as the Axman, the Son of Sam and the Zodiac killer. It is almost as if he wrote the handbook for the would-be notorious serial killer—a handbook followed by even fictional fiends like Batman's nemeses the Riddler and the Joker.

In any event, the Axman went to work in grisly fashion in the dead of night on May 22, 1918, killing a grocer, Joseph Maggio, and his wife, Catherine, in the bedroom of their house on the corner of Upperline and Magnolia streets. Joseph's brother Jake lived in an adjoining set of rooms and was awoken by groans at four a.m. He roused the third Maggio brother, Andrew, and the two of them went to investigate. They saw immediately that there had been a break-in—a chisel had been left behind—and in the bedroom they found Joseph, breathing his last, with Catherine draped across him, very much dead. Also found on the scene were an ax and a straight razor, both of which had been employed in the double murder. The razor, which had quite nearly beheaded

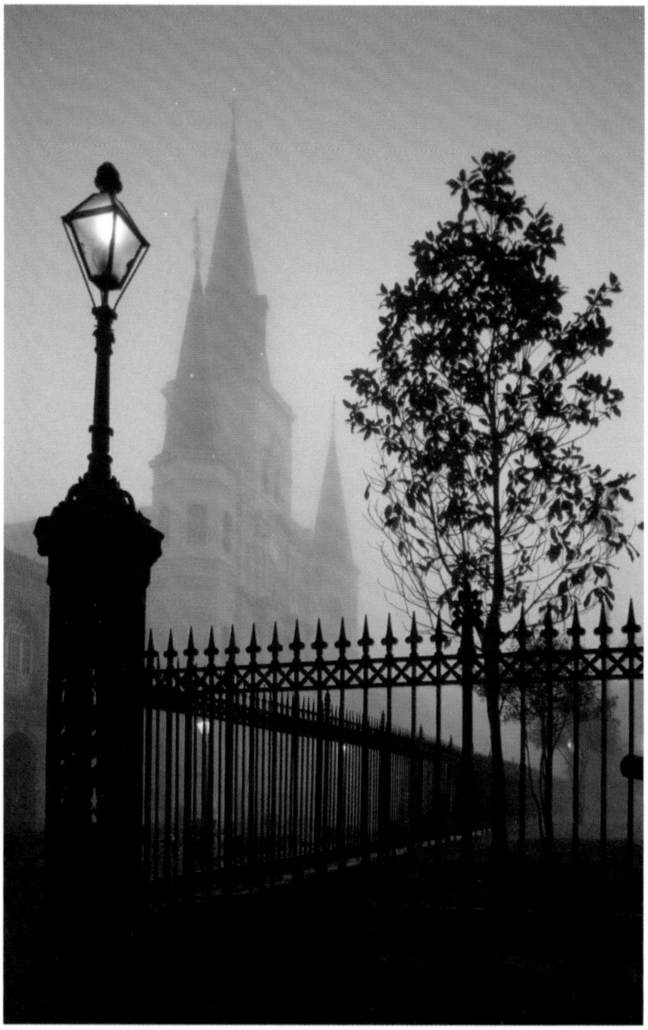

PHILIP GOULD/CORBIS

The Axman worked New Orleans's famous French Quarter (opposite) among other precincts, and today ghost tours of the neighborhood are popular with tourists. Legend has it that the piece represented by this sheet music cover (right) was composed specifically for the night targeted by the Axman and was performed lustily throughout the city.

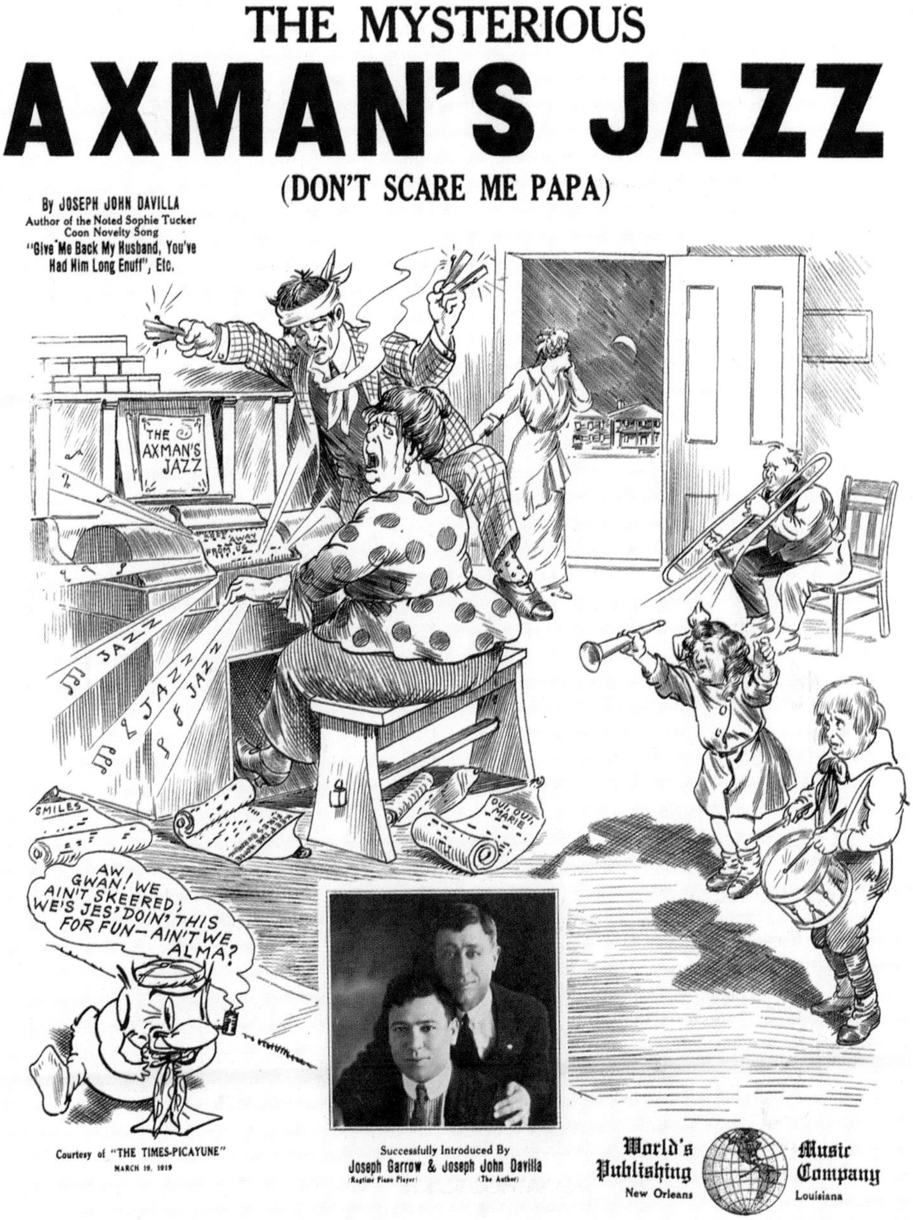

THE MYSTERIOUS
AXMAN'S JAZZ
(DON'T SCARE ME PAPA)
By JOSEPH JOHN DAVILLA
Author of the Noted Sophie Tucker Coon Novelty Song
"Give Me Back My Husband, You've Had Him Long Enuff", Etc.
THE AXMAN'S JAZZ
JAZZ
JAZZ
JAZZ
SMILES
OUI OUI, MARIE
AW GWAN! WE AIN'T SKEERED; WE'S JES' DOIN' THIS FOR FUN—AIN'T WE, ALMA?
Courtesy of "THE TIMES-PICAYUNE" MARCH 19, 1919
Successfully Introduced By
Joseph Garrow & Joseph John Davilla
(Ragtime Piano Player) (The Author)
World's Publishing Music Company
New Orleans Louisiana

THE HISTORIC NEW ORLEANS COLLECTION

Catherine, had belonged to Andrew. He was arrested but released before long for lack of evidence.

Other early suspects in the Axman murders—which resumed two weeks later with a second bedroom attack on a anothergrocer, Louis Besumer (who survived), and his mistress, Anna Lowe (who did not)—included members of the New Orleans branch of the Black Hand, a vicious Mafia organization. But then the cast of victims began to diversify—an eight-months-pregnant woman was attacked with an ax on August 5, an elderly man was attacked five days later—and fear spread generally. On March 10, 1919, the Axman went to the suburbs, to Gretna, and killed a father and his two-year-old daughter, while wounding the mother. Three days after that ghastly act riveted the city's attention, a letter was sent to the newspapers claiming that at 12:15 a.m. on March 19 a murder would be committed, but that the Axman would spare any citizen who was in an establishment where jazz was playing. This grandiose, ghoulish and obviously New Orleans–flavored flourish served to pack the jazz clubs, but no one was killed in the city that night. Three more were attacked before the year was out, however, and then the Axman retired, his anonymity secure at the time—and to this day.

A letter was sent to the newspapers claiming that at 12:15 a.m. on March 19 a murder would be committed, but that the Axman would spare any citizen who was in an establishment where jazz was playing.

Who Murdered William Desmond Taylor?

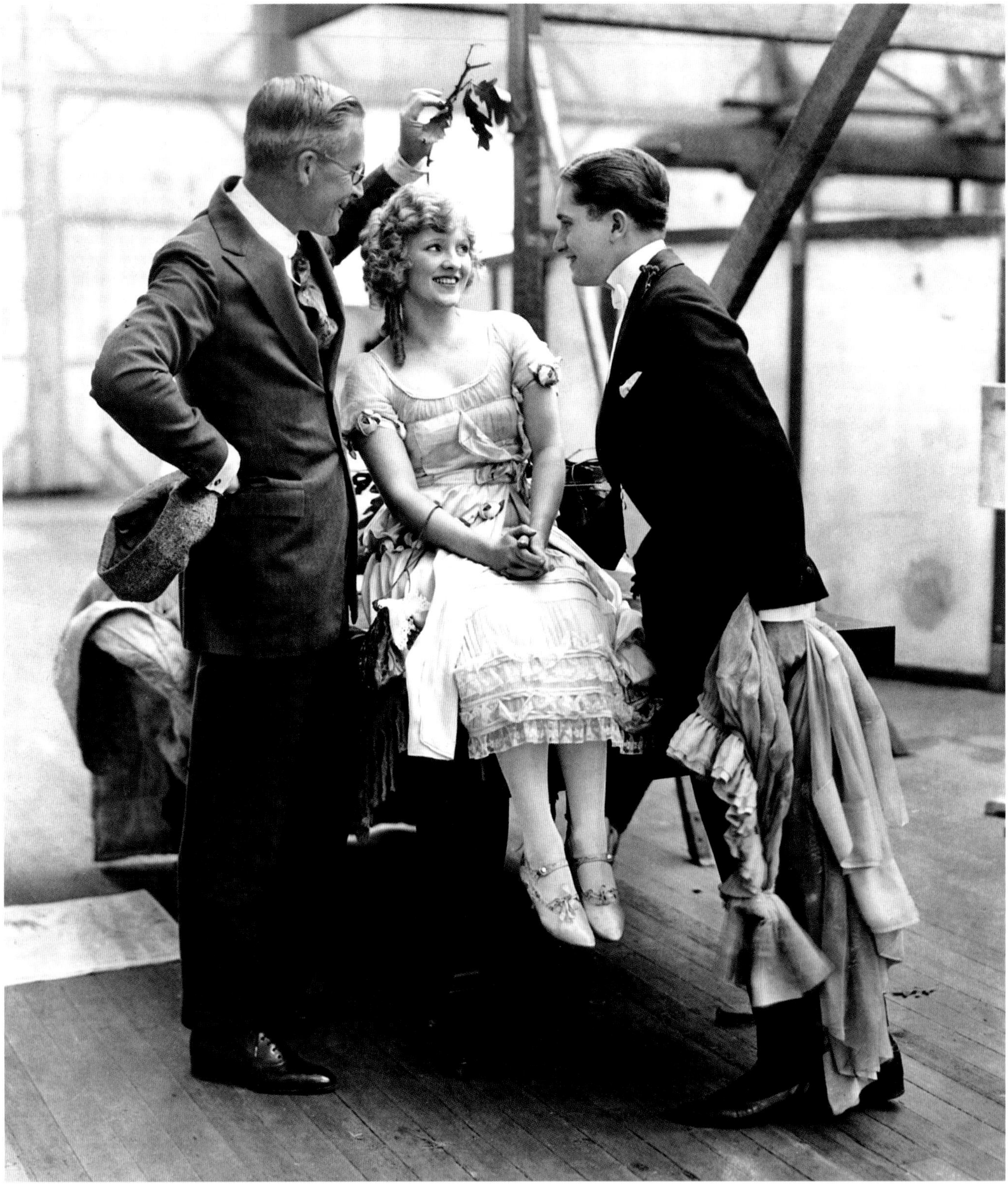

NELSON EVANS/KOBAL COLLECTION

There has been no shortage of Tinseltown trauma through the years, from the Fatty Arbuckle rape and murder trial (which led to an acquittal but ruined the comedian's career) to the Black Dahlia murder (which we will learn about shortly) to the O.J. Simpson case. But few scandals have blended more sordid ingredients than did the murder of William Desmond Taylor, a handsome director and actor of the silent-screen era who was shot once in the back at his Hollywood bungalow in February 1922. Sex and drugs are part of this story, as is a potential studio cover-up. Suspects have included everyone from an anonymous gangland hit man to an obsessed starlet to an overwrought stage mother. This story would seem outlandish enough as a movie script, but it was played out in real life. And someone got away with murder.

Taylor was a shady figure even before he landed in L.A. Born in Ireland in 1872, William Cunningham Deane-Tanner immigrated to the U.S. in 1890 and got early work as a bit player on the Broadway stage. He married the daughter of a wealthy Wall Street broker and, with his new father-in-law's funding, opened an antique-furniture firm. One day in 1908, "Pete" Tanner went to lunch and never looked back, abandoning his wife, Ethel, and his young daughter, Daisy.

Cut to: Ethel and Daisy in a movie theater, watching the 1914 film *Captain Alvarez*. Mother tells daughter that the actor in the title role is her father. Tanner had gone West and, landing in L.A. in 1912, changed his name and found film work. Just as he had been in New York society, he was a popular figure at Paramount Studios. Among his dearest friends was the lovely comic actress Mabel Normand, who unfortunately was a $2,000-a-month cocaine and opium addict. Taylor was vigorous in his support of her, urging her into rehab, serving as the head of an antidrug commission and going to the feds to urge them to stop the pushers who were Normand's suppliers. Not so close to Taylor as Normand but hopelessly infatuated with him was Mary Miles Minter, a 20-year-old actress who would steal away to Taylor's place when her mother was asleep and plead with him to accept her advances. Minter's mom was Charlotte Shelby, who reportedly had threatened another director, James Kirkwood, with a gun. Shelby believed her daughter had become pregnant by Kirkwood—a pregnancy ended by an abortion she had paid for.

On the opposite page, Taylor, left, is seen with Mary Miles Minter, who loved him only too well, and fellow actor-director Allan Forrest. The photograph was taken in 1921, a year before Taylor's death. Above: Two players in real-life melodramas, Mabel Normand and Fatty Arbuckle, at play in the 1916 comedy *He Did and He Didn't*.

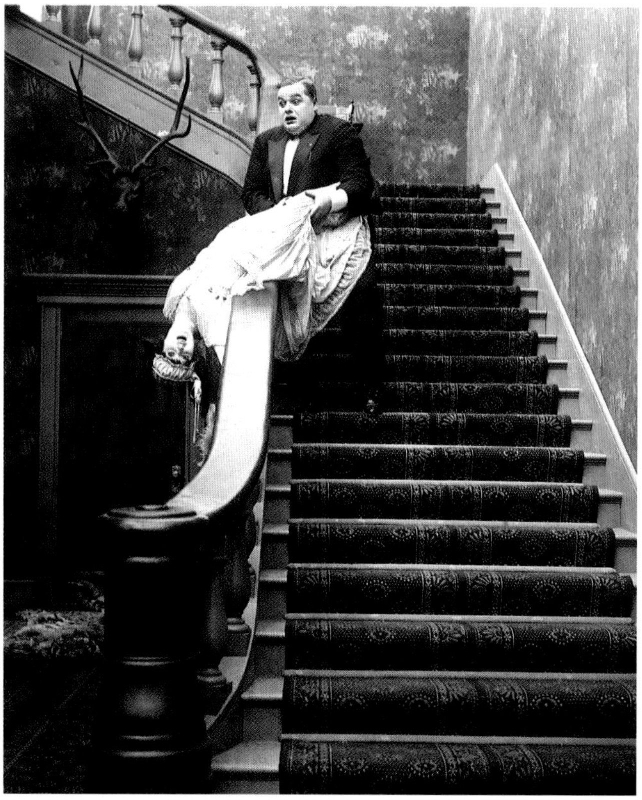

KEYSTONE FILMS/KOBAL COLLECTION

Sex, drugs, a studio cover-up: What a script it would make! And someone got away with murder.

Sometime prior to eight p.m. on February 1, 1922, Taylor's neighbors heard a noise that sounded like a backfire. Looking out their windows, at least two of them saw someone leaving Taylor's house. Was it a killer from the drug trade, protecting his interests? Was it Minter, the spurned lover? Was it Shelby, who'd been to Taylor's at least once before, searching for Minter?

Taylor was found the next morning by his houseman, and Paramount Studios was called before the cops were. Panic ensued; Hollywood was already under siege by the decency police squads after the Arbuckle scandal the previous year, and more tabloid headlines just wouldn't do. Minions were dispatched, and they grabbed letters and other possible evidence. By the time investigators arrived, the crime scene had been thoroughly compromised. A grand jury was convened in the case, but no one was charged.

It is said that when frail Mabel Normand, who had costarred in hit movies alongside Arbuckle, died of tuberculosis in 1930 at age 37, among her last words were "I wonder who killed poor Bill Taylor?"

Did Mallory and Irvine Conquer Everest?

N. E. ODELL

The most famous fact in the annals of mountaineering is that in 1953, New Zealand beekeeper Edmund Hillary and his Sherpa companion, Tenzing Norgay, climbing with a British expedition, became the first men to set foot on the summit of the world's tallest peak, 29,029-foot-high Mount Everest on the border of Nepal and Tibet.

But were they actually the first?

Prior to the 1953 triumph, there had been 32 years of expeditions and at least 13 lives lost in the attempt to conquer Everest.

In Everest lore and legend, no name is writ larger than that of George Herbert Leigh Mallory—not even Sir Edmund Hillary's. Mallory was a brave and dogged climber, the man who had to try Everest "because it's there."

Two of those who died were Englishmen Sandy Irvine and George Mallory, who were last seen stunningly close to the summit on June 8, 1924. They vanished, then perished. The question that lingers: Did they die after having given up or during their descent after reaching the top?

In Everest lore and legend, no name is writ larger than that of George Herbert Leigh Mallory—not even Hillary's. A British schoolteacher, Mallory was a brave and dogged climber. By 1924, he had already participated in two earlier Everest expeditions, and had, with Guy Henry Bullock, found the approach over the East Rongbuk Glacier to the North Col. On June 4, 1924, during the third expedition, group leader Lieutenant Colonel Edward Felix Norton established a new record by reaching an altitude of 28,126 feet. The big question brought back by the survivors of that

JOHN NOEL

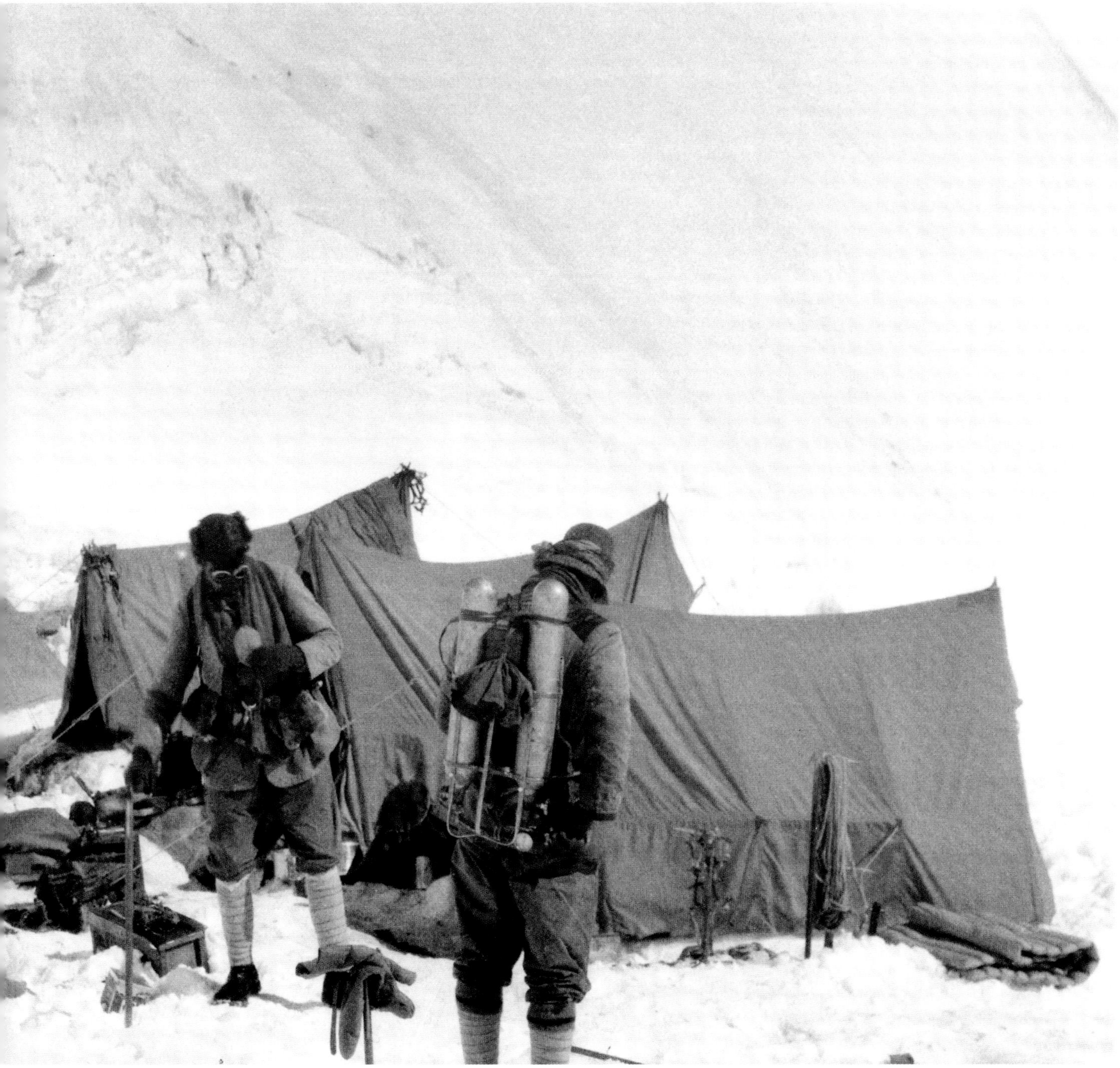

expedition was: Did Mallory eclipse Norton's achievement four days later, perhaps?

Opposite: The 1924 British team is pictured with Sandy Irvine standing at left with George Mallory immediately beside him. Above: Noel Odell took this last picture of Mallory (left) and Irvine a day before they disappeared.

On that day, along with his climbing partner, Andrew Comyn "Sandy" Irvine, a 22-year-old engineering student, Mallory set off for the summit just 2,000 feet away. At 12:50 p.m., teammate Noel Odell saw the two men as "black spots" below the peak, moving forward with due speed. Mallory and Irvine disappeared into the clouds, "going strong for the top." They were never seen alive again. An ice ax belonging to one of the men was found by the fourth British expedition, which nine years later reached the same height as Norton had. The discovery of the ax did nothing to solve a mystery that, at intervals, devolved into an unpleasant controversy: Does the glory belong to Hillary and Norgay or to Mallory and Irvine? Hillary partisans insist the earlier climbers wouldn't have had time that day to reach the summit. The position of the Mallory supporters was poetically expressed early on by Tom Longstaff, a friend of both Mallory and Irvine, who had climbed with the British team in 1922: "It was my good luck to know both of them: such splendid fellows . . . Mallory wrote in the last

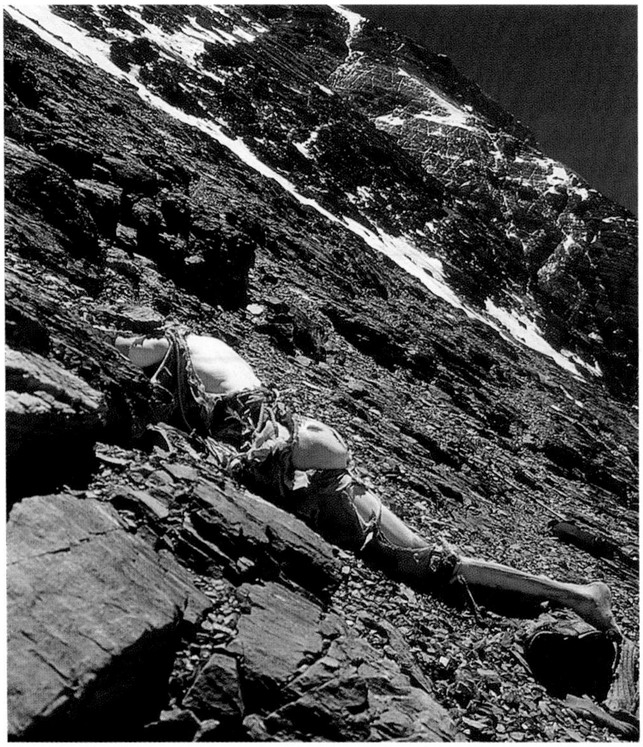

JAKE NORTON/MALLORY & IRVINE/GETTY

In 1999, Mallory's body (left) was found at 26,800 feet. In his pockets were (below) glacier glasses, a broken altimeter and a pocketknife that was closed when discovered. Opposite: Before leaving for home, the 1924 expedition built a cairn at base camp that commemorated those who had died in British attempts since 1921. The rocks have long since been taken by souvenir hunters.

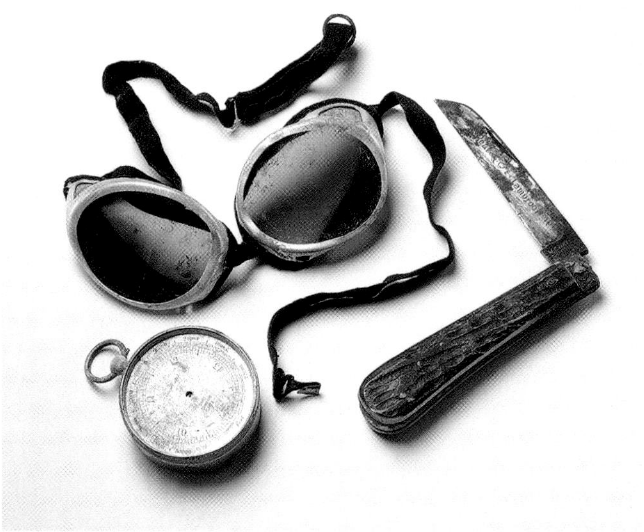

JIM FAGIOLO/MALLORY & IRVINE/GETTY

letter I got from him, 'we are going to sail to the top this time and God with us—or stamp to the top with our teeth in the wind.' I would not quote an idle boast, but this wasn't—they got there alright. Somehow they were 4 hours late, but at 12:50 they were less than 800 ft below and only a quarter of a mile away from the summit: Odell reports them moving quickly: therefore the oxygen was working well; nothing could have stopped these two with the goal well in their grasp at long last."

The two men disappeared into the clouds "going strong for the top." They were never seen alive again. The big question: Did they die before reaching the summit or while descending from it?

Such strong boosterism is not, of course, proof—and it was long thought that proof would never be forthcoming. Then, on May 1, 1999, the Mallory and Irvine Research Expedition, an operation led by American mountain guide Eric Simonson, found Mallory's frozen corpse on a wind-scoured ledge at nearly 27,000 feet—several hundred feet below where the ice ax, identified as Irvine's, was found in 1933. Mallory, still in a fur-lined leather helmet and hobnailed boots, a frayed rope around his waist, lay facing upslope, his body frozen into the earth. A leg was broken, an elbow injured. On his forehead was a puncture that exposed part of his brain. On May 17, expedition members found a 1924 oxygen bottle 65 feet above the site of the ax; evidence seemed to be pushing Mallory and Irvine ever farther up the hill. The 1999 expedition, spurred by its finds, continued to search—but discovered nothing conclusive. They were particularly disappointed not to find the camera, which might contain pictures of the men on the summit.

To most experts, it is clear from the evidence that Mallory fell to his death. Some analysts of the scene maintain that we now know the two climbers were descending when Mallory, in the lead, took a tumble. Irvine likely tried to arrest the fall, but then the rope that connected them snapped, and Mallory plummeted. Though Irvine's body has never been recovered, it is surmised that he, alone and exhausted, with little or no oxygen remaining, perished during the bitter night.

It's all conjecture still. From where were they descending? The summit? The Second Step, a wall of rotten rock that took ace rock climber Conrad Anker an hour to climb during the Mallory and Irvine Research Expedition? If the "black spots" Odell saw on the ridge at 12:50 p.m. were Mallory and Irvine, they probably could not have reached the summit until seven p.m. Wouldn't they have turned back much earlier, knowing that an overnight in the Everest cold would almost surely kill them?

"The mystery of Mallory and Irvine therefore lives on," wrote Peter Firstbrook, a member of the research expedition, in *The Search for Mallory & Irvine*. "In death, as in life, they remain together on the mountain; they are in every sense, *the* men of Everest."

JOHN NOEL

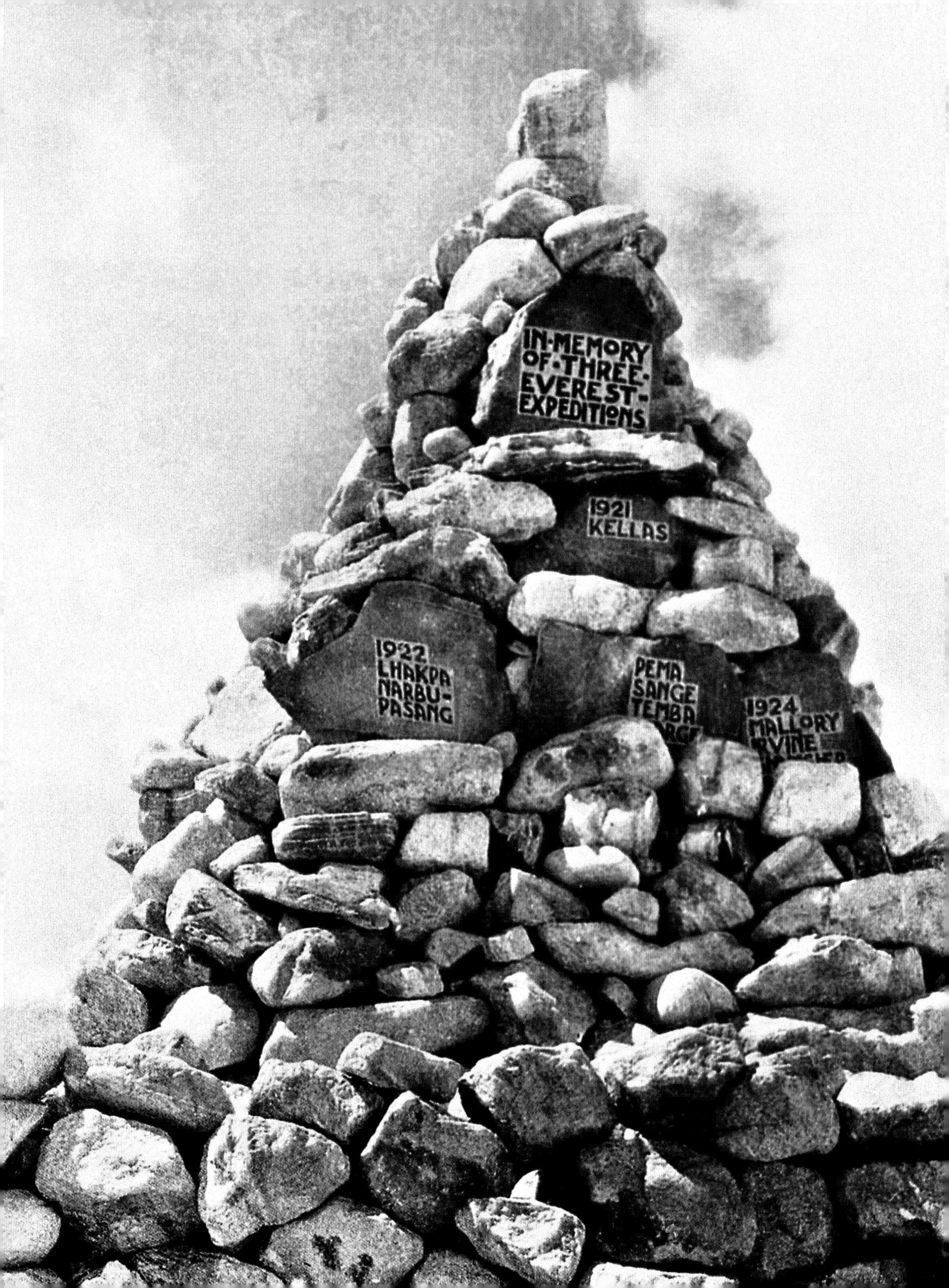
IN·MEMORY OF·THREE· EVEREST· EXPEDITIONS
1921 KELLAS
1922 LHAKPA NARBU- PASANG
PEMA SANGE TEMBA
1924 MALLORY

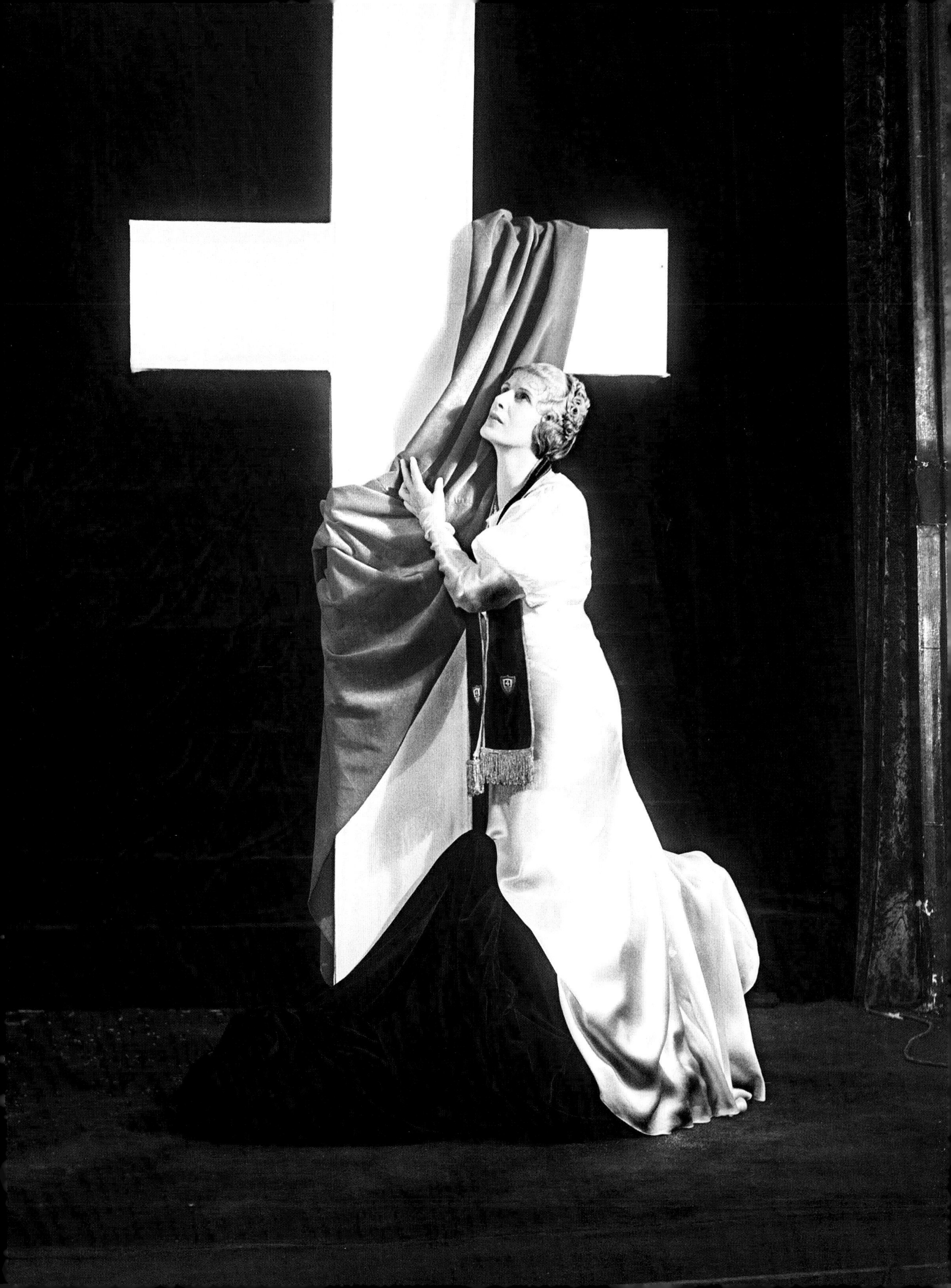

Where Did Aimee Semple McPherson Go?

The year 1926 was a banner one for famous women disappearing and reappearing, as first America and then England were gripped by the unexplained absence of two ladies with large and devoted followings. As we will see in these next two chapters of our book, a relationship with a man was quite possibly the crux in both cases. One of these women remained vehement her whole life that this was not the case, while the other kept decorously mum.

Aimee Semple McPherson was the one who was vigorous in presenting an alternative theory, and perhaps this was because she was a religious leader—Sister Aimee—and had much to lose to a scandal of the flesh. Born Aimee Kennedy in Ontario, Canada, in 1890, as a girl, she played at being a Salvation Army missionary and would arrange her dolls attentively and preach to them, according to biographer Matthew Avery Sutton. She married Irishman Robert Semple, a world-traveling Pentacostal minister, at the age of 17. When he died a mere two years later, having contracted malaria during a tour of Asia, she returned to the United States and worked alongside her mother for the Salvation Army. She then married accountant Harold Stewart McPherson and took up the late Semple's mantle and fashioned herself as an evangelist, tirelessly touring the U.S. and Canada and attracting a rabid following; during one not atypical revival meeting,

She published a magazine, built a huge radio audience and was filling the pews of her 5,300-seat church thrice daily, seven days a week. And then, in 1926, she vanished.

the National Guard had to be deployed to control the fervor of an audience of 30,000 in San Diego. Her relationship with her husband suffered due to her constant traveling, and she and McPherson divorced in 1921.

Aimee, too, eventually sought to get off the road and saw an

Talk about a drama queen! In the photograph opposite, the evangelist McPherson stirs the masses during a pageant at her Angelus Temple, the central house of worship of the International Church of the Foursquare Gospel in the Echo Park district of Los Angeles. Below: She performs a reenactment of her dramatic escape from kidnappers.

opportunity to do so in the burgeoning city of Los Angeles, where she based her International Church of the Foursquare Gospel. She published a magazine, built a radio audience—in fact, built her own radio station, KFSG—and, by the mid-1920s, was filling the pews of her 5,300-seat church thrice daily, seven days a week. She had an empire that was her era's equivalent of Rick Warren's Saddleback Church today.

On May 18, 1926, McPherson went to Ocean Park Beach for a swim. She did not return to officiate at her scheduled church service, and from the pulpit, her mother, Minnie Kennedy, announced to the shocked flock, "Sister is with Jesus!" There was, as might be expected, wailing and lamentation—and frantic searches and tearful prayer vigils near the Pacific Ocean. As May gave way to June, most of the country had resolved itself to a sad conclusion: Aimee Semple McPherson had drowned.

Her version was that she had fled her captors and made a 13-hour exodus through the desert. So how come her shoes were grass stained instead of all beat-up?

And then, on June 23, 1926, the lost evangelist reappeared at a border town in Mexico and announced she had been seized in California, chloroformed, then held and tortured at a shack in Mexico. She had escaped and made a 13-hour exodus through the desert. Problems with this story were immediately apparent: She was wearing clothes she hadn't possessed at Ocean Park Beach, her grass-stained shoes hardly looked like they had been employed in a 13-hour desert trek, etc. Then reports started to surface that McPherson had

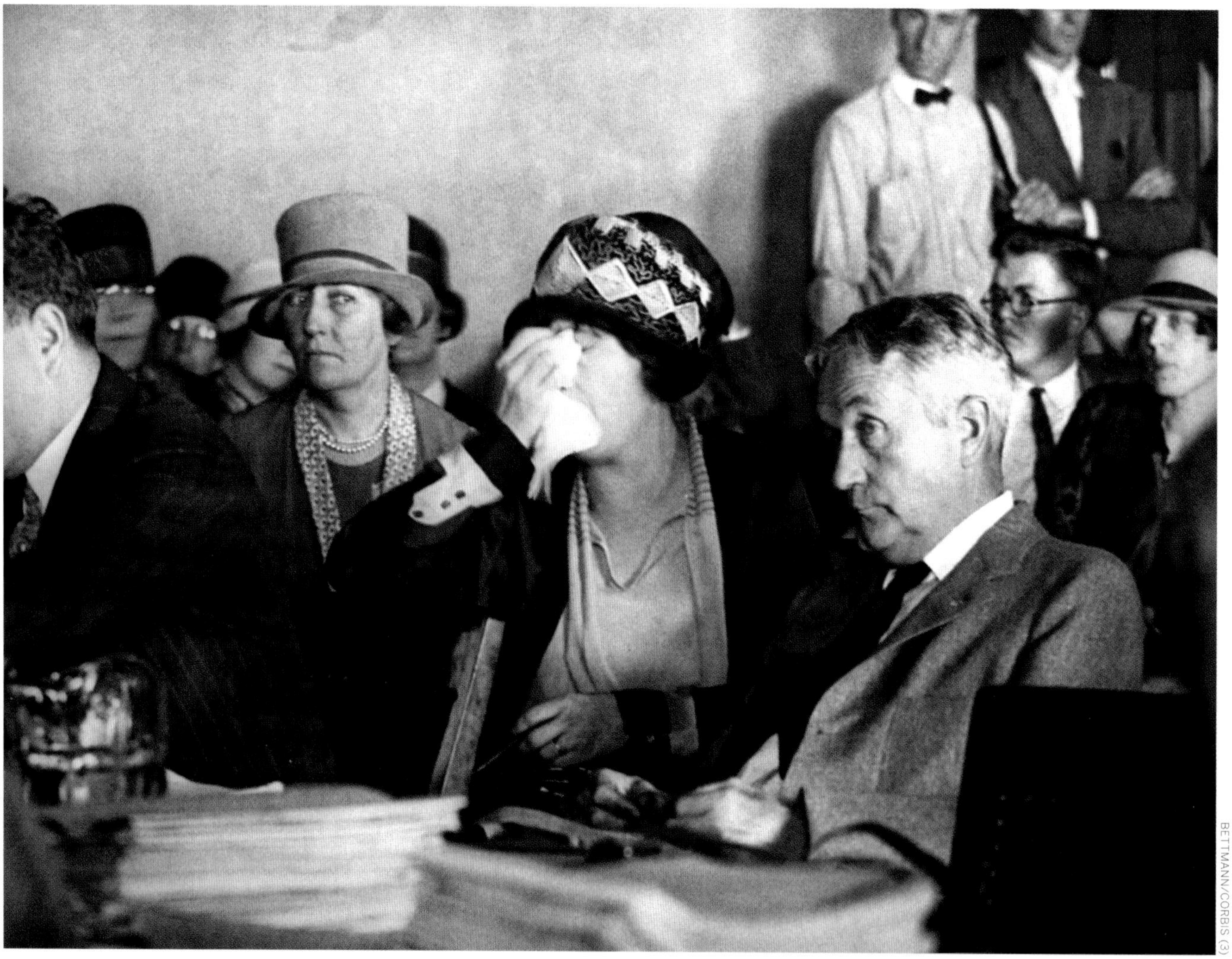

BETTMANN/CORBIS (3)

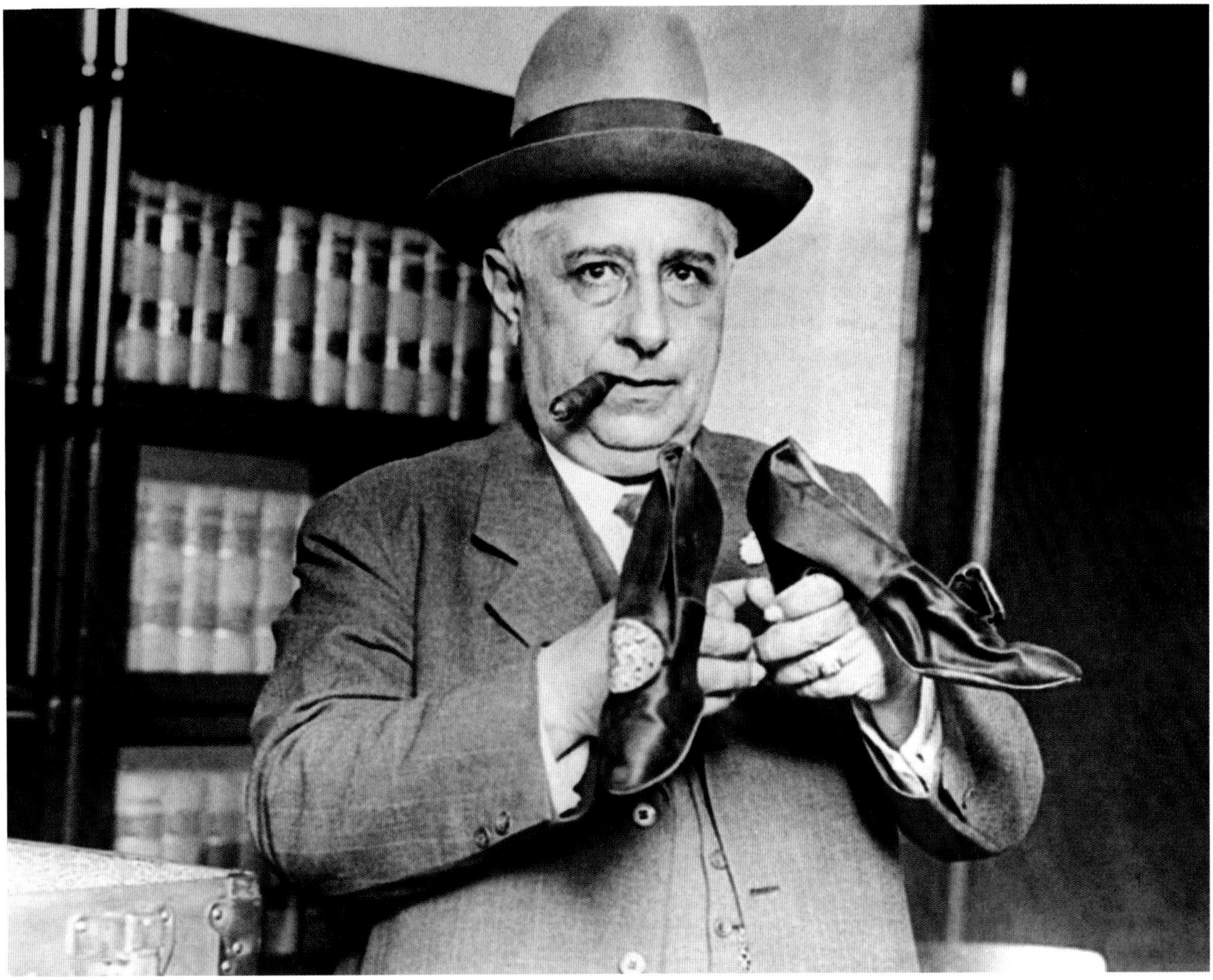

been spotted during her walkabout at a cottage in charming Carmel-by-the-Sea in the company of Kenneth Ormiston, a married man who worked as an engineer at the church's radio station. A grand jury was twice convened in the summer of '26, but while a judge at one point cited McPherson and her mother for obstruction of justice, McPherson never stood trial for any crime.

Opposite: During a preliminary hearing, McPherson sobs as she listens to the testimony of the Angelus Temple's manager, Blanche Rice, who is describing the abject grief of McPherson's mother when she learned that her daughter had probably drowned. (That's Mom herself, left, just behind McPherson—and Lord knows what she's thinking.) On this page: Los Angeles County Chief of Detectives Ben Cohn peruses garb and footwear that indicate McPherson was fashionably dressed during her ordeal.

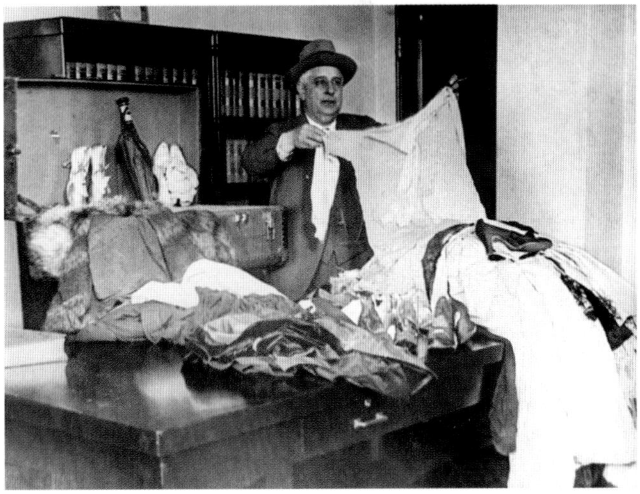

Sister Aimee's popularity did take a hit, though her church continued to be strong (today, Foursquare has eight million parishioners worldwide). McPherson, who went on to marry a third time, divorce a second and have a brief affair with comedian Milton Berle, clung to her account of the disappearance until her death in an Oakland hotel room in 1944, possibly from a sedative overdose. Some of her adherents certainly believed her to the end, though many Americans went along with the conclusions reached in "The Ballad of Aimee McPherson," a folk song made popular by Pete Seeger, which argued that you just couldn't ignore that "the dents in the mattress fitted Aimee's caboose."

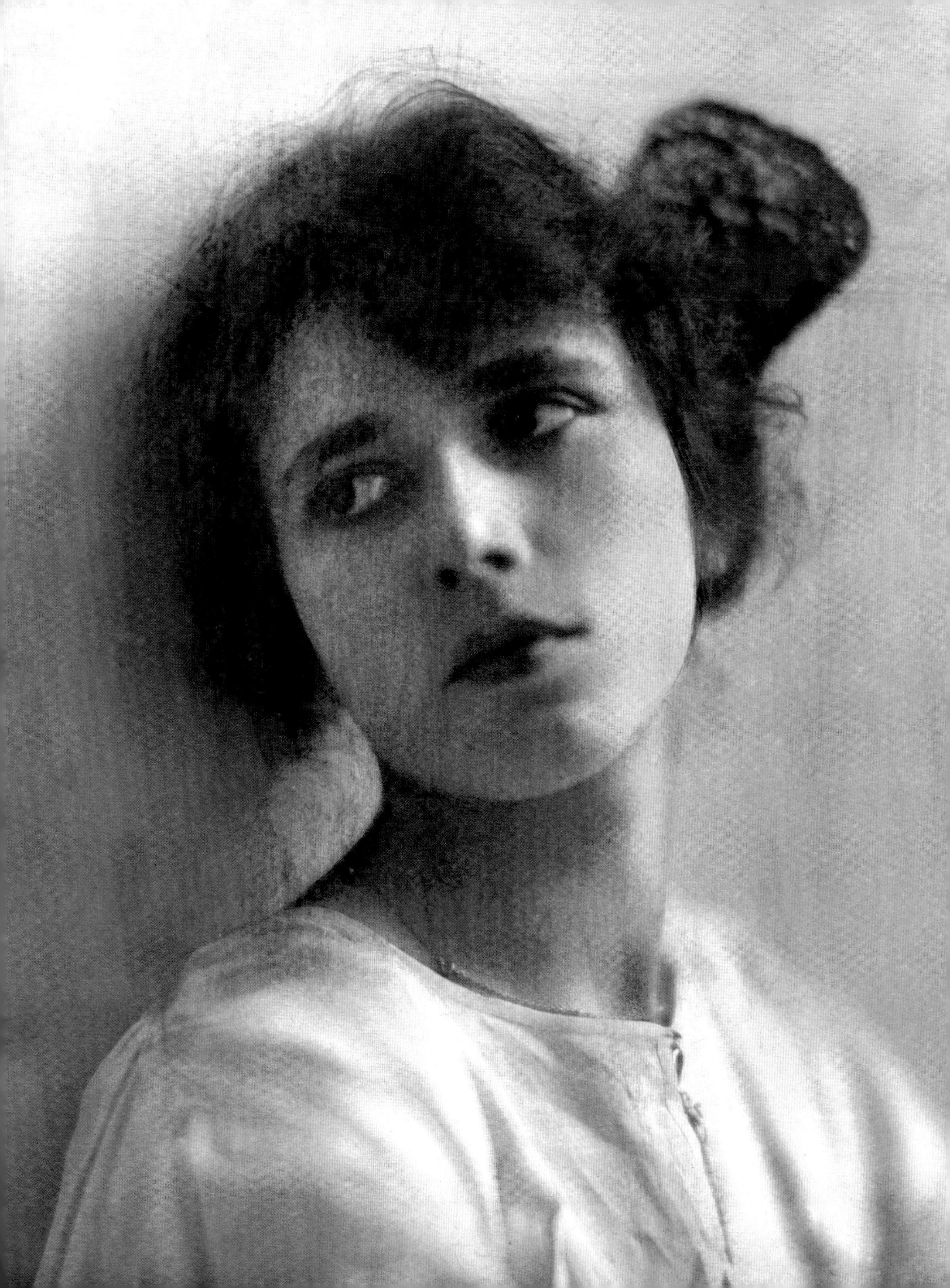

An Agatha Christie Mystery?

The best-selling author ever, Great Britain's Dame Agatha Christie wrote 80 novels and short-story collections that have sold an estimated four billion—that's *billion*—copies in some 50 languages worldwide. She also wrote hit plays, including *Witness for the Prosecution* and *The Mousetrap*, which is the longest running play in history, still going strong in London after more than a half century. Of the multitude of mysteries Christie spun during her long and illustrious career, not one of them was true.

Or maybe there was one.

She created it, even if she didn't write it down.

This was the British version of the Aimee Semple McPherson case: On Friday evening, December 3, 1926, Agatha Christie, already a well-known novelist as the creator of detective Hercule Poirot, went upstairs in the family house in Sunningdale, Berkshire, and kissed her seven-year-old daughter, Rosalind, goodnight. At 9:45, she got into her car and drove away. She would not be seen for 11 days, and her legion of fans was confronted with a quandary of much more consequence than any Poirot faced in Christie's fictions: What happened to Agatha?

The car was discovered abandoned several miles from the house, with many of her personal belongings in disarray within. The writer was nowhere to be found.

At 9:45, she got into her car and drove away. She would not be seen for 11 days, and her fans were confronted with a quandary of more consequence than any in Christie's fictions: What happened to Agatha?

The search was large and frantic; headlines ran in bold type throughout the land. The creator of Sherlock Holmes, Sir Arthur Conan Doyle, was consulted for any insights, as was Christie's sister in crime writing, Dorothy L. Sayers. Truth was quite literally yielding a story stranger than fiction.

Agatha had been married since 1914 to Archibald Christie, who had been an aviator in the Royal Flying Corps. Their courtship had been tumultuous and so, too, at times, was their marriage. Late in 1926, Archie told Agatha that he was in love with his mistress, Nancy Neele, and had asked for a divorce. Before Agatha went

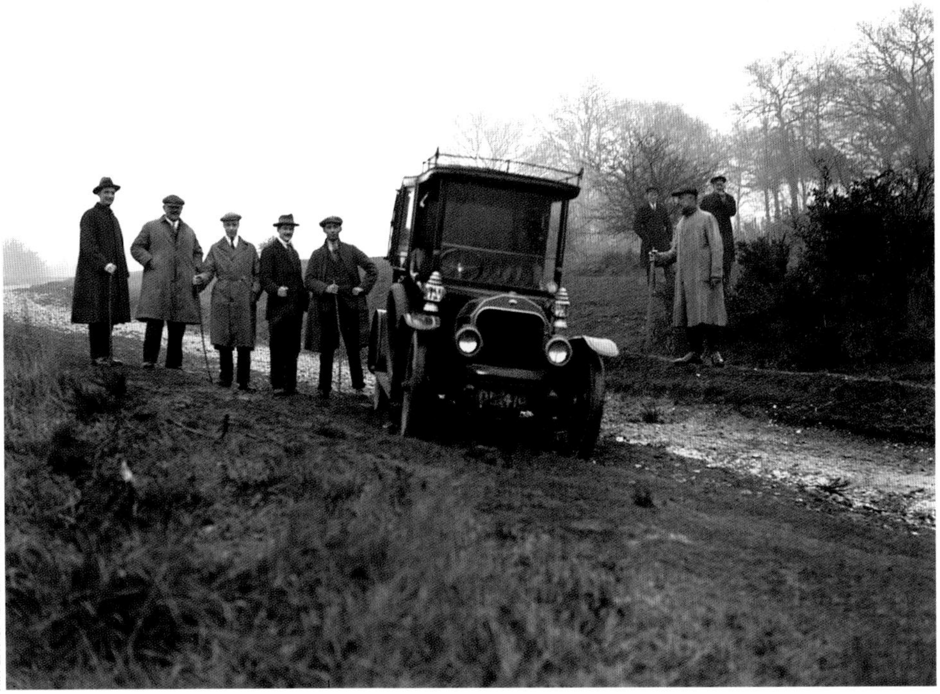

Opposite: The already famous author, in a portrait made in 1926, the year she would go missing. Right: On December 6, her car is found abandoned near Newland's Corner, Guildford, Surrey—but there's no sign of Agatha.

SV-BILDERDIENST/THE IMAGE WORKS

H.F. DAVIS/TOPICAL PRESS/GETTY

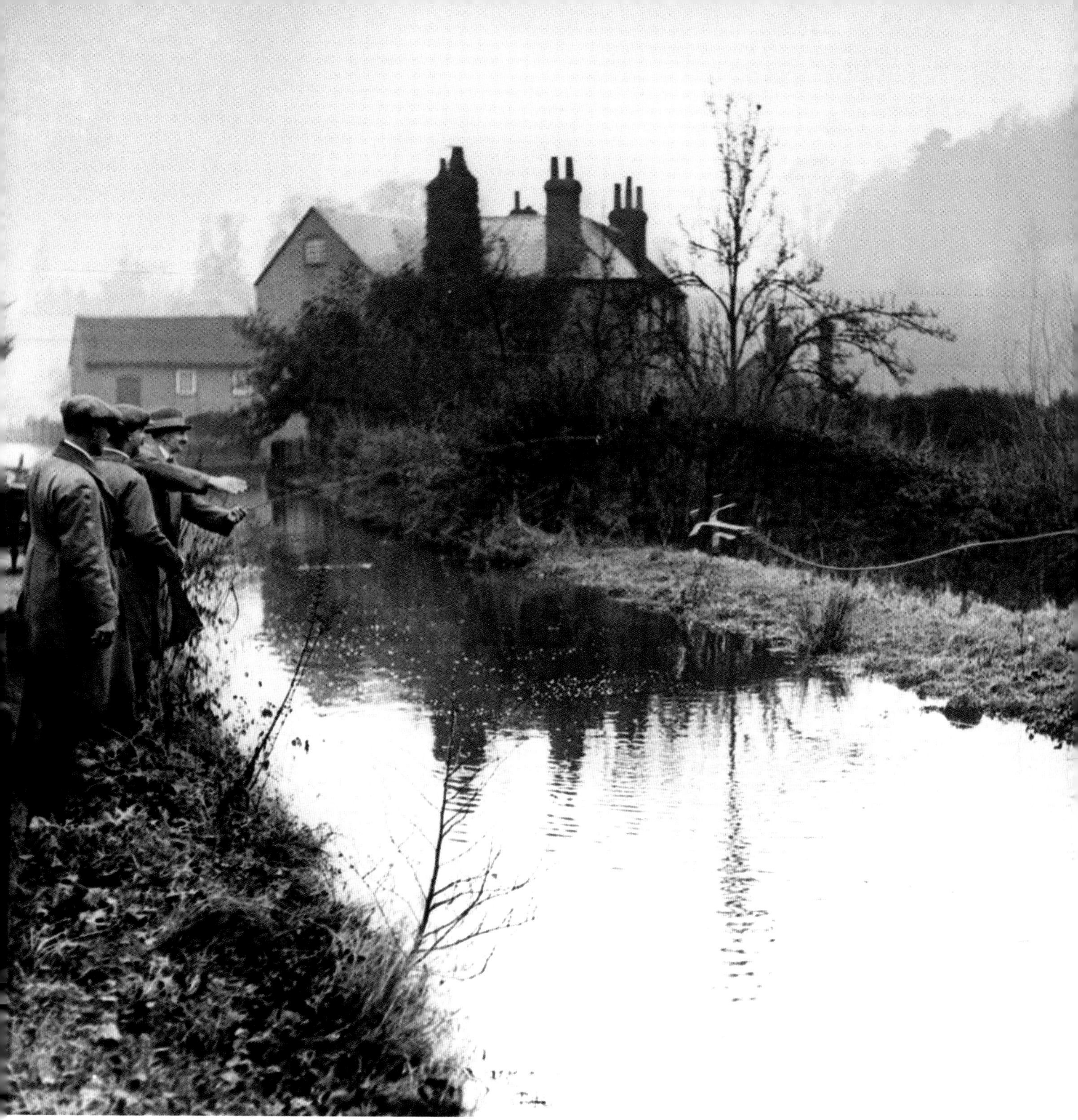

Sir Arthur Conan Doyle was consulted for any insights, as was Christie's sister in crime writing, Dorothy L. Sayers. Truth was quite literally yielding a story stranger than fiction.

upstairs to kiss Rosalind on that fateful Friday night, there had been a row. Archie fled Sunningdale to spend the weekend with Neele, and Agatha wrote a letter to her secretary indicating that she, too, was leaving for a time—headed for Yorkshire.

When some of these details emerged, and with Agatha still missing, the cries for Archie's head grew general: He had done her in or driven her to suicide.

On December 14, Agatha was found in Yorkshire—identified

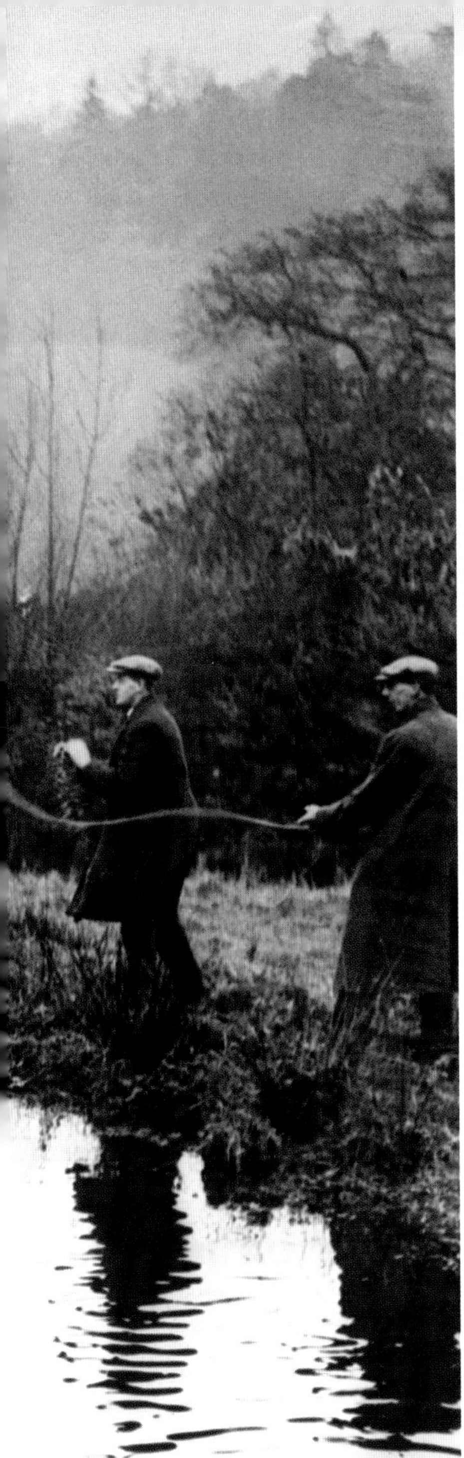

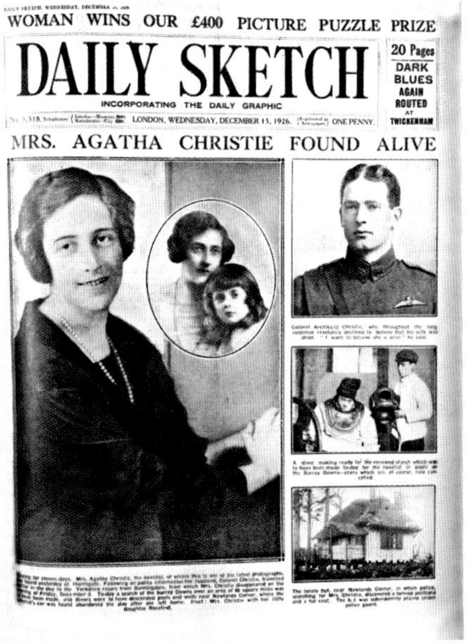
WOMAN WINS OUR £400 PICTURE PUZZLE PRIZE

DAILY SKETCH

INCORPORATING THE DAILY GRAPHIC

20 Pages

DARK BLUES AGAIN ROUTED AT TWICKENHAM

LONDON, WEDNESDAY, DECEMBER 15, 1926. ONE PENNY

MRS. AGATHA CHRISTIE FOUND ALIVE

HULTON/GETTY (2)

Far left: Near where Christie's car was found, searchers drag a waterway in hopes of finding evidence and with dread that they will find a body. They come up empty. But then the writer turns up alive and the tabloids trumpet the news (left). Below: The huge crowd at King's Cross Station in London presses in against the train that is bringing Agatha and her husband, Archie, back to the city. Archie is safe from prosecution but hardly back in the good graces of his wife or the British public.

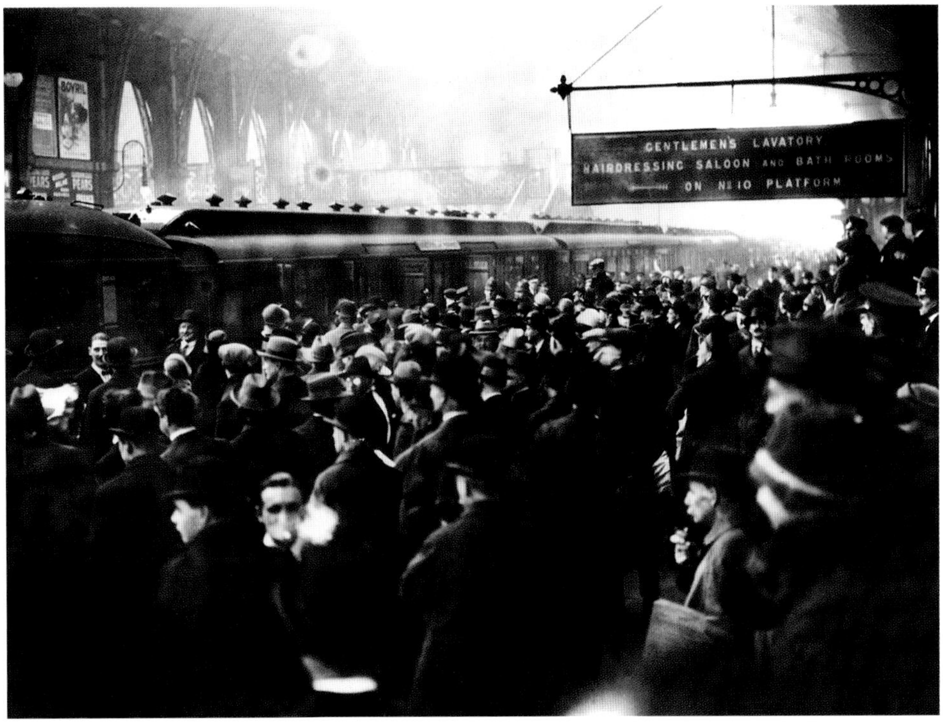
BOVRIL
GENTLEMENS LAVATORY
HAIRDRESSING SALOON AND BATH ROOMS

BETTMANN CORBIS

as one of the guests at the Swan Hydropathic Hotel. She was using an alias closely resembling Neele's name. The police and Agatha's family indicated she was suffering from amnesia.

With Agatha safe, the reaction was clamorous and divided. One theory was that the whole thing was a big publicity stunt. Another was that she was trying to embarrass Archie by drawing attention to his infidelity or even to have him persecuted and perhaps prosecuted as her killer. And the third is that she indeed suffered a nervous breakdown upon learning of her husband's affair, and amnesia might have resulted. Agatha never said what had really happened. Or did she?

She sometimes wrote under the pseudonym Mary Westmacott. The 1934 Westmacott novel *Unfinished Portrait* dealt with a female writer driven to the brink of suicide after her husband asks her for a divorce. How much of that book was fact and how much was fiction will, like so much in this curious case, never be known.

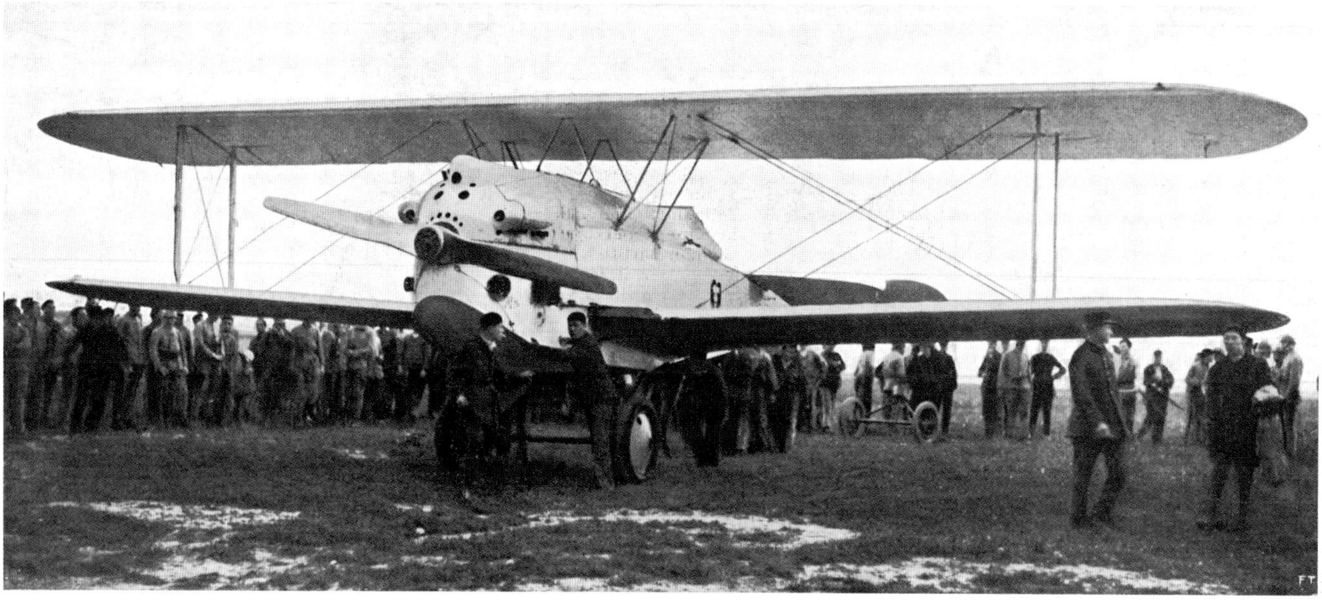
MARY EVANS PICTURE LIBRARY/THE IMAGE WORKS(2)

Did the *White Bird* Beat Lucky Lindy Across the Atlantic?

The custom-built, wide-winged, fuel-laden biplane (above) bore the rather chilling World War I emblem of its pilot, Nungesser (who is seen to the right of his emblem on the opposite page; his partner, Coli, is at left).

Charles Lindbergh's first successful solo nonstop transatlantic airplane crossing in 1927 is seen today as such a thunderous historic event—up there in aviation lore with the Wright Brothers' triumph at Kitty Hawk or Neil Armstrong's first step on the lunar surface—that it is not often noted that Lucky Lindy's feat was achieved in response to a contest. That's right: In 1919, New York hotelier Raymond Orteig, who was after all in the tourist business, put up a prize of $25,000 for any crew or individual making a nonstop flight between New York and Paris in the next five years. None had taken up the challenge by 1924, but Orteig left the money on the table, and as technology advanced, several pilots stepped forward. One of them, a French World War I ace named François Coli, had started planning a transatlantic crossing in 1923, and by 1925, he and fellow war veteran Paul Tarascon had the Orteig Prize in their sights. But the next year, their biplane crashed and Tarascon was injured. His place as Coli's pilot was taken by Charles Nungesser, yet another Legion of Honor veteran with more than 40 kills during the war. The two comrades began collaborating with engineers on the design of a new aircraft, and by 1927, the *White Bird* was ready for takeoff.

It was quite a construction. Built principally of lightweight plywood and canvas, and based on a military reconnaissance plane, it had a wingspan of 48 feet, and its cockpit was widened to allow Coli and Nungesser to sit side by side. All available space was given to fuel tanks—three of them, holding 1,056 gallons of gasoline, which could keep the *Bird* flying for more than 40 hours (since the French team would be flying west against the prevailing winds, the trip would take longer than an eastbound flight). The single-engine biplane, which fully fueled weighed in at 11,000 pounds, was painted white and bore two emblems: the French tricolor and Nungesser's wartime symbol—a black heart with a skull, crossbones, candles and a coffin.

On May 8, 1927, the *White Bird* took flight in the dusky dawn of Le Bourget Field and headed northwest over the English Channel. Reliable sightings were made in Ireland as the plane continued out over the Atlantic. The plan was to proceed across the ocean, then head down over Newfoundland and New England to New York and touch down near the Statue of Liberty (the craft had been designed for water landings). A crowd gathered in lower Manhattan to witness the great event.

Even as press accounts in Paris shouted of a triumph, the crowd grew wary, then worried. Once it became clear the gas supply would have been expended, frantic searches began in Canada and along the northeastern U.S. coast. When nothing was found, it was assumed Coli and Nungesser had met their end in the frigid Atlantic. The fate of the *White Bird* more fully fixated the world's attention on the effort of Lindbergh in his monoplane the *Spirit of St. Louis* later in May. And when Lindy touched down at Le Bourget Field, he was mobbed by 150,000 Frenchmen celebrating his success even as they mourned their countrymen.

A curious thing happened in the aftermath of the *White Bird*'s disappearance. Rumors started circulating that villagers in Newfoundland and Maine had heard a plane pass over. There were reports—all unconfirmed—that a wrecked aircraft had been seen by hunters, that the engine had been found in Maine, that the pilots had survived and were living with Canadian Indians. Then, in 1980, an article in *Yankee* magazine, quoting one of the old-timers who'd sworn they had heard the plane, spurred new investigations by such as the French government, the TV show *Unsolved Mysteries* and even the author Clive Cussler. Today many believe that the *White Bird* may well have made it to North America before it crashed.

There are intriguing footnotes to this story: Had the *White Bird*, which may have come so very close, actually succeeded, then Lindbergh might have turned his attention to a pioneering trans-pacific crossing or even an around-the-world mission, and Amelia Earhart, who disappeared in 1937 during just such an effort (and whom we will meet in these pages shortly), might have lived to a ripe old age. Also: If Lindy had not triumphantly landed in Paris, the U.S. aeronautics industry might not have been jump-started as it was, and what consequences this might have had for the world when America entered the war against fascism are chilling to ponder.

What Happened to Judge Crater?

J udge Crater, call your office!" That was a surefire punch line for Depression-era comics after the 1930 disappearance of "The Missingest Man in New York," Joseph Force Crater, an associate justice of the state's supreme court who had been appointed in the spring of that year by Governor Franklin D. Roosevelt. The married "Good Time Joe" Crater was a 41-year-old man about town with a taste for showgirls and known associations at the political den of thieves Tammany Hall. Therefore he was fair game for the humorists—even if his fate may have been tragic. "Pulling a Crater" became a catchphrase for vanishing into

thin air, and a magazine cartoon had Lassie finally finding the judge. It was pure fun to track the rumored sightings of Crater: riding a burro as a gold prospector in California; wielding a staff as a shepherd in the valleys of the Pacific Northwest; rolling the dice at a crap game in Georgia; calling the numbers at a bingo game in—get this!—North Africa.

Most likely, Crater wasn't around to appreciate the humor of the situation. Though we'll never know for sure.

What we do know is that he was vacationing in Maine with his wife, Stella Mance Wheeler, when, in late July of 1930, he received a phone call that left him visibly distressed. He told Stella that he had to rush back to New York "to straighten those fellows out." Upon arriving back in the city, he went to his apartment on Fifth Avenue and told the maid she could have the next few days off. Whom he might have straightened out during this visit to Gotham is unclear, as he next took a quick side trip to Atlantic City with his mistress, the showgirl Sally Lou Ritz, then returned to his wife's embrace in Maine on August 1. Two days later, he headed back to New York, telling Stella he would return to celebrate her birthday on the ninth. She later said that he had been chipper as he departed, and the same was reported of the judge by his two dinner companions at Billy Haas's Chophouse on August 6—Sally Lou and a lawyer friend of his.

"Pulling a Crater" became a catchphrase for vanishing into thin air, and a magazine cartoon had Lassie finally finding the judge. It was fun to track the rumored sightings of Crater: riding a burro as a gold prospector in California, rolling the dice at a crap game in Georgia …

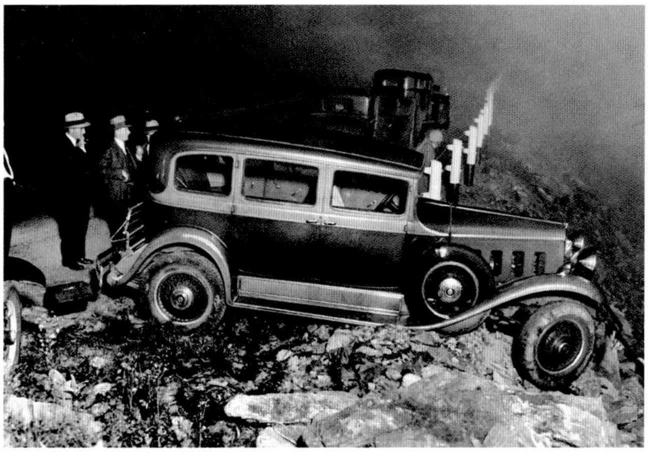

NEW YORK DAILY NEWS

The judge seems at ease with his wife in Maine three days before his disappearance (opposite), but life in New York was clearly more complicated. After Crater's car was found in Brooklyn more than a year after he disappeared (left), the search was called off. As late as 1959, however, people were still curious; that year, a story circulated that he was buried behind a house in Yonkers, just north of New York City. The homeowner allowed LIFE to search there (below). Nothing.

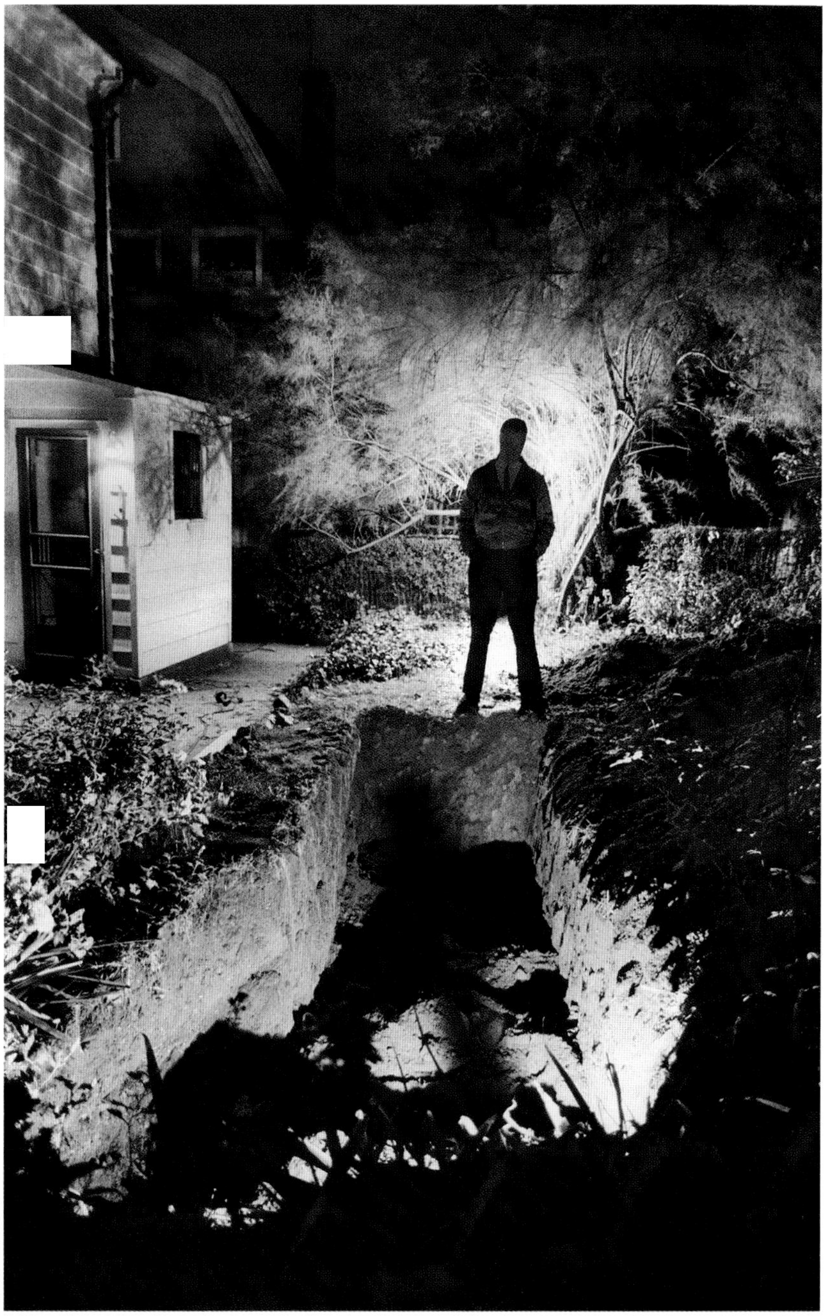

WALTER SANDERS

Earlier that day, Crater had behaved in a fashion that, subsequently, appeared mighty suspicious: He spent two hours going through personal files at the courthouse office; he had his assistant cash two checks for him totaling $5,150; and he withdrew a further $20,000—nearly a year's salary—from campaign funds. He also bought a single ticket to the Broadway comedy, *Dancing Partner*, and when he hailed a cab after dinner, his companions thought he was off to the show. Whether he ever got there—or even intended on going—cannot be known. He was never seen again.

Did the judge, cash in hand, run off with another of his paramours? Did he commit suicide? Was he straightened out by whomever he was going to straighten out? Was the driver of the taxi Frank Burns?

Frank Burns was the brother of New York City cop Charles Burns, who by chance had been the bodyguard of Murder Inc. hit man and turncoat Abe "Kid Twist" Reles, who by chance had fallen from a sixth-floor window while under Burns's care, just before Reles was set to testify against his old cronies. What do the Burns brothers have to do with Judge Crater? Well, on April 2, 2005, a 91-year-old woman named Stella Ferrucci-Good died in Queens, New York, and left behind a handwritten letter in an envelope marked DO NOT OPEN UNTIL MY DEATH. In the letter, Ferrucci-Good said that her late husband, Robert Good, a parks department supervisor, had teamed with the Burnses in rubbing out Crater. She wrote that the judge was buried in Brooklyn's Coney Island, under the boardwalk near West Eighth Street. Authorities confirmed that several bodies had been found there during a construction project in the 1950s but said that the bones had been reinterred in a pauper's field with those of hundreds of anonymous others.

Where Judge Crater rests, and how and why he died, remains a mystery. And it is clear that, all these years later, he's not calling in.

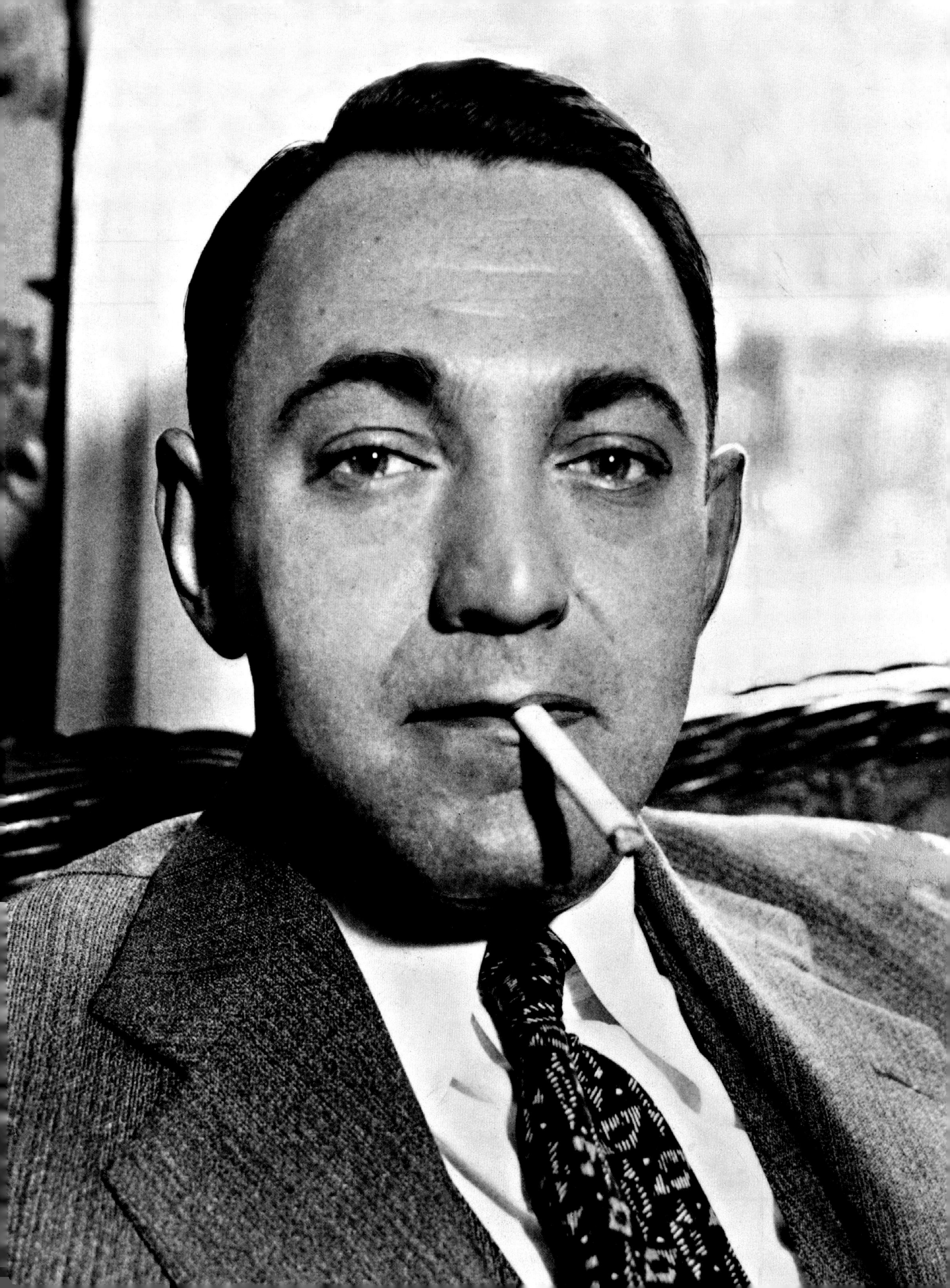

Where Is Dutch Schultz's Loot?

"Like anyone else who ever knew him, I disliked him intensely," said Willie Sutton. The famed bank robber was referring to Arthur Flegenheimer, who was born in the Bronx to German Jewish parents. His doting mother tried to bring him up to be a religious boy, but the grammar-school dropout followed more readily in the footsteps of his saloon-keeper father. Before too long, Arthur had recast himself as Dutch Schultz because "it was short enough to fit in the headlines."

Schultz knew that there was easy money to be made in a thirsty Prohibition era, and after some mentoring by crime genius Arthur Rothstein, he was on his way to earning the title Beer Baron of the Bronx. He got there by being very rough—he took on Mad Dog Coll and Legs Diamond—very mean (the notorious madam Polly Adler said, "He seemed to have no more warmth or need for human companionship than a machine") and so cheap that, according to Lucky Luciano, "here was a guy with a couple of million bucks and he dressed like a pig... His big deal was buyin' a newspaper for two cents so he could read about himself." One result of the Dutchman's pecuniary nature was that, as you'd expect, the loot piled up.

Schultz was such an abhorrent figure that he ended up an anachronism. As Prohibition persisted, most other gangs formed partnerships, but he was unable to get in on these lucrative pacts. As a freelancer moving beyond the beer biz, ruthlessly taking over the Harlem numbers racket and building a slot machine empire to boot, Schultz was putting himself in peril, and in the end, his aggression proved too much for other criminal kingpins.

In 1935, he became the primary focus of New York special prosecutor Thomas E. Dewey. When Schultz's income was threatened, he told a recently formed national crime syndicate, "Dewey's gotta go! He's my nemesis. I'm hitting him myself and in 48 hours." On October 23, the syndicate, fearing public reprisal, sent hit men to the Palace Chop House and Tavern in Newark, New Jersey, where Schultz was shot by Charles "the Bug" Workman. Schultz survived into the next day. Toward the end, he began to ramble incoherently, and the police kept a stenographer at his bedside to glean useful information. They could make nothing of the monologue, but literary figures William S. Burroughs and E.L. Doctorow later used the bizarrely poetic transcript in their fictions. In Doctorow's *Billy Bathgate*, the deathbed soliloquy contained coded clues as to where Schultz's fortune was stashed.

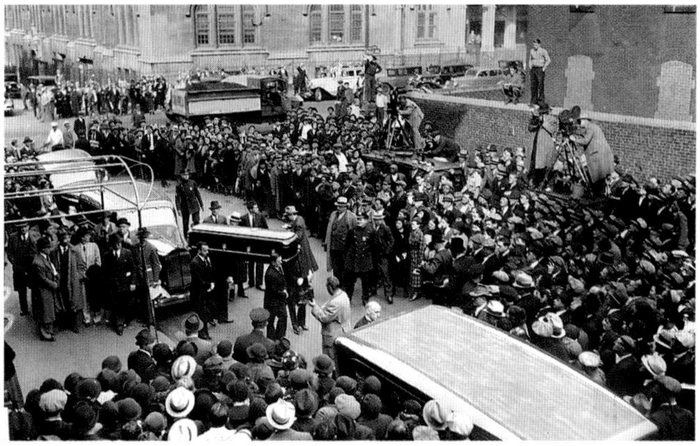

NEW YORK DAILY NEWS

The Dutchman (opposite) had few friends in life, but a vast throng turned up outside Daniel F. Coughlin Brothers Funeral Parlor at the corner of 58th Street and 10th Avenue in Manhattan to see him off (above). Below: Does the treasure lie near the Esopus Creek in upstate New York? Good question.

Yes, for with Dewey closing in and the prospect of incarceration looming, Schultz had put between $5 million and $7 million in cash and bonds (some versions add gold and jewels) in an airtight safe (some versions say steel suitcases) and, with the help of bodyguard Bernard "Lulu" Rosencrantz, buried the treasure somewhere in the Catskill Mountains of upstate New York. Rosencrantz, too, was nixed at the Palace Chop House, and so the secret died with that rubout. It is said that several of Schultz's many enemies, Luciano among them, exhausted themselves digging for the safe. Still today, amateur sleuths return to the hills each summer—an area along Route 28 between the road and the Esopus Creek, a tributary of the Hudson River, is a favorite target—and search for the booty. If anyone's found anything, they're not telling.

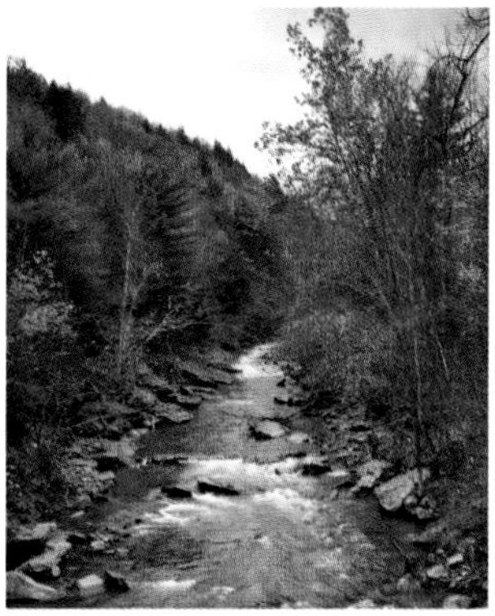

KATE KUNATH/GETTY

REX USA

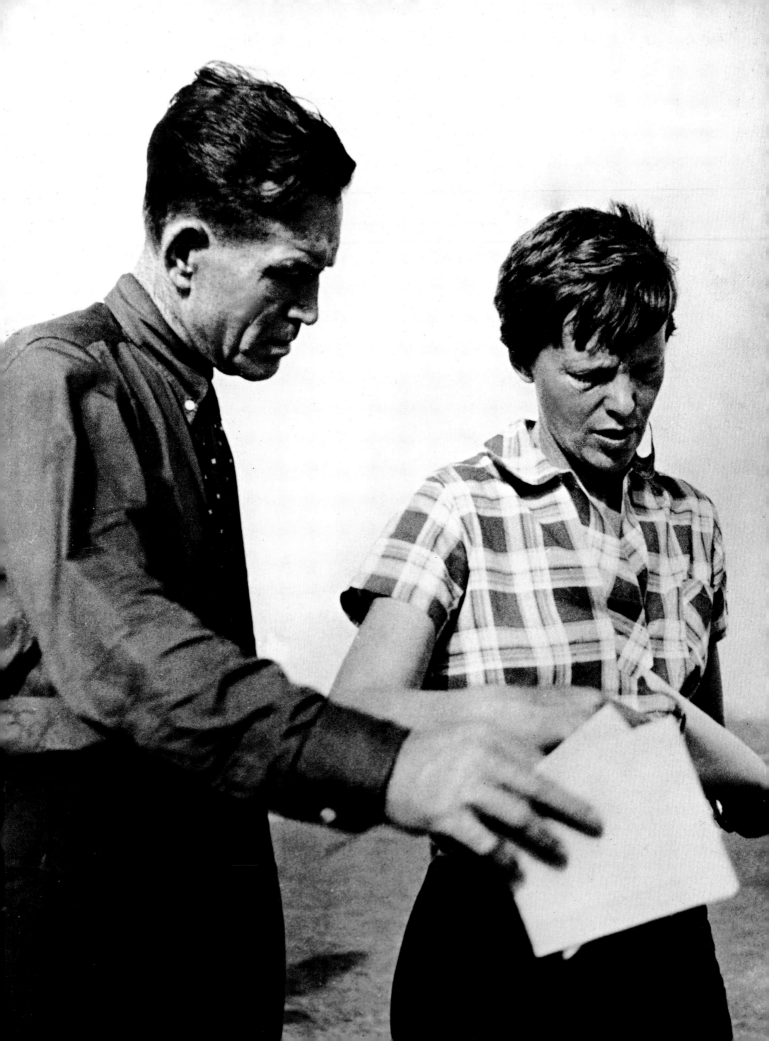

Whither Amelia Earhart?

"Nothing scares Amelia," her sister, Muriel, said, and the words appear to be true. For after numerous crash landings and knowing that 10 pilots had already died in the attempt, Amelia Earhart, in 1937, determined to become the first woman to fly around the world.

There were some who disagreed with Muriel, saying that Amelia wasn't necessarily fearless, merely reckless. Legend has it that as a child she steered her speeding sled between the legs of a galloping horse. In 1904, after returning from a family trip to the World's Fair in St. Louis, the seven-year-old designed and built a roller coaster in her Atchinson, Kansas, backyard. When she was 23, she got $10 from her father and paid for a thrilling 10-minute flight at a local airfield. Right then Earhart decided she would be a flier, and later that day she announced the news. In her memoir, *The Fun of It*, she wrote: "'I think I'd like to fly,' I told the family casually that evening, knowing full well I'd die if I didn't."

She again went to her dad, this time for $500 to purchase flying instruction. Miss Neta Snook, one of only a handful of women pilots and herself only 24, took Earhart under her wing in 1920—for a dollar a minute. Less than a year later, for $2,000, Earhart bought her first plane, a Kinner that she named *The Canary*.

In 1937, she told the *New York Herald Tribune* that she had "just one more good flight left in my system" and said she would become the first woman to fly around the world.

Earhart quickly crashed her *Canary*, repaired it and set her first record by flying to 14,000 feet—higher than any woman before her. In 1928, she became the first woman to cross the Atlantic in an airplane. Four years later she made the crossing again, piloting solo, thus becoming the first woman to do

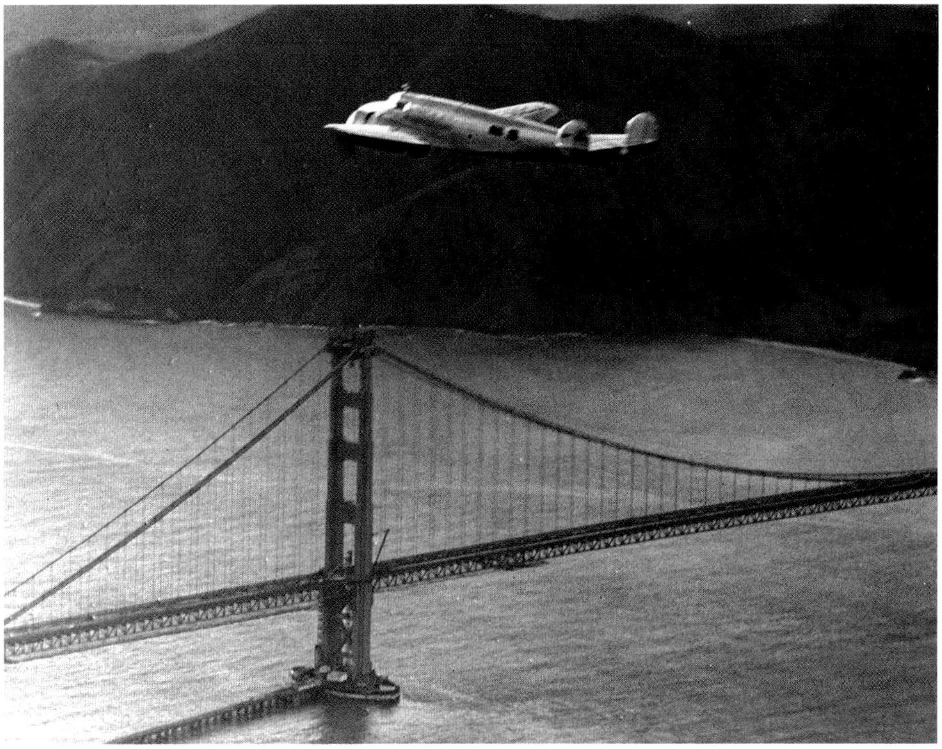

Right: During Earhart's first attempt to fly around the world, she soars west over San Francisco's Golden Gate Bridge toward Honolulu. During her next takeoff, in Hawaii, she crashes, and one of her navigators quits the team, leaving her partnered with only Noonan (opposite) for the second, fateful effort.

BETTMANN CORBIS (2)

She and Noonan had been heading for Howland Island, a speck of land barely two miles long that had an airstrip. They didn't make it.

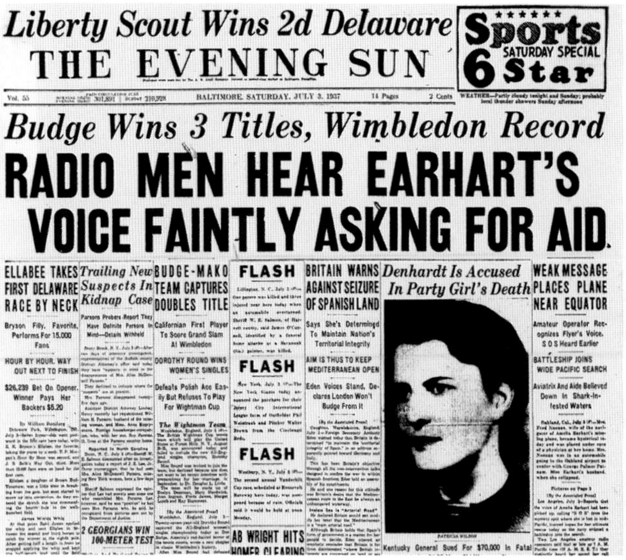
Liberty Scout Wins 2d Delaware

THE EVENING SUN

Sports SATURDAY SPECIAL 6 Star

BALTIMORE, SATURDAY, JULY 3, 1937

Budge Wins 3 Titles, Wimbledon Record

RADIO MEN HEAR EARHART'S VOICE FAINTLY ASKING FOR AID

ELLABEE TAKES FIRST DELAWARE RACE BY NECK

Bryson Filly, Favorite, Performs For 15,000 Fans

HOUR BY HOUR, WAY OUT NEXT TO FINISH

$26,239 Bet On Opener, Winner Pays Her Backers $5.20

Trailing New Suspects In Kidnap Case

Parsons Probers Report They Have Definite Persons In Mind—Details Withheld

2 GEORGIANS WIN 100-METER TEST

BUDGE-MAKO TEAM CAPTURES DOUBLES TITLE

Californian First Player To Score Grand Slam At Wimbledon

DOROTHY ROUND WINS WOMEN'S SINGLES

Defeats Polish Ace Easily But Refuses To Play For Wightman Cup

The Wightman Team

FLASH

FLASH

FLASH

AB WRIGHT HITS HOMER CLEARING

BRITAIN WARNS AGAINST SEIZURE OF SPANISH LAND

Says She's Determined To Maintain Nation's Territorial Integrity

AIM IS THUS TO KEEP MEDITERRANEAN OPEN

Eden Voices Stand, Declares London Won't Budge From It

Denhardt Is Accused In Party Girl's Death

PATRICIA WILSON

Kentucky General Sued For $70,000 In Fatal

WEAK MESSAGE PLACES PLANE NEAR EQUATOR

Amateur Operator Recognizes Flyer's Voice, S O S Heard Earlier

BATTLESHIP JOINS WIDE PACIFIC SEARCH

Aviatrix And Aide Believed Down In Shark-Infested Waters

Pictures on Page 3

CORBIS

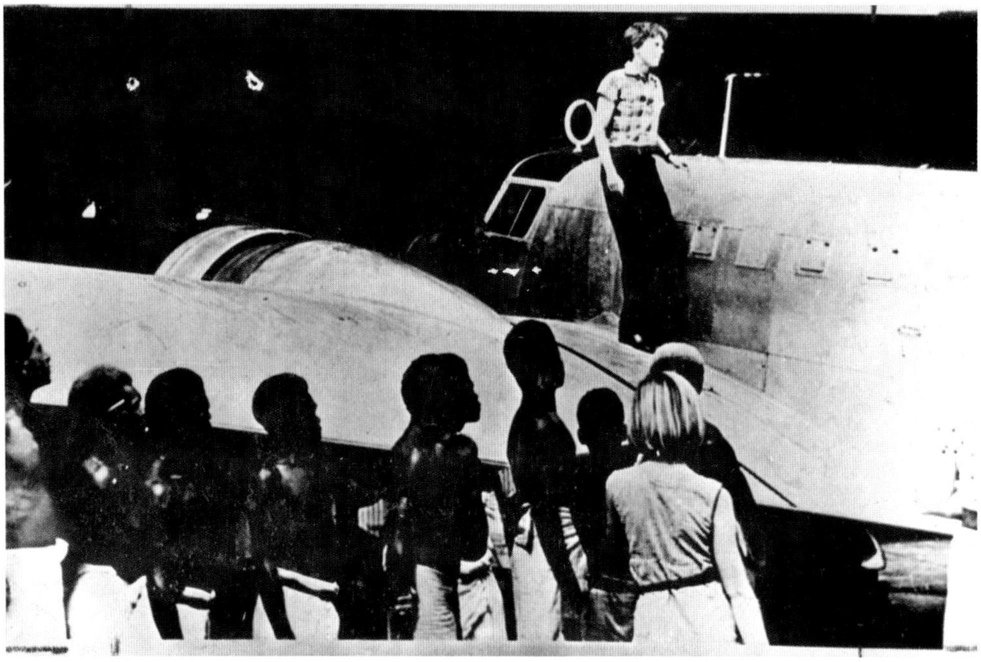

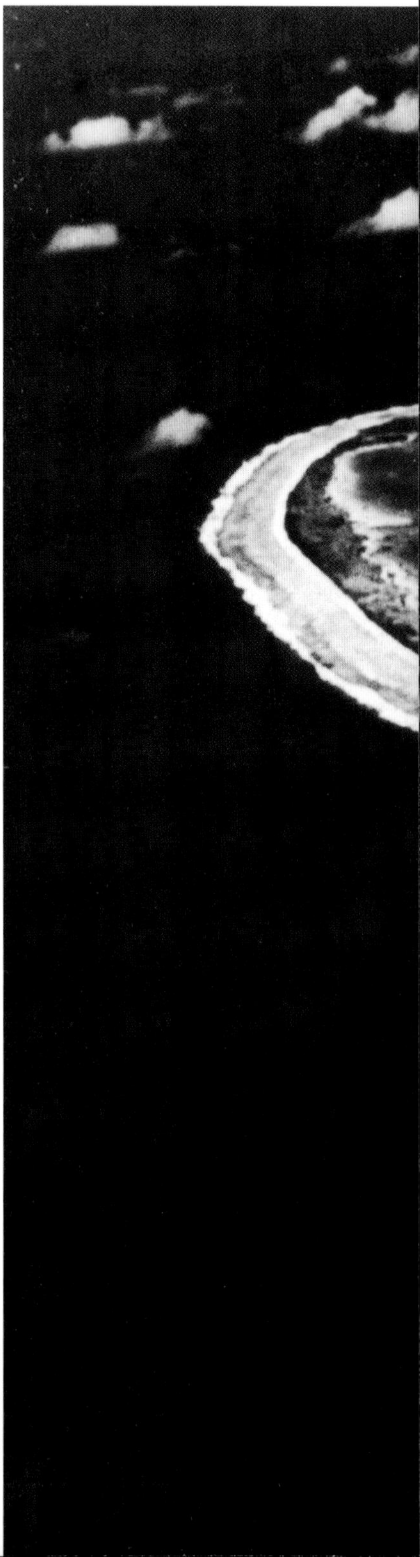

that. She was almost killed on that trip when her Lockheed Vega went into a spin, hurtling toward "whitecaps too close for comfort" before she could pull the plane up. But Earhart survived the plummet and 14 hours and 54 minutes after taking off from Newfoundland, she landed in Northern Ireland: Lady Lindy.

By the late 1930s, thanks to the PR efforts of her husband, George Palmer Putnam, and her continuing successes—she was the first woman to fly solo from Hawaii to California, and to go it alone across the United States—Earhart was a national hero. With her serene beauty and inherent charisma, she became a trendsetter in matters of style, as well as an early feminist icon.

In 1937, she told the *New York Herald Tribune* that she had "just one more good flight left in my system" and said she would become the first woman to fly around the world.

The world followed her progress with its collective breath held, as the headline in the July 3, 1937, Baltimore *Evening Sun* illustrates (top). Above: This is a photo—proven fraudulent—that was supposedly found on the body of a Japanese soldier killed on Okinawa during World War II. It purports to show Earhart alive and in captivity. The Nikumaroro atoll (right), 1,800 miles south of Hawaii, may in fact be where she wound up—and yet another expedition to the island seeking evidence will be mounted in 2010.

NATIONAL ARCHIVES

On her first attempt, Earhart completed the leg from Oakland, California, to Honolulu, then crashed during the subsequent take-off. One of her two navigators, Harry Manning, resigned, blaming the accident squarely on Earhart's lack of ability as a pilot. But Earhart was not deterred. On June 1, 1937, with only one navigator, Fred Noonan, she took off from Miami, this time heading east. Amelia Earhart flew 22,000 miles—three quarters of the way around the world—before disappearing into clouds above the Central Pacific. Her last words, as recorded by the ship *Itasca*, were "We must be on you, but cannot see you, but gas is running low, been unable to reach you by radio, we are flying at altitude 1,000 feet." She and Noonan had been heading for Howland Island, a speck of land barely two miles long that had an airstrip. They didn't make it. Did they ditch at sea and subsequently sink? Did they make it to then uninhabited Gardner Island (now called Nikumaroro), where certain artifacts that *might* have been from Earhart's plane have been found? Much more wildly, was Earhart spying on the Japanese in the Pacific? Were she and Noonan captured by them and executed after their plane crashed on Saipan Island?

Questions . . . but no answers.

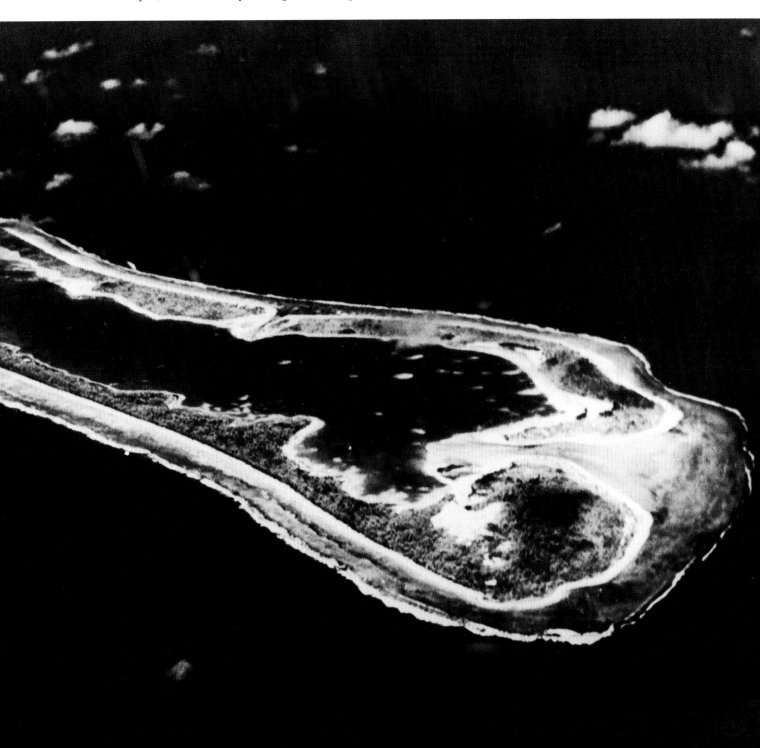

Who Killed Sir Harry Oakes?

During his undergraduate days at Bowdoin College, Harry Oakes, who was born in 1874 in Sangerville, Maine, told a classmate that he would become a millionaire one day and subsequently die a violent death, though he had no reason to expect either eventuality. This unfortunate sage was only too accurate in his foretelling.

The money was sought, first, in the Yukon, after the ambitious Oakes, having graduated from Bowdoin and spent some time at Syracuse University Medical School, determined that the Klondike Gold Rush was a better bet than doctoring. Oakes's big hit would not come in Alaska, however; in fact, his experience there was fraught. After hacking away at rock in temperatures as cold as 60 below, to make ends meet he took a job as a medical assistant treating frostbite victims. In 1906, he was aboard a ship that foundered off the coast, and he was taken prisoner by the Russians, then released. That was enough of Alaska, and he boarded another ship, this one bound for Australia, where again Oakes struck out

DANIEL E. SCHERMAN

When it came time to suspect someone, the locals were happy to suspect the count, who had swept up Harry's daughter and eloped with her, and who had started winning their yacht races.

as a prospector, as he would do next in New Zealand and then in California. It was in Canada in 1911—at Kirkland Lake in Ontario—that Oakes finally hit pay dirt. Did he ever. His Lake Shore Mine at Kirkland grew to be the second richest in North America after the Homestead Mine in the Dakotas' Black Hills, and Oakes was earning $60,000 a day. Before the decade was out, Oakes was said to be the wealthiest man in Canada.

He married Eunice MacIntyre, a shy woman 26 years his junior, and for tax reasons the couple settled on the island of Nassau in the Bahamas. He became Nassau's most famous benefactor, building a golf course, a waterworks, a bus service, an airline service for medical emergencies, a program that delivered free milk to kids and another to assist unwed mothers. Now a subject of the English Crown, Oakes was named a baronet by King George VI in 1939.

Oakes's wife and four of their five children were away vacationing at their summer home in Bar Harbor, Maine, in early July 1943; Oakes was to join them on the ninth, but on the night of the seventh, an intruder or intruders brutally murdered Oakes in his bedroom, shattering his skull with four blows to the head according to one account, shooting him in the head four times according to another. A fire had been set in the bedroom, presumably to eliminate evidence. Oakes was found by his longtime business associate Harold Christie, a close friend with whom, it was said, there had been a recent falling out.

Suspicion fell on Oakes's son-in-law Count Alfred de Marigny, who was disliked by Oakes

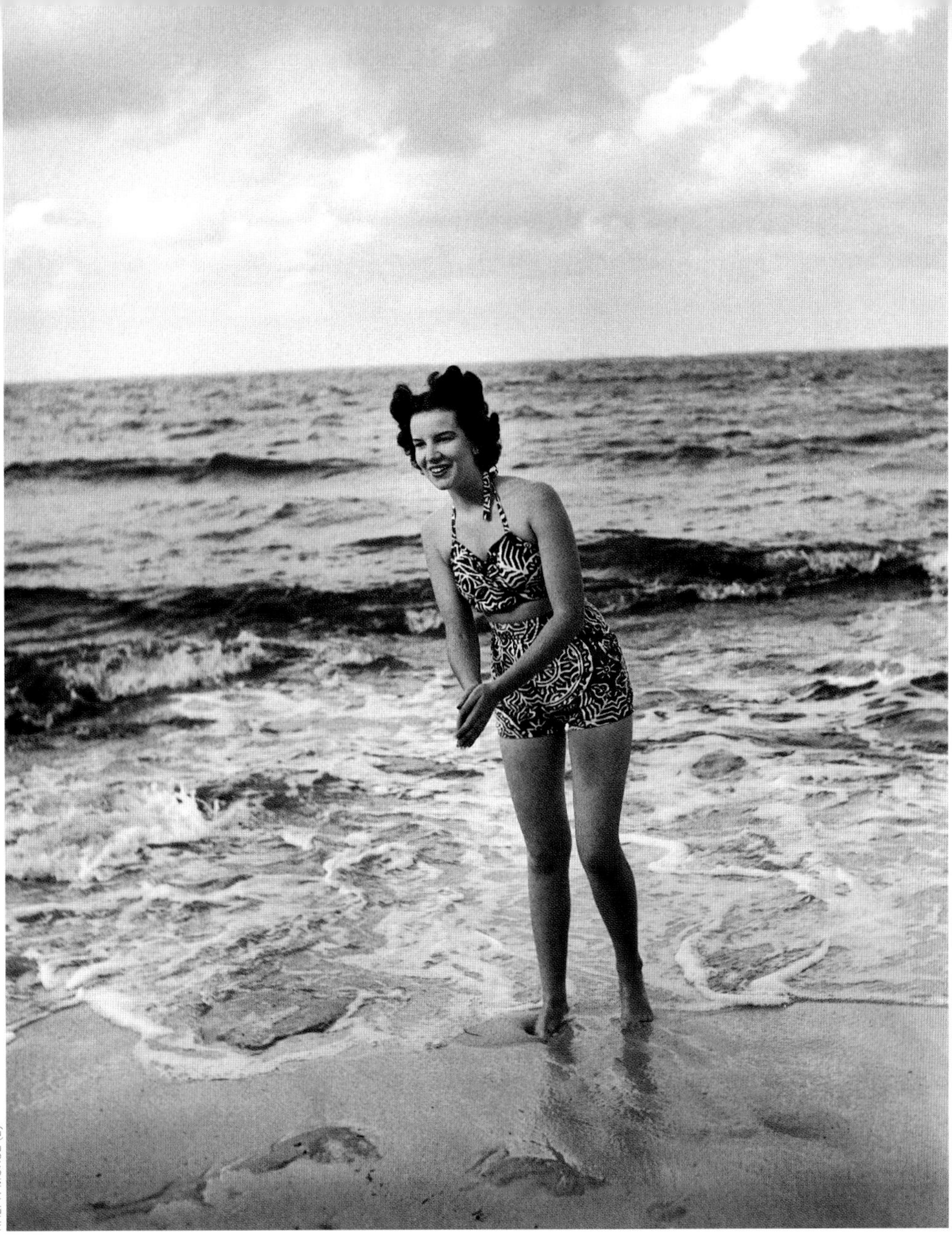

RALPH MORSE (2)

Opposite: Sir Harry relished his standing as a larger than life personality; some saw him as an eccentric, especially when he was brandishing that sword. Left: His beautiful daughter Nancy was popular on the island of Nassau, but the same could not be said for her husband, Count Alfred de Marigny, who in the picture below is arriving at the courthouse during his trial.

and most of Nassau society. De Marigny had arrived on the island a year earlier, scooped up Oakes's eldest daughter, Nancy, and eloped with her as soon as she turned 18. He had further irked the locals by winning their yacht races. De Marigny was arrested and charged with murder. The trial created a tabloid sensation worldwide; however, the investigation had been conducted incompetently in the extreme, and the acquittal took less than two hours.

Years later, de Marigny pointed the finger at Christie, forwarding the shooting theory and saying he had found a witness—a watchman—who had heard the gunfire and seen Christie and two others fleeing in a sedan. One version had it that the killers were from the mainland, sent by Mob boss Meyer Lansky to ice Oakes because he had been opposing efforts to build casinos on Nassau. Many today still suspect that de Marigny was the perpetrator after all.

The case has never been retried, nor has Oakes's tomb ever been opened to see if, perhaps, there are four bullets in his head.

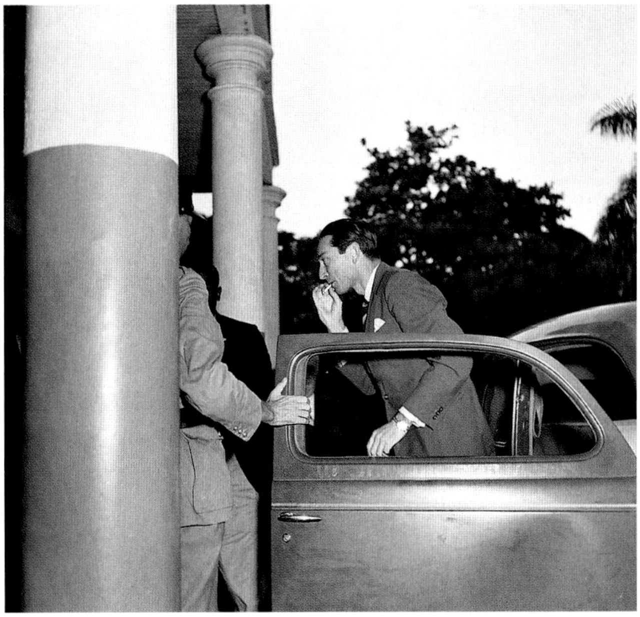

What Happened to the Nazi Gold?

This is the story of one of history's largest-ever heists and largest-ever hunts—a treasure hunt that will never end. The perp was, of course, Adolf Hitler. The hunters have included individuals and nations from around the world.

At the outset of World War II, the German economy was depressed and hardly capable of underwriting the continental and then global offensive Hitler was imagining. The modus operandi

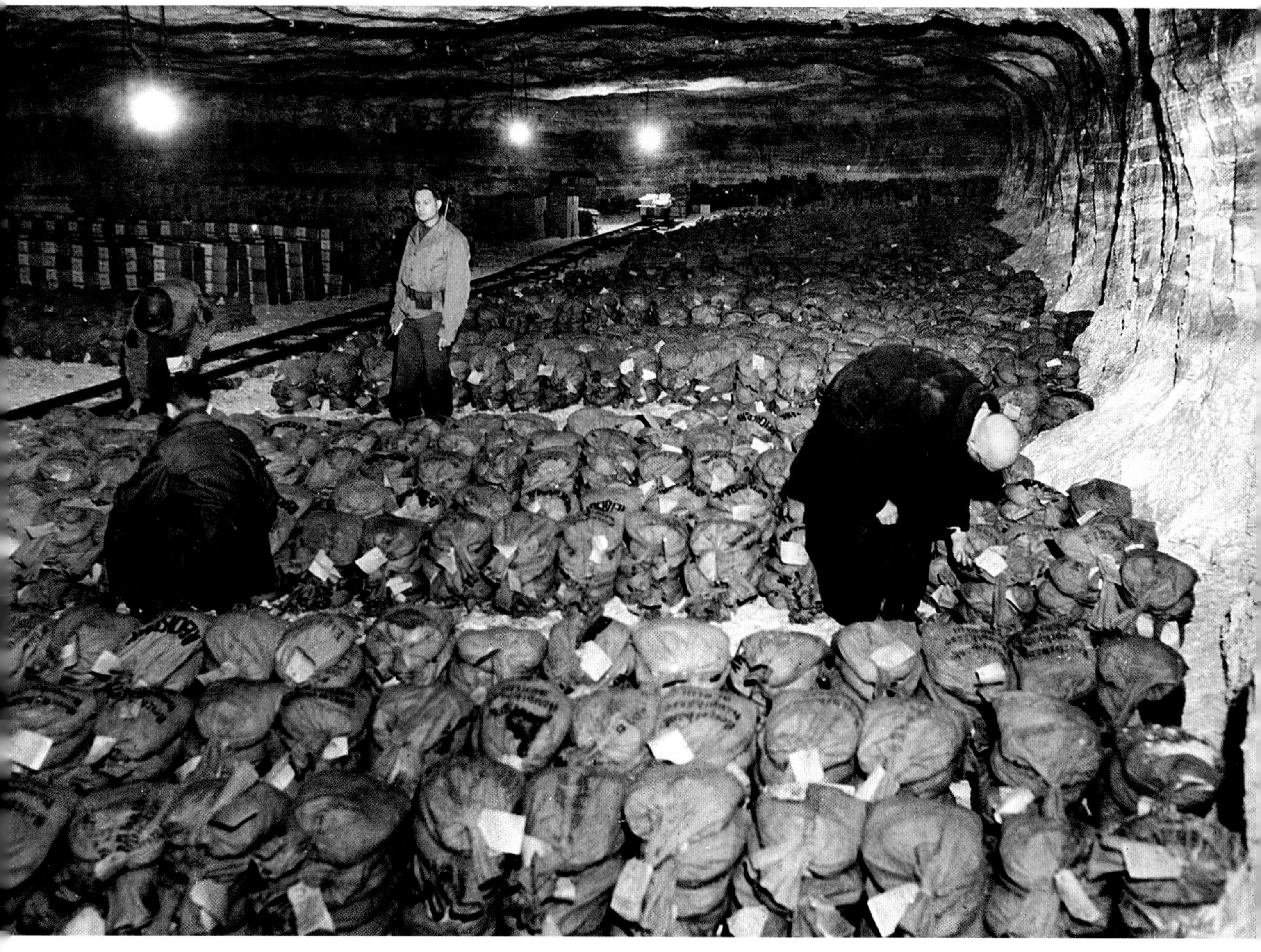

When the Allies closed in, fleeing Nazis scrambled to hide what riches they could. In lakes within the mountains of Austria, watertight casks full of Nazi gold were sunk to the bottom.

of the Nazis thus became to loot gold, jewelry, artworks and all other riches from the countries they conquered. For instance, the exercise of control over Czechoslovakia, Austria and Danzig between 1937 and 1939 wound up boosting Germany's gold reserves by more than $70 million. According to the U.S. State Department, during the course of the war the Germans stole more than $400 million in gold from occupied nations and more than $140 million from individuals. One of the most infamous, horrific war atrocities the Nazis committed was the extraction of gold fillings from the teeth of concentration camp inmates. More than half a billion dollars in all—and that was just the gold. Museums and private residences in Berlin were filled with ill-gotten masterworks, and when there was no more room in the capital, Hitler filled castles in remote Alpine realms with the overflow.

When the Allies closed in near the war's end, fleeing Nazis sought to hide what riches they could. A large supply of gold—as much as 100 tons—that was being kept in the Reichsbank was moved by rail when bombs started falling; some of it was stashed in a potassium mine 200 miles southwest of Berlin. This was recovered by Patton's troops when workers at the mine told them what lay within, but much more has yet to be found. Gold and currency that had already made its way into accounts in neutral countries such as Switzerland simply kept moving; a U.S. Treasury agent's report that was filed in 1946 (and declassified 50 years later) indicated that millions of dollars in gold coins wound up in a numbered Swiss account belonging to the Vatican, and in January 2000, a civil suit was filed against the Vatican Bank, the Franciscan order and other defendants. The Mob may have grabbed a share: Lucky Luciano and Meyer Lansky had strong connections to the Swiss National Bank, and it has been reported that hundreds of millions of dollars in gold may have been laundered into their anonymous accounts. Well before the war ended, Hitler henchman Martin Bormann was trucking his horde of riches across France to Spain, where it was transferred to U-boats and shipped to Argentina. Juan and Eva Peron are said to have gained control of much of this plunder and to have subsequently deposited more than $800 million in numbered Swiss bank accounts.

And then, in lakes within the mountains of Austria, watertight casks full of Nazi gold were sunk to the bottom.

New discoveries are made every year—in the lakes, in the mountains, in the most circumspect banks (for instance, in the Bank of England, where seven tons of Nazi gold were found in 1996). Investigations are constant, as are lawsuits.

It is a certainty that the ledger will never be closed, but there is a holy grail for the treasure hunters, one thing they desperately hope to find: the Amber Room. When Hitler's army invaded the Soviet Union in 1941, they stole, among other valuables, the interior of a room from a St. Petersburg palace that was made entirely of amber and gold. Perhaps the panels were lost at sea, as is rumored. Perhaps they were blown to bits by bombs. Perhaps they are buried in a cavern in Deutschkatharinenberg, Germany, as a 2008 dig—which failed—speculated.

Until the Amber Room is found, the world has only a reproduction of it that has been constructed in Ekatermininsky Palace in Pushkin, a village near St. Petersburg. In its extravagance, its loudness and its brazenness, it fairly shouts of Nazi greed: They dismantled *this*, they spirited it away, they sought to steal all that they could. They sought to rule the world.

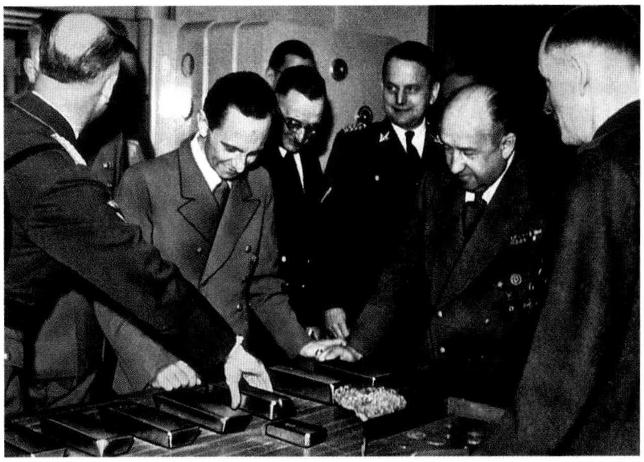

Opposite: Patton's Third Army has taken control of the many tons of gold that was hidden in the potassium mine 200 miles from Berlin. Right: Before the fall of the Third Reich, Hitler's minister of propaganda, Joseph Goebbels (second from left), examines gold bars made of plunder taken from Jewish victims of the Holocaust.

BETTMANN/CORBIS

Who Murdered the Black Dahlia?

We would be happy to solve the legendary Black Dahlia murder case—perhaps the most noir of all the noir crimes in Hollywood history— over the next several paragraphs. Alas, we're no closer to fingering the culprit than Los Angeles law enforcement was more than 60 years ago. The case remains open and perhaps always will.

During her lifetime, Elizabeth Short was, in all likelihood, not called the Black Dahlia, though some accounts claim that she was. Short probably received her exotic nickname in death, since the investigation of this raven-haired beauty's grisly demise followed close upon the release of the 1946 Raymond Chandler crime film, *The Blue Dahlia*. Likely, some inspired ink-stained wretch working for one of L.A.'s tabloids channeled Chandler and anointed Miss Short with her immortal moniker.

She called herself Beth; friends and family knew her as Betty. She was born on July 29, 1924, and grew up during the depths of the Depression in a working-class neighborhood of Medford, Massachusetts, outside of Boston. Beth found an occasional escape from the drudgery of the real world at the movie theater and was determined to become a star.

In pursuit of her dream, she wound up in Hollywood. At one point during World War II, she worked as a cashier at a local military base, where she won the title "Camp Cutie of Camp Cooke."

On January 9, 1947, she was seen in the lobby of L.A.'s Biltmore Hotel. She was making phone calls while she waited for her sister, who was supposed to meet her there. According to the official version, she was never seen alive again—except by her killer.

Elizabeth Short is on the left in the beach photo, while on the opposite page is a letter purportedly from the killer (some think it was assembled by reporters trying to keep the story alive). Taking a lie detector test is one of the many suspects in the case, Robert "Red" Manley, a married man who had dated Short.

AP

No one has ever been charged in the case, although scores have been suspected. Over the years, this list has included such luminaries as Norman Chandler, a publisher of the *Los Angeles Times;* the folksinger Woody Guthrie; and the film titan Orson Welles.

TOPHAM/THE IMAGE WORKS

to Los Angeles Herald-Express
I Will GivE UP IN
Dahlia KILLing if I Get
10 Years
DON'T TRY TO Find Me

INTERNATIONAL NEWS PHOTO/HULTON/GETTY

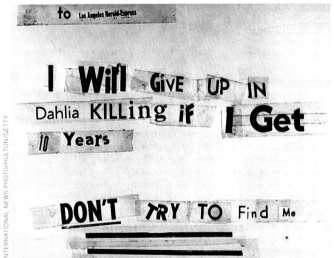

A number of people subsequently claimed to have spotted Short here or there, in the company of various people, during the six days that passed between her disappearance from the Biltmore and the discovery of her brutally mutilated corpse. On January 15, Betty Bersinger was walking with her three-year-old daughter when they stumbled upon what Bersinger first thought to be a discarded department-store mannequin— a "broken doll"—in a vacant lot. It turned out to be the body of Elizabeth Short, severed at the waist, naked, and posed with the legs spread and the corners of the mouth cut so that they extended to each ear thus forming a frightful smile. The police soon determined that Short had been bound, tortured and killed elsewhere, then dumped. The hunt was on.

And it still is, because no one has ever been charged, although scores have been suspected. Over the years, this list has included such as Norman Chandler, a publisher of the *Los Angeles Times;* the folksinger Woody Guthrie, who once wrote sexually explicit letters to some California women he knew; and Orson Welles, thanks to a theory forwarded by Mary Pacios, a former neighbor of the Shorts in Medford, who wrote a book about the case in 1999.

Pacios's is only one of many books and movies that have dealt with the Black Dahlia mystery. Incredibly, two separate nonfiction accounts make the case that each of the authors' fathers was responsible. In one of these tomes, Steve Hodel's *Black Dahlia Avenger,* the former murder investigator claims that his dad, Dr. George Hodel, whom cops had looked at in 1949, was indeed the killer. James Ellroy, author of the classic crime novel *The Black Dahlia,* said of Hodel's book in 2004: "It's divine providence that a mad doctor spawns a son who becomes an LAPD homicide detective. And it turns out that his old man did the job . . . I dig it."

In that interview with *CBS News,* Ellroy theorized about why the case has endured and, in his estimation, will last forever: "She's a ghost and a blank page to record our fears and desires. A postwar Mona Lisa, an L.A. quintessential."

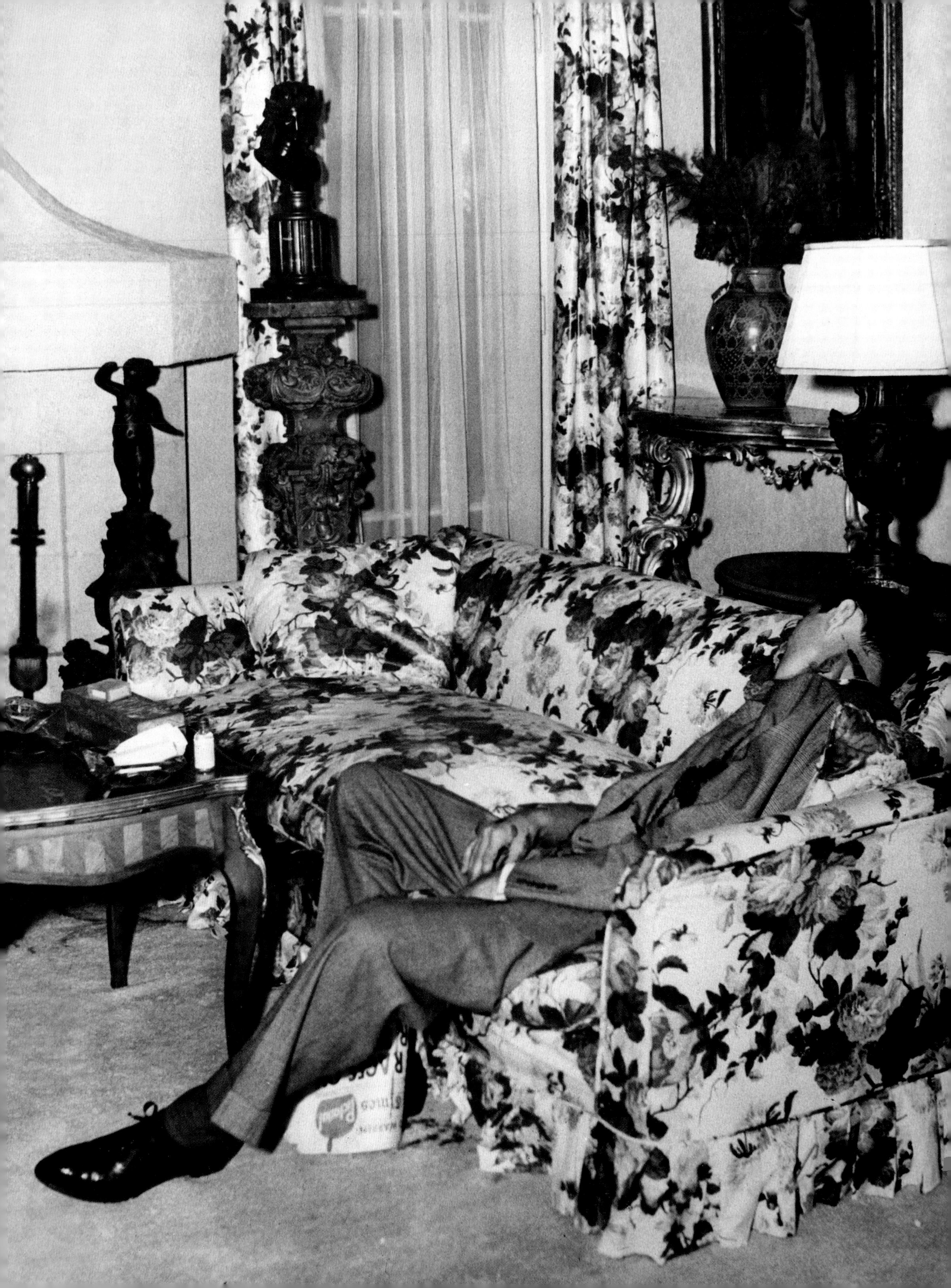

Who Offed Bugsy Siegel?

The answer to that question is surely: the Mob. Or maybe: his associates. Or perhaps more specifically: Meyer Lansky, though the rap was never pinned on him.

As we have seen, mobsters and gangsters have already made appearances in the pages of this book—in the Dutch Schultz case, even in the disappearance of the Nazi loot. This makes sense. The Mob works in shadowy ways and doesn't always get caught, and so it would be expected to figure in lots of unsolved mysteries.

Benjamin Siegel was very hands-on in the evolution of organized crime. He was born to poor Russian Jewish immigrants in Brooklyn in 1906. As a boy, he preyed on pushcart vendors. If they didn't pony up, he doused their carts with kerosene and torched them. That low flashpoint gave him his nickname, the mere mention of which set him off. Bugsy had a serious yen for violence. Even in his later years, when he was a crime royal, he liked to be in on the dirty deed and was personally responsible for several rubouts. When Lucky Luciano and Lansky launched their syndicate in the early '30s, they needed muscle to carry out their plans, so Lansky created Murder Inc., a pack of killers siphoned mainly from Jewish gangs, and handed the reins to Siegel. Murder Inc. was strictly "professional." Its members didn't work for outsiders nor were they sicced on politicians; it would attract too much attention. As Siegel once said, allaying a businessman's fears, "We only kill each other." Murder Inc. marked the inception of contract killing, in which the gunmen have no obvious link to the victim and therefore are difficult to catch. Of the 500 or so murders committed, Lansky, Luciano and/or fellow boss Frank Costello probably signed off on every one.

By the mid-'30s, things were plenty hot for Siegel. He had made a ton of enemies and had frequent run-ins with the police (though he would never serve time). Luciano and Lansky were tired of his "acting without thinking," so they sent him to California to goose the rackets out there and infiltrate the Hollywood scene. Luciano sent a minatory missive to his boys in Los Angeles: "Ben is coming West for the good of his health and health of all of us."

Bugsy, no garden-variety psychopath, was made for L.A.: charming, witty, handsome. He couldn't keep his paws off the ladies, and they hardly minded.

Bugsy was perfect for his new job. As a Jew, he was able to mingle comfortably with the Hollywood moguls. And he wasn't your garden-variety psychopath but was charming, witty and handsome, with blue eyes and black hair. He couldn't keep his paws off the ladies, but then most of them seemed to like the arrangement.

Siegel rented a mansion and was shown the ropes by boyhood pal George Raft, the veteran portrayer of screen gangsters. Raft introduced Bugsy to the ravishing Countess Dorothy Di Frasso. Reputedly, she took Siegel to her estate in Italy, where he met Hermann Goering and Joseph Goebbels. The two Nazis irked Siegel in some way, and the contessa had to beg him not to kill them.

In the mid-'40s, Bugsy, either acting on his own or at the behest of Lansky, carved out a plan for a lavish casino in the innocuous desert town of Las Vegas. The Flamingo was a fiasco, beset particularly by cost overruns—caused mainly by Bugsy's skimming syndicate money, which his moll, Virginia Hill, stashed in Europe. It was a reckless endeavor. Finally, even Lansky agreed that Siegel had to be killed. On June 20, 1947, he was reading in Hill's living room—she was conveniently away at the time—when shells from an Army carbine burst through the window and ripped into Bugsy. They found his left eye in the next room.

An unsolved mystery? Well, no one was ever charged. It seems to come down to that adage: They only kill each other.

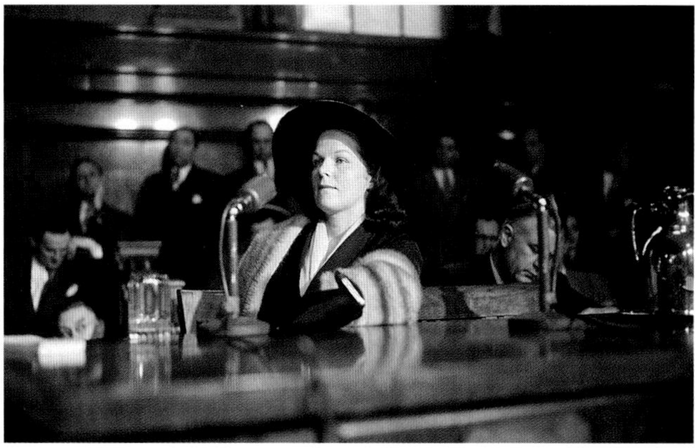

BETTMANN/CORBIS

Bugsy's in a bad way on Hill's couch (opposite), while, at right, Hill is on the hot seat, testifying—but keeping pretty much mum—before a U.S. Senate committee investigating organized crime.

AP

Where Did Richard Colvin Cox Go?

When one thinks of the U.S. Army's military academy at West Point, one thinks of strength, fortitude, courage, security and, finally, exemplary, forthright behavior. Therefore, anomalous events concerning West Point really do stand out. When it was a fort during the Revolutionary War, the traitor Benedict Arnold tried to turn it over to the British. This is still the most infamous incidence of treachery in American history, not least because it concerned such a hallowed place. Men and women associated with West Point do not turn traitor, and another thing they do not do is disappear. But one of them did, and so he is remembered today. Richard Colvin Cox remains the only West Point cadet ever to vanish from the campus and not turn up either alive or dead.

After graduating from high school in Ohio in 1946, Cox enlisted in the Army and served in an intelligence unit near the newly created border between West and East Germany. Also serving in Cox's section was an Army official who went by the name of George. According to a 1996 book about the case by 1949 West Point graduate Harry Maihafer, this George apparently told Cox he was a former ranger and bragged that he had not only killed Nazis during the war but he had also impregnated a German girl and then murdered her to cover up the relationship. The depth of Cox and George's association at the time is unclear, but in any event: In 1947, Dick Cox applied for admission to West Point and was accepted. He arrived there in January 1948.

On Saturday, January 7,

> "Well, look, when he comes in, tell him to come on down here to the hotel . . . Just tell him George called—he'll know who I am."

1950, at 4:45 p.m., the phone rang in Cox's barracks. Cadet Peter Hains was assigned to answer incoming calls, and he did so. He later remembered that the caller's "tone was rough and patronizing, almost insulting." Informed that Cox was out, the caller told Hains: "Well, look, when he comes in, tell him to come on down here to the hotel . . . Just tell him George called—he'll know who I am. We knew each other in Germany. I'm just up here for a little while, and tell him I'd like to get him a bite to eat."

The call touched off a strange week in the life of Richard Colvin Cox—a week that was, perhaps, his last. He did meet George later on the evening of the seventh in the visitors' area of Grant Hall, the great stone pile on Thayer Road where Cox's company B-2 was

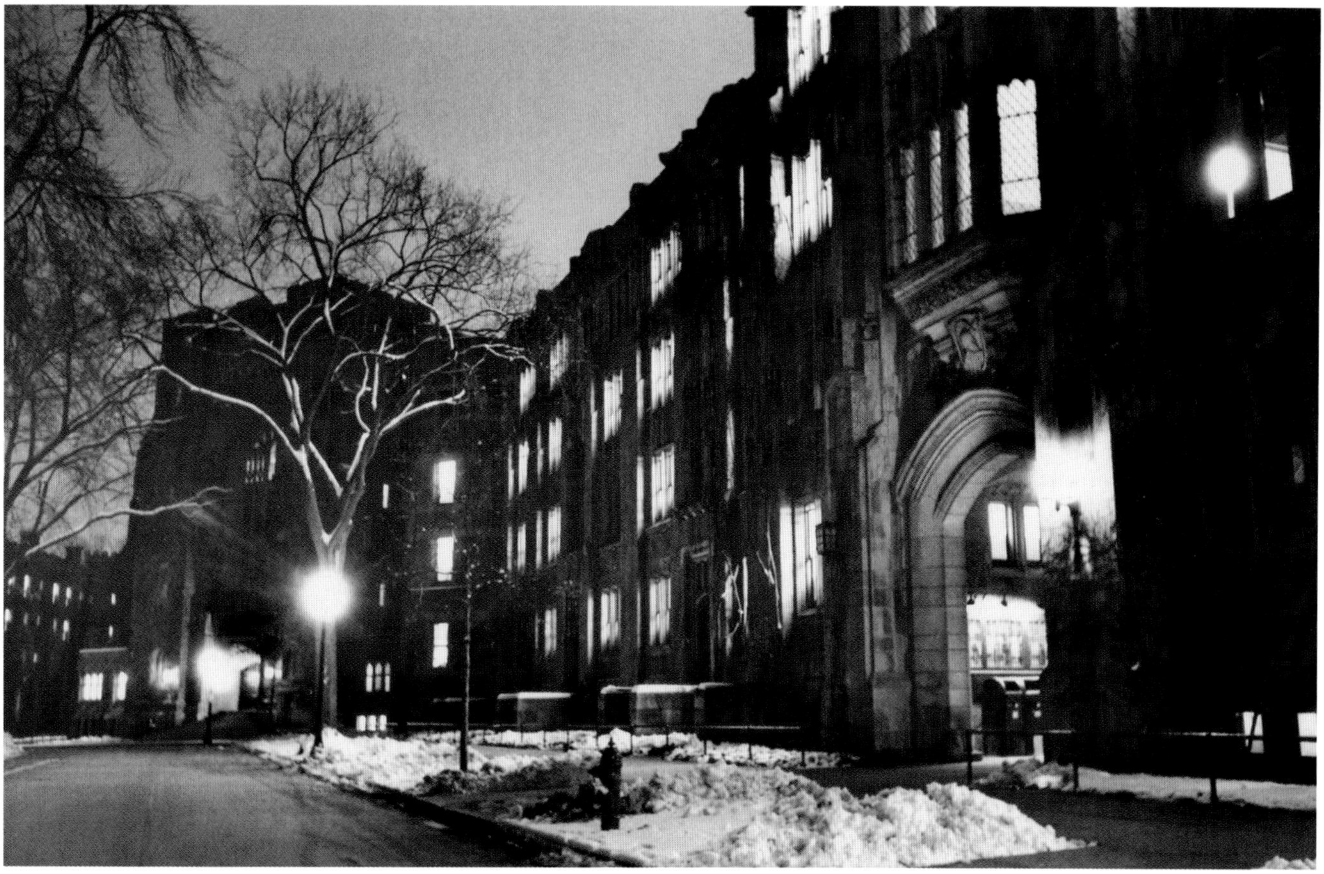
DAN WEINER

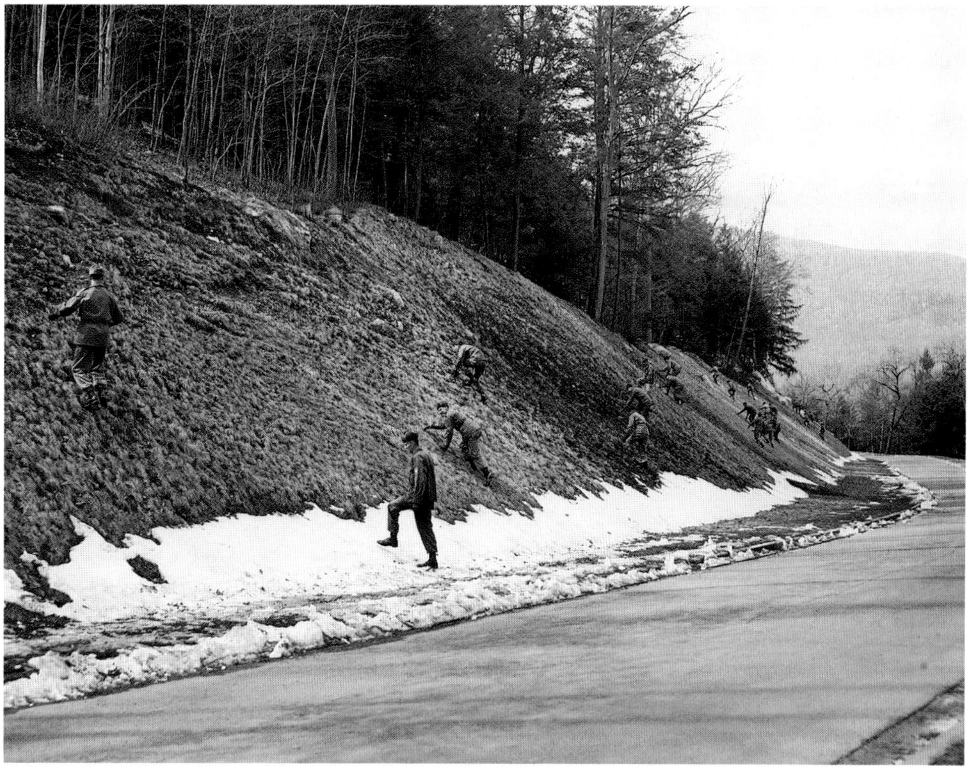
INP/CORBIS

Opposite: After Cox went missing, this portrait was sent to all law enforcement agencies and Army posts in the U.S. and Germany under the heading: WANTED FOR ABSENCE WITHOUT LEAVE. Above: Grant Hall in the North Barracks, where Cox lived in a room on the top floor and where he met George. Right: The West Point campus is scoured for evidence.

quartered. The two men went to George's car and shared a bottle of whiskey. Back in Grant Hall later, Cox bothered to alter the time that he had earlier written in the B-2 departure book to make it seem like he had been at the 6:30 p.m. supper formation, which he had in fact missed.

George visited Cox again the next day. Maihafer writes: "During the next few days, Dick Cox mentioned his visitor a few times, but never by name, even when asked." George visited a third time on the evening of Saturday, January 14. Cox apparently left the campus with him that night, for he was not seen again. West Point had never experienced an incident remotely like the one involving cadet Cox and hasn't seen anything remotely like it since.

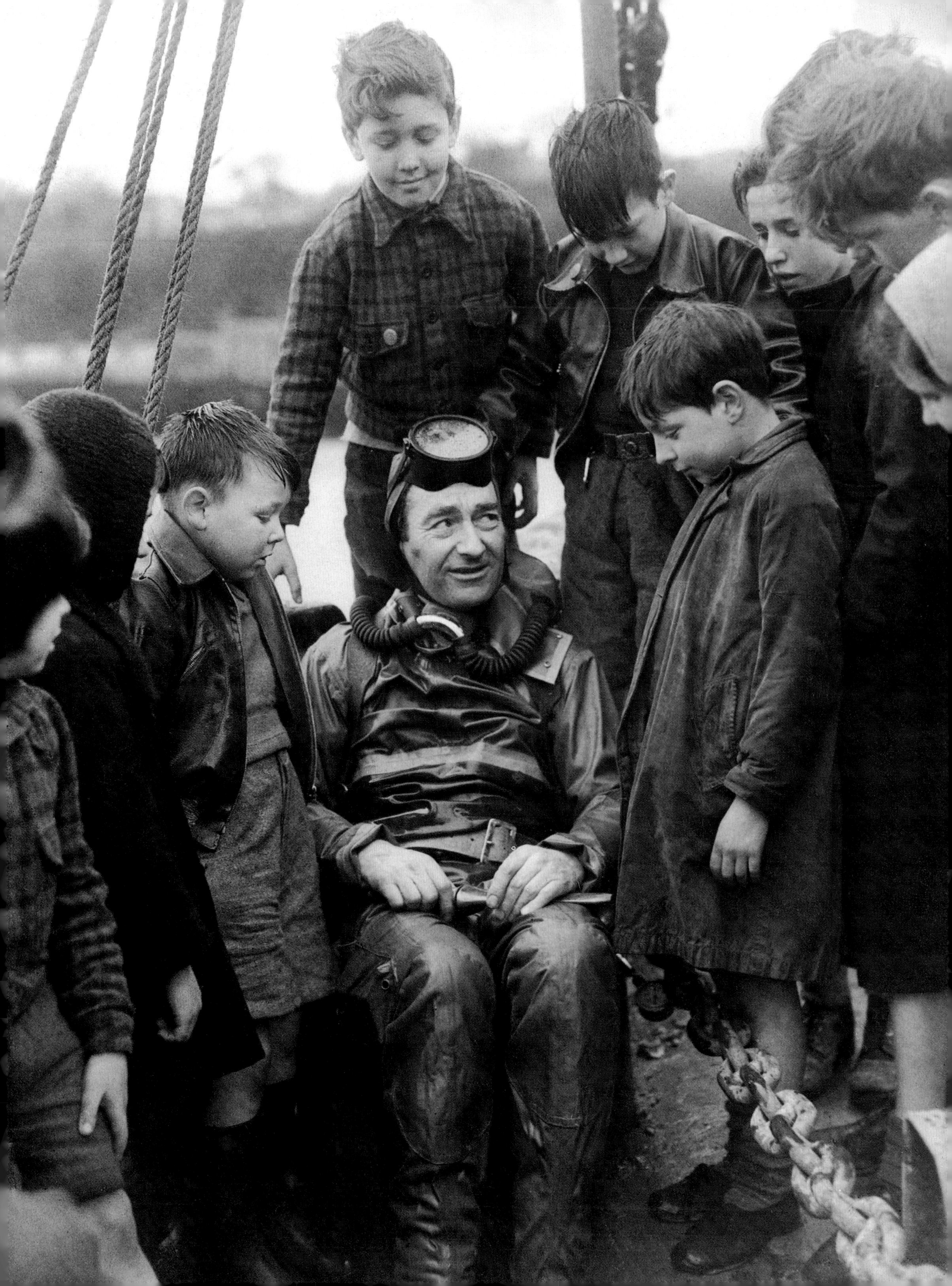

Did the Soviets Kill Commander Crabb?

The man who was said to be one of Ian Fleming's models for the superspy James Bond earned his legend during World War II, searching beneath the waves for limpet mines. But even when the war ended, Crabb was not done serving his country.

The British naval hero Commander Lionel "Buster" Crabb was so intrepid during his service in World War II and subsequently that it was said he was one of Ian Fleming's models for the superspy James Bond. Crabb earned his legend as a frogman, searching beneath the waves for limpet mines during the war. He was awarded several high military laurels before retiring from the Royal Navy in 1955.

Crabb was not done serving his country, however. In 1956, he was contacted by Lord Mountbatten, Great Britain's First Sea Lord, and asked if he would help with a top secret mission being planned in conjunction with the intelligence agency MI6. Soviet leaders Nikolai Bulganin and Nikita Khrushchev were coming to England on a diplomatic mission, and while their ship, the cruiser *Ordzhonikidze*, was docked in Portsmouth Harbour, some espionage could be enjoyed. It would be dangerous business, Crabb was candidly told, but he was the man for the job. On April 19, Crabb dived into the bay and made his way toward the *Ordzhonikidze*. He never returned.

With Crabb having vanished, the Admiralty had to come up with something, and 10 days after the failed spy mission, it announced that the fabled commander had gone missing in Stokes Bay while conducting "trials of certain underwater apparatus." Meantime, Prime Minister Anthony Eden learned for the first time what MI6 had been up to and went ballistic. As hazy details began to leak out, Eden did nothing to stanch the flood of rumors concerning the incident when he said that it would "not be in the public interest" to discuss the true circumstances of Crabb's death. Said Eden: "[W]hat was done was done without the authority or knowledge of Her Majesty's ministers." He canned the head of MI6.

From: L K P Crabb

Thank you for a very delightful lunch & break

Marshall tells me that the photo is to come back.

Lots of trouble here. Chaos complete.

L K P Crabb

BRIAN SEED

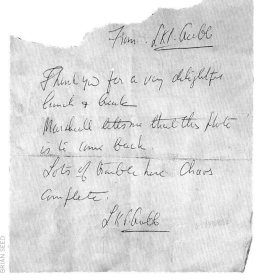

Opposite: The hero frogman with young admirers in 1950. Right: In the days before his last dive, Crabb told an associate he wasn't sleeping well as he was concerned about a "little job" and wrote a letter to the publisher of his forthcoming biography, ending ominously, as we see: "Lots of trouble here. Chaos complete."

KEYSTONE/GETTY

Fourteen months after Crabb disappeared, the body of a man in a frogman suit was discovered floating near Pilsey Island in Chichester Harbour, which is near Portsmouth. Positive identification proved impossible since the corpse had neither head nor hands. Crabb's ex-wife said she couldn't be sure, and his girlfriend said she thought the body was not his, but the coroner made a formal announcement that he was satisfied Crabb had been found.

Another person who viewed the remains, Sydney Knowles, who had been one of Crabb's diving buddies,

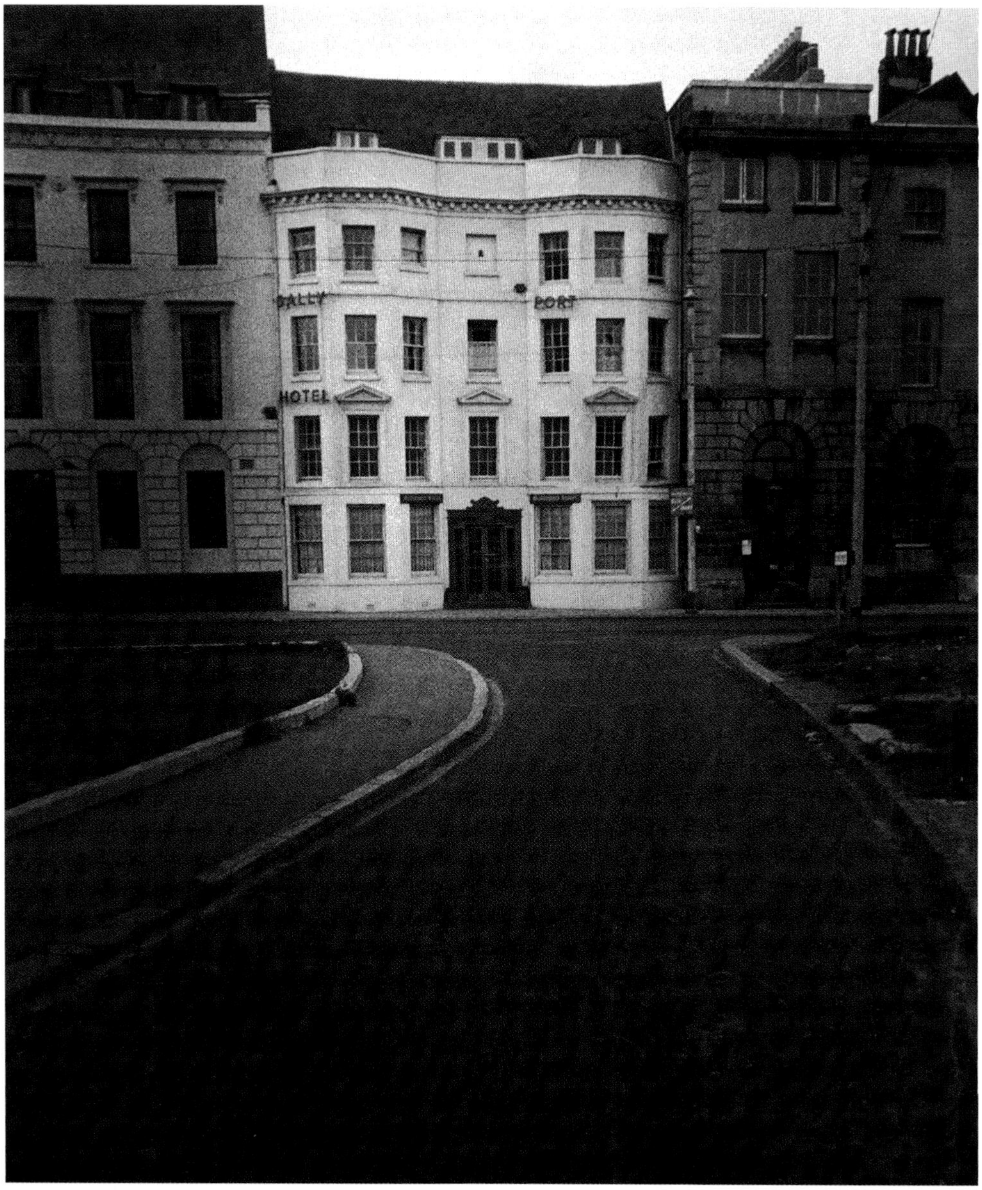

said at the time that he thought, because of a scar on the left knee, the body was that of the late commander. But years later, Knowles told a writer that he had been coerced into identifying the body, which he felt sure was not Crabb's, by the British intelligence unit MI5. He said further that Crabb had indeed been killed during the *Ordzhonikidze* operation, but not by the Russians. Knowles said MI5 had learned that Crabb intended to defect to the Soviet Union, and so it had sent a diving partner into the harbor with the legendary commander to kill him.

Wow.

But that was just one story on the table . . . then there was the one about how Crabb had been shot in the water when discovered by the Soviets . . . and the one about how he had been captured and taken to the USSR, where he was tortured and imprisoned, with the Soviets later dumping the headless torso of some other poor schmuck in Chichester Harbour . . . and the one about how Crabb had been brainwashed and then assigned to train Soviet frogmen . . . and the one about how he had indeed defected and become an officer in the Soviet Navy.

In 2007, Eduard Koltsov, a retired Russian sailor, said he had been serving on the *Ordzhonikidze* back in '56 and had slipped into the sea to investigate the sighting of a frogman near the ship. "I saw a silhouette of a diver who was fiddling with something at the starboard, next to the ship's ammunition stores." Koltsov said he swam closer and cut Crabb's throat.

Koltsov's testimony was received with skepticism in Great Britain, where many feel the truth will never be known—not least because the government has long wanted it not to be known.

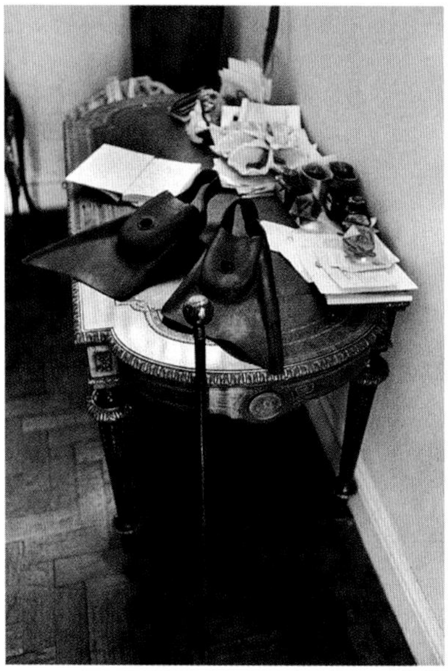

BRIAN SEED (2)

Crabb, who is pictured opposite in the depths where he was usually so comfortable, last stayed at the Sallyport Hotel (above) on a drab street near the docks in Portsmouth. With his disappearance, only a few mementos remained (left): a pair of flippers and his sword cane embossed with a crab.

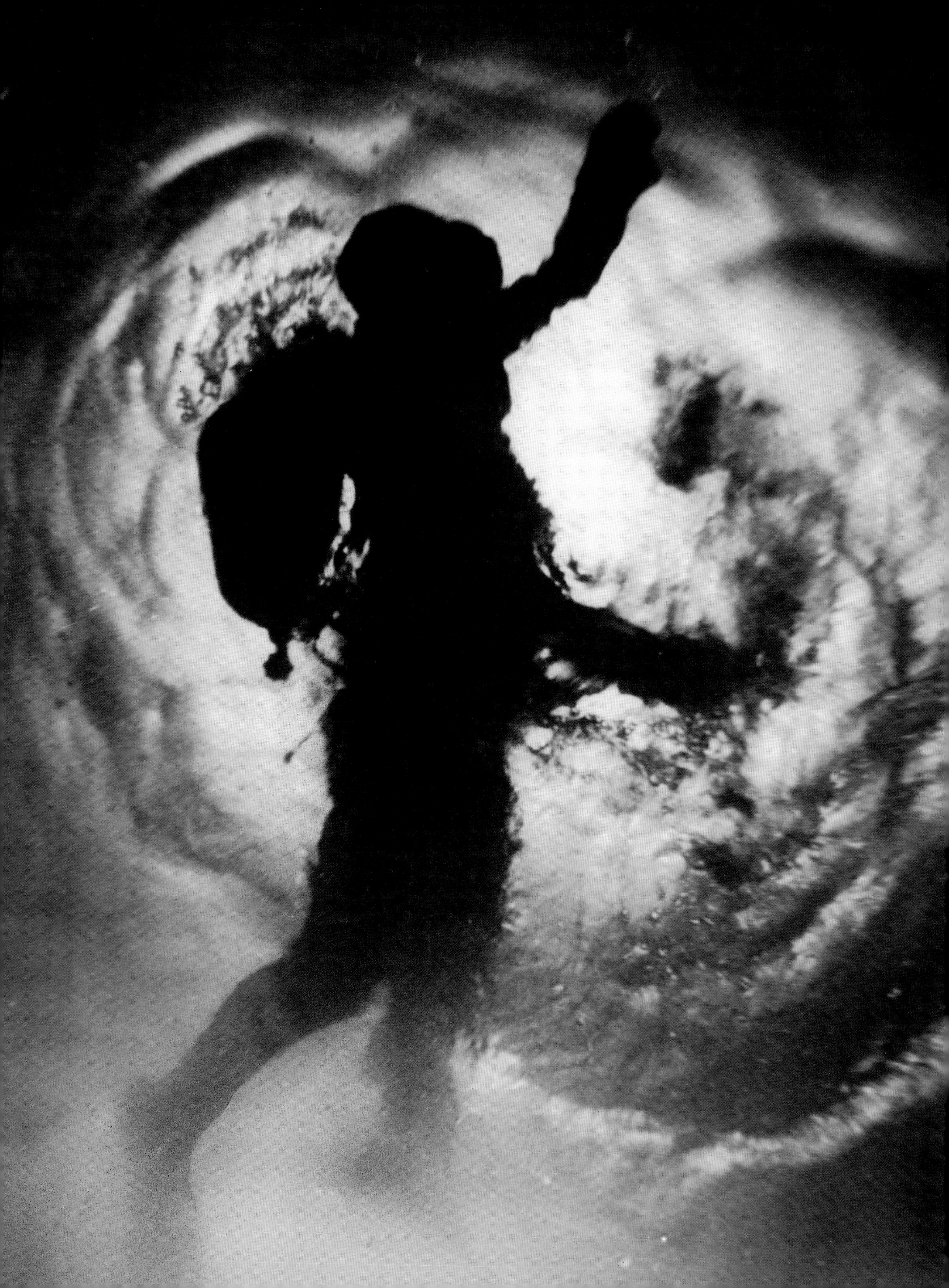

Was Dag Hammarskjöld Assassinated?

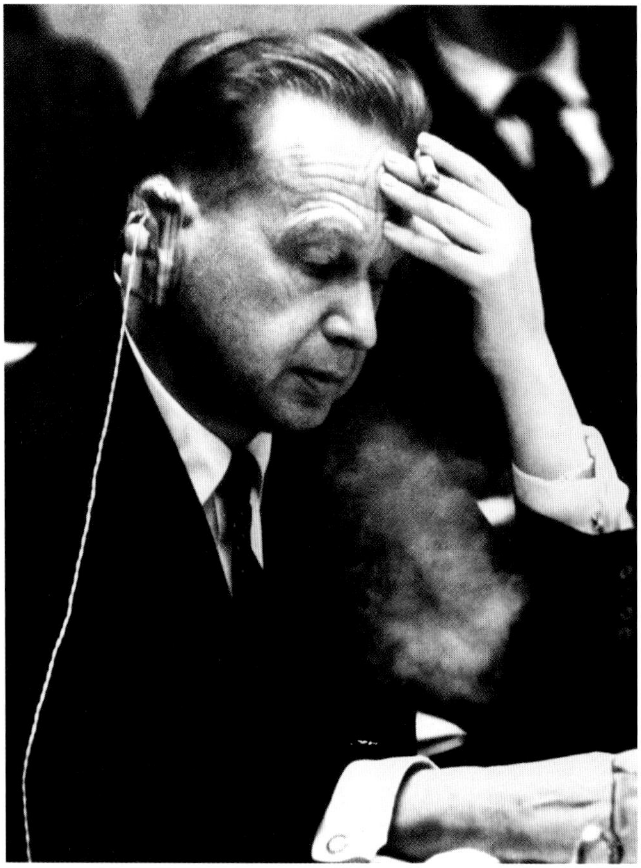

AP

Above: In February of 1961, the crisis in the Congo is growing as Hammarskjöld listens during a meeting at the U.N. headquarters. Opposite: Before the year is out, he will be dead in the plane crash, a fact announced by President Kennedy.

John F. Kennedy saluted this preeminent diplomat, who died in an airplane crash in 1961, as the "greatest statesman of our century." Born into a family that had been involved in Swedish government since the 17th century—his father was elected prime minister in 1914—Dag Hammarskjöld came by his calling naturally. In the 1930s and '40s, he served his country in a wide variety of posts, and in the early 1950s, he took a leadership role with Sweden's delegation to the United Nation's General Assembly in New York City. When the U.N. Secretary General Trygve Lie stepped down in 1953, the Security Council surprised Hammarskjöld by choosing him for the post. He was reelected in 1957.

He was a proactive leader, involving the U.N. in efforts to build better relations between Israel and the Arab States, in the Suez crisis of 1957, and in the successful negotiation with China for the release of 15 U.S. pilots who had been captured during the Korean War. The mission that led to his death had to do with the Congo, which had, in 1960, solicited the U.N.'s assistance in quelling civil upheavals. In September of that year, he ordered a noncombatant emergency force to the region but denied Prime Minister Patrice Lumumba's request that the U.N. help force a rebel province to rejoin the Congo. Lumumba then asked the Soviet Union if it might assist with the rebels.

A year later, in September 1961, Hammarskjöld left for Africa in hopes of brokering a cease-fire in the Congo; his U.N. forces had indeed become engaged in fighting with soldiers of the rebel province. There were 16 aboard the DC-6B, which had filed no flight plan for security reasons. According to a police report, a bright flash was seen in the sky over the Ndola Airport at one a.m. on

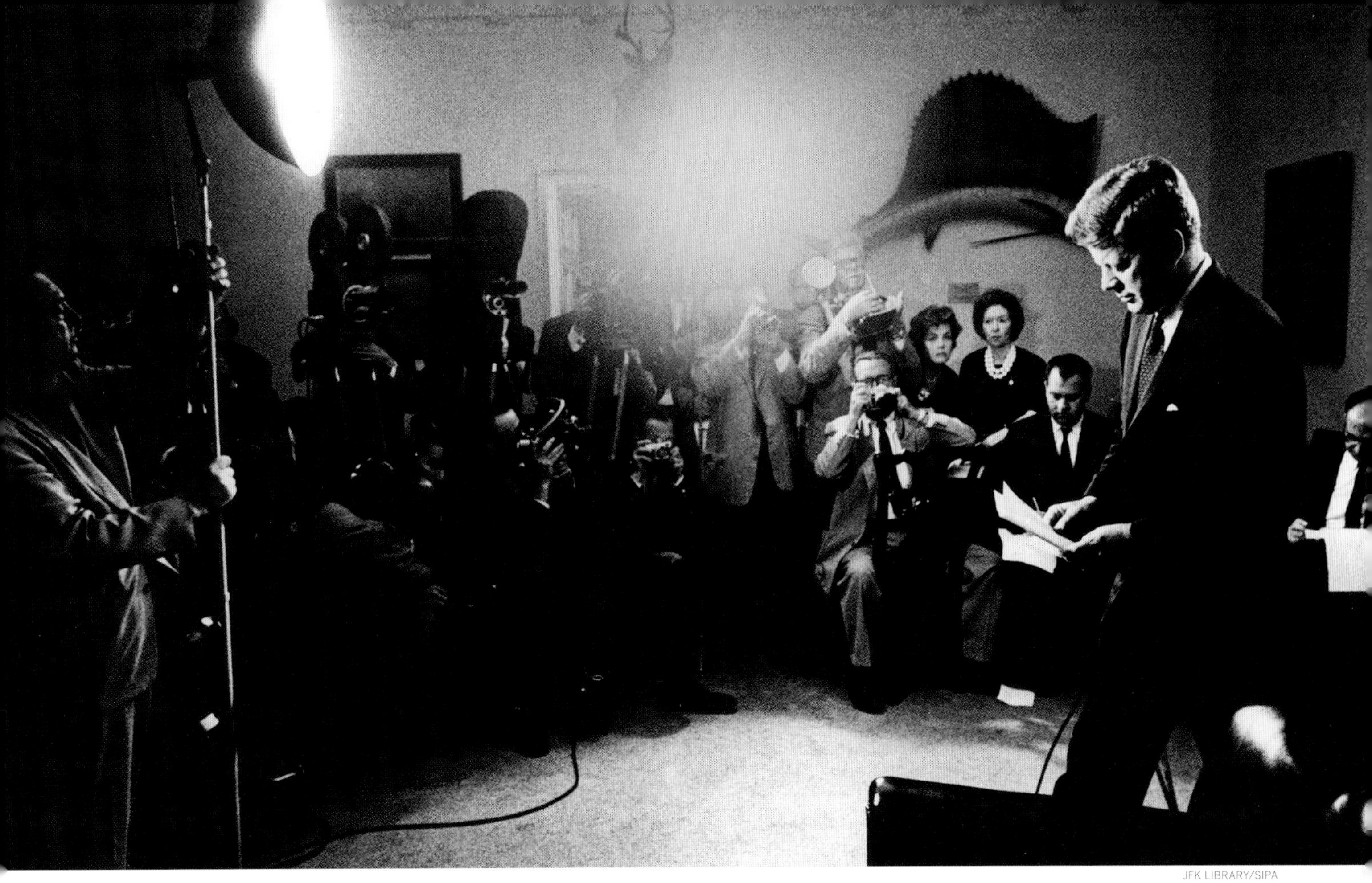

JFK LIBRARY/SIPA

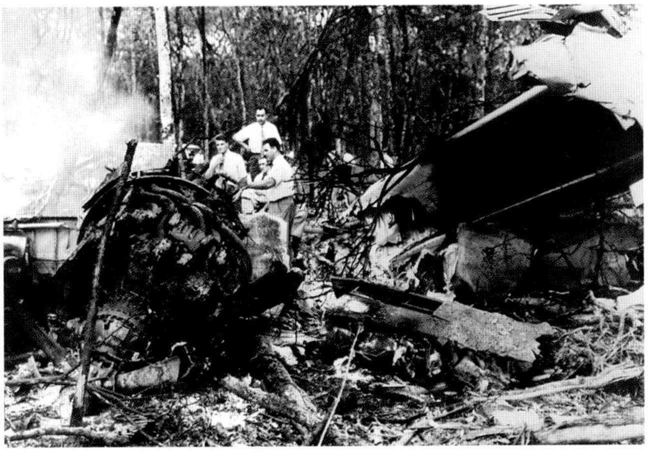

TOPHAM/THE IMAGE WORKS

September 18. The sole survivor of the incident, Sergeant Harold Julien, later said that a series of explosions preceded the crash.

The Congo had recently achieved independence from Belgium, and several countries were meddling in its internal, unstable political situation. Years later, Archbishop Desmond Tutu's Truth and Reconciliation Commission would say that it had found letters (whose veracity it admittedly could not verify) implicating Great Britain's intelligence agency, the United States' CIA and the South African intelligence services in the crash. There were concerns in some Western nations about the nationalization of the Congo's copper industry, and clearly Prime Minister Lumumba thought that a nefarious act had been

There was grass in Hammarskjöld's hands, indicating he was scrambling from the wreckage when he died. Had he been shot dead after the crash?

committed when he immediately issued an edict stating that "in order to pay a tribute to this great man, now vanished from the scene, and to his colleagues, all of whom have fallen victim to the shameless intrigues of the great financial Powers of the West, and in order to demonstrate publicly our indignation at the scandalous interference in our affairs by certain foreign countries, the Government has decided to proclaim Tuesday, 19 September 1961 a day of national mourning."

If there had been a bomb on the plane, as a theory holds, it still might not have caused Hammarskjöld's death. Norwegian Major General Bjørn Egge was the first U.N. official to see the body. He later recalled in 2005 that there was a bullet hole in Hammarskjöld's forehead and grass in his hands, indicating he was scrambling from the wreckage when he died. And in 2007, an anonymous retired mercenary claimed that another mercenary, from South Africa, had once told him that he had shot Hammarskjöld.

Former President Harry S Truman, for one, certainly thought that there had been no accident: "Dag Hammarskjöld was on the point of getting something done when they killed him. Notice that I said, 'when they killed him.'"

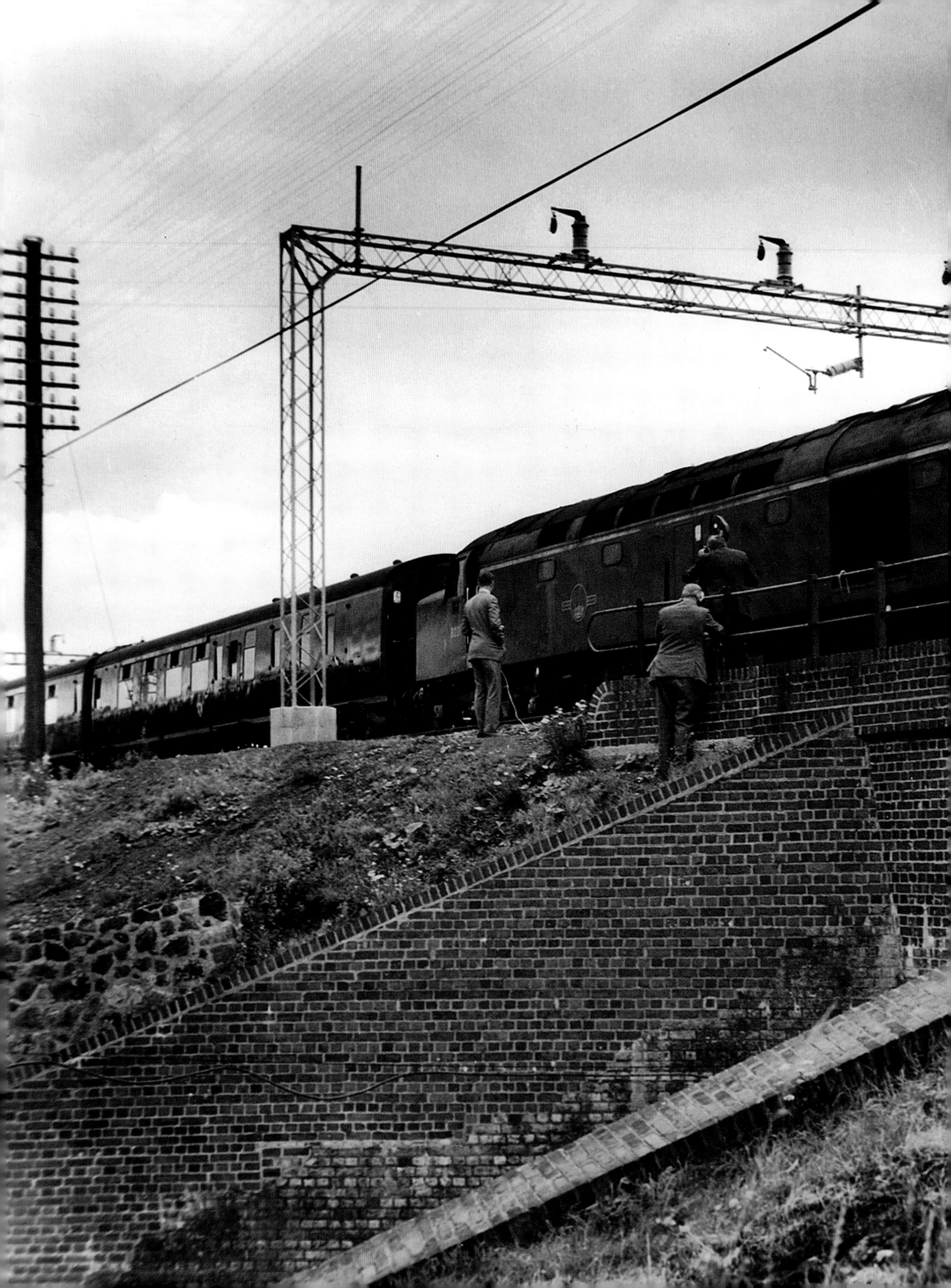

Where Is the Money from the Great Train Robbery?

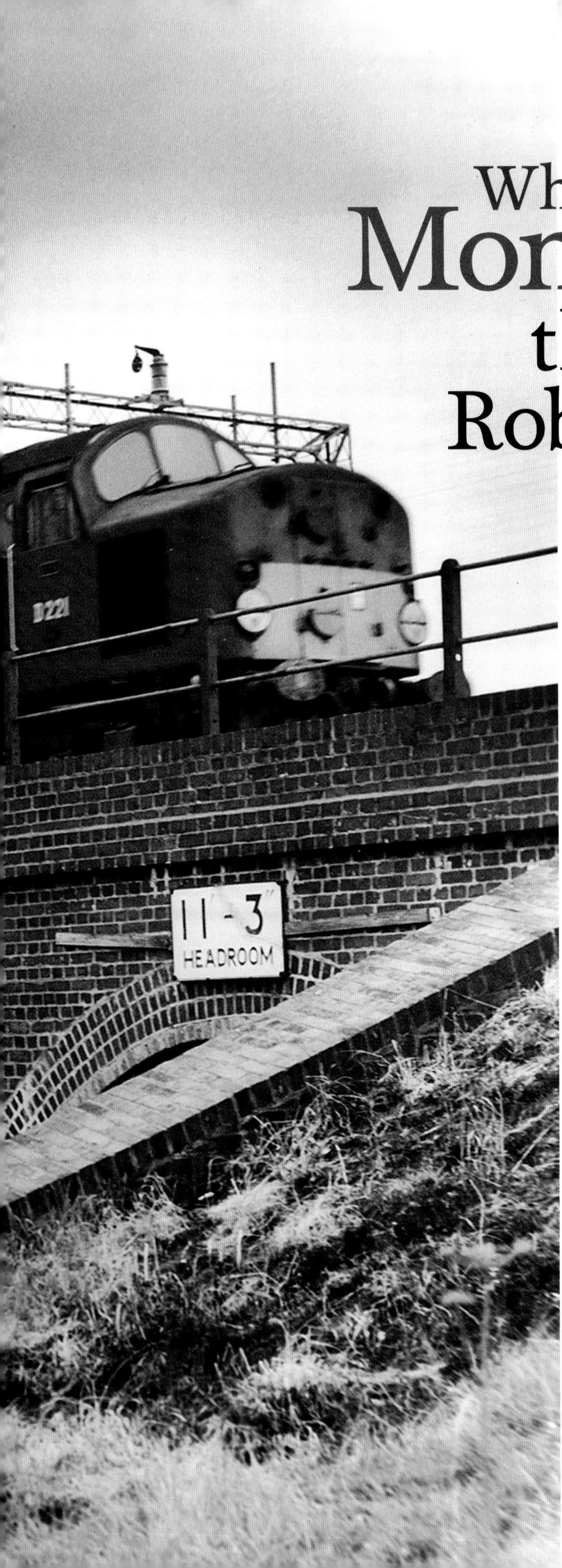
D221
11'-3"
HEADROOM

In the land that cherishes the legend of the outlaw Robin Hood, a modern-day heist of tremendous proportions was carried out with no intention of robbing the rich and giving to the poor, but rather with lining the thieves' pockets. The Great Train Robbery made folk heroes out of a 15-member gang of robbers, and one small-time criminal in particular who didn't play much of a role in the crime.

The heist made folk heroes out of a 15-member gang, and one small-time criminal in particular, Ronnie Biggs, who really didn't play much of a role in the crime.

It's not clear who came up with the idea for this robbery in the early 1960s, but it seems the gang for which it was designed passed on the plan as being too ambitious. A member of that gang, serving time in prison for another crime, shared the details with a fellow inmate, the London antiques dealer and master thief Bruce Reynolds. After serving out his sentence, Reynolds discussed the possibilities with his associates in the South West gang. They were certainly intrigued, but it seemed too large an operation, so it was decided to invite in Reynolds's friend, Ronald Edwards, and his confreres in the South East gang. During this period, Reynolds was approached by another buddy of his, Ronnie Biggs, who, after a short career as a nickel-and-dime hood, was trying to go legit with a construction business and was looking for a loan of a few hundred pounds. Reynolds said he didn't have the dough to loan, but that Biggs could earn a share worth £40,000—a mind-boggling sum—if he signed on with this new enterprise. The condition

On the morning after, police inspect the train at the Bridego Railway Bridge (left), where the culprits' cars awaited it.

PAUL POPPER/POPPERFOTO/GETTY

was that Biggs had to find and enlist someone who could drive a diesel locomotive. He knew just such a fellow, a man later referred to as "Stan Agate," and the team was complete.

On August 8, 1963, the Glasgow-to-Watford traveling post office train stopped when the driver saw a red light at Seers Crossing in Buckinghamshire, England. The light had been jimmied and was being powered by a small battery while a glove was being held over the green light. The gang took over the train, and "Stan Agate" was put behind the controls. He proved unable to pilot the train to the nearby Bridego Railway

The operation did not go smoothly. The perps left prints everywhere, including in the hideout, where they played Monopoly using real money.

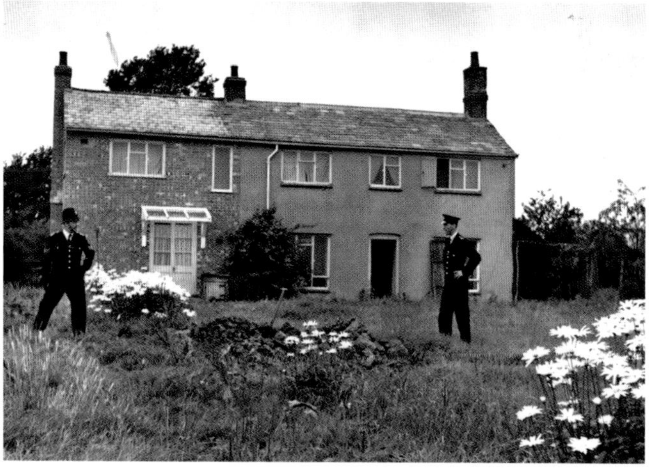

KEYSTONE/HULTON/GETTY

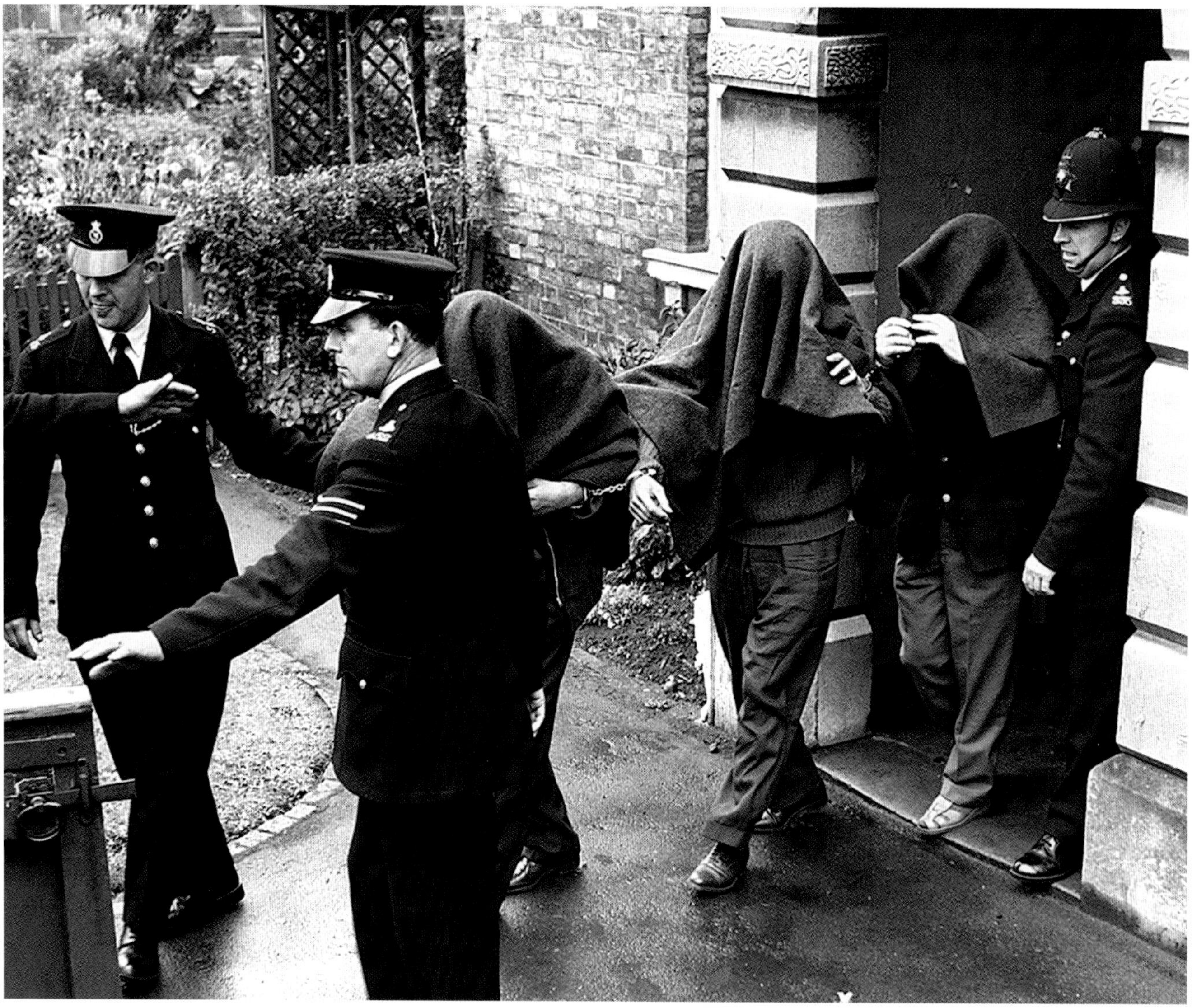

HULTON-DEUTSCH/CORBIS

Bridge, where the gang's Land Rovers were parked, and so the real driver was coerced with an iron bar to the head into moving the train forward. "Agate" and his keeper, Biggs, were therefore sidelined from the action, except to help load the bags into the getaway vehicles—bags containing £2.6 million in notes, the equivalent of nearly $60 million today.

It was not a smooth operation. The perpetrators left fingerprints everywhere, including in their temporary hideout at Leatherslade Farm, where they had played Monopoly using real money. It was details like this, romanticized by the British tabloids, that transformed the Great Train Robbery from a story of sordid fact into one of fanciful, romantic legend.

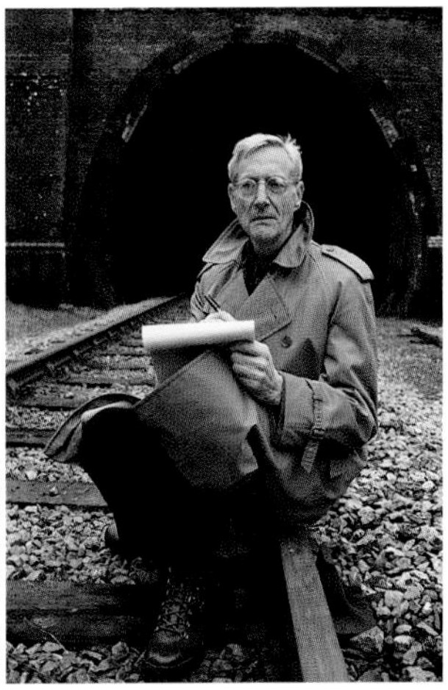

PENNY TWEEDIE/CORBIS

Opposite: The gang's hideout hardly helped, and eight days after, arrests are made (bottom). Left: Reynolds is at liberty once more, having finished his prison sentence in 1979. Below: Biggs raises a glass in Rio in 1987. Fourteen years later, he returned to England, and to prison. Soon after his release on humanitarian grounds in August 2009, Biggs celebrated his 80th birthday in the hospital and said he hoped to live until Christmas. Reynolds said of his old mate's reprieve that he was "overjoyed for Ronnie."

Thirteen of the 15 bandits were caught and convicted; they were sentenced jointly on April 16, 1964. Then, 15 months into his prison term, Biggs escaped during an exercise period, scaling a 30-foot wall with a ladder that had been thrown over from the outside. He fled to France, changed his name and his face, slipped away to Australia, lived there quietly for years, then continued on to Rio de Janeiro, where he went about his business openly because Brazil had no extradition agreement with Great Britain. The British press followed his every move, including reported clandestine returns to his beloved England, turning Biggs into a bona fide celebrity. The punk band the Sex Pistols recorded in Rio and asked Biggs to sing backup vocals on two tracks, one of which, "No One Is Innocent," climbed to No. 6 on the British charts.

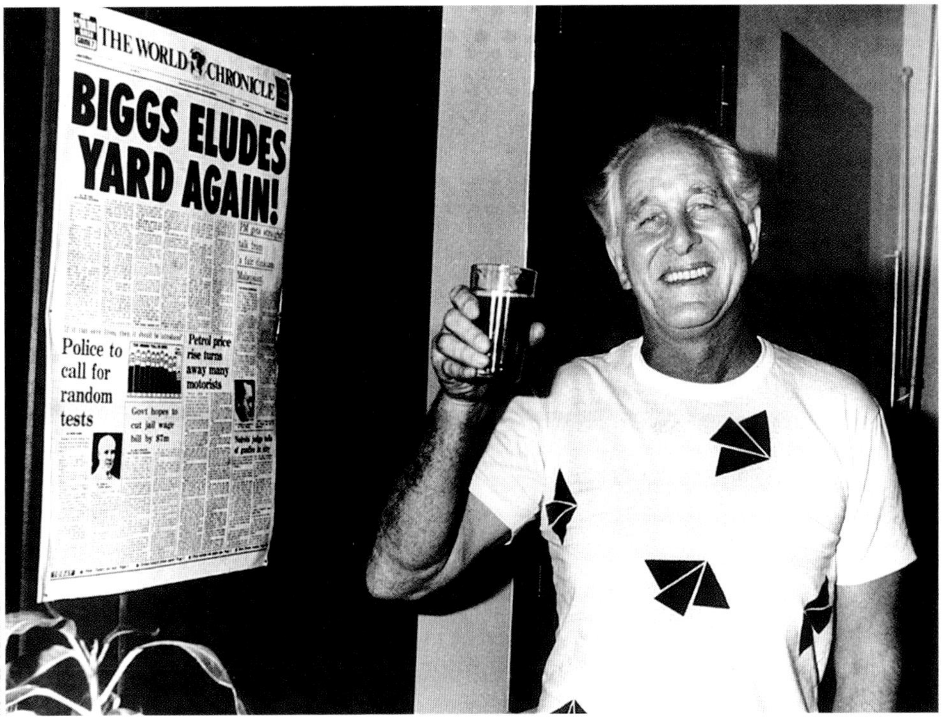
THE WORLD CHRONICLE
BIGGS ELUDES YARD AGAIN!
Police to call for random tests
Petrol price rise turns away many motorists

RONALD SIEMONEIT/SYGMA/CORBIS

In 2001, Biggs, 71, came back to England with a professed desire to "walk into a Margate pub as an Englishman and buy a pint of bitter." In fact, he was thought to be returning home to find better medical treatment, as he was ailing. He was promptly rearrested and reincarcerated. He spent eight years in prison before being released on August 6, 2009. Biggs, now very ill, was freed on humanitarian grounds to live his last days with his family.

The overarching mystery in this case remains, however: Most of the Great Train Robbery loot has never been found.

The British press followed every move that Biggs made—from jail to France to Australia to Rio de Janeiro—and turned him into a bona fide, rock star celebrity.

Why Was Mary Pinchot Meyer Murdered?

Buckle your seat belts, JFK-conspiracy theorists. It's going to be a wild ride!

Largely forgotten today amid all of the Marilyn Monroes and Judith Exners is Mary Pinchot Meyer, a brilliant blonde beauty who also had an affair with John Fitzgerald Kennedy and whose story is arguably as intriguing (and murky) as any.

Mary Pinchot was born in 1920 in Pennsylvania into a family of wealth, influence and left-wing politics. Her father was a lawyer, her mother a journalist, and their associates included Mabel Dodge, Louis Brandeis and Harold Ickes. Mary was educated at the Brearly School and Vassar College, and it was during a dance at the elite Choate School in the late 1930s that she first met John F. Kennedy.

At Vasser, she proved to be her parents' daughter, showing an interest in liberal and even radical politics. After graduating college, she joined the American Labor Party, which assured her a dossier in J. Edgar Hoover's FBI files in Washington, D.C.

She married Cord Meyer, a Marine officer who had lost an eye in World War II and would become, like her, a politically minded young person. Stunned by the events that ended the war, Cord commissioned a film, *The Beginning or the End*, about the perils posed by the nuclear age. The Meyers moved from Cambridge, Massachusetts, to Washington, where they were immediately accepted as part of Georgetown's liberal circle. Cord, however, was becoming disillusioned with his associates on the left, and he started to work on assignment for the CIA, an organization he eventually joined formally. And then, Senator Joseph McCarthy, in full witch-hunt mode, accused him of being a Communist. The politics were flying every which way.

In the summer of 1954, Jack and Jackie Kennedy bought Hickory Hill, an estate just down the road from the Meyers' place in Langley Commons, Virginia. Jackie and Mary became fast friends. But tragic things were beginning to happen. On December 18, 1956, the Meyers' nine-year-old son, Michael, was struck and killed by a car on a curve by their house where, two years earlier, the family's golden retriever had been similarly struck and killed. After the incident with their dog, Cord had presciently expressed concern to his colleagues that the same might happen to a member of his family.

She began her affair with JFK in the fall of 1961 and told friends she was keeping a journal about the relationship. After her very untimely death, the diary was handed over to the CIA.

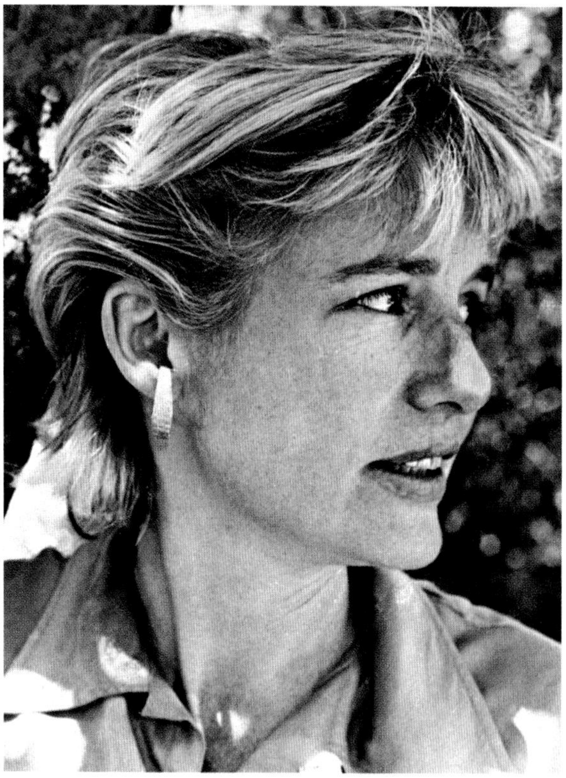

AP

The Meyers divorced in 1958; JFK and Jackie moved to the White House in 1961, and Robert F. Kennedy and his family became Mary's new neighbors at Hickory Hill. Mary began her affair with the President in the fall of 1961. She told her friends she was keeping a journal about the relationship. In

BETTMANN/CORBIS

1962, Mary got some LSD from Timothy Leary, the Harvard professor who was notoriously promoting the drug as an enlightenment tool. She perhaps shared her supply with JFK before their lovemaking: These details were supposedly in her diary, which was recovered by her sister Antoinette during a search of Meyer's rooms after her death. Antoinette handed over the diary to the CIA's James Angleton, and it was reportedly burned.

What pillow talk might there have been between Mary and the President? Mary was smarter than most. Had they had high-level discussions? Did she know secrets?

The murder of Mary Pinchot Meyer occurred on October 12, 1964, not quite a year after JFK's assassination—an event that had prompted Mary to express fear for her own well-being. She was shot twice at close range while walking on a towpath in Georgetown. No one has ever been convicted of the crime.

In 2001, Mary's former husband, Cord Meyer, granted an interview to the writer C. David Heymann. Meyer was asked who had killed Mary. His answer was succinct, if chilling and, at bottom, somewhat cryptic: "The same sons of bitches that killed John F. Kennedy."

> Not quite a year after the Kennedy assassination, Meyer, too, was felled by a gunman's bullets while walking along the Chesapeake and Ohio Canal in Georgetown.

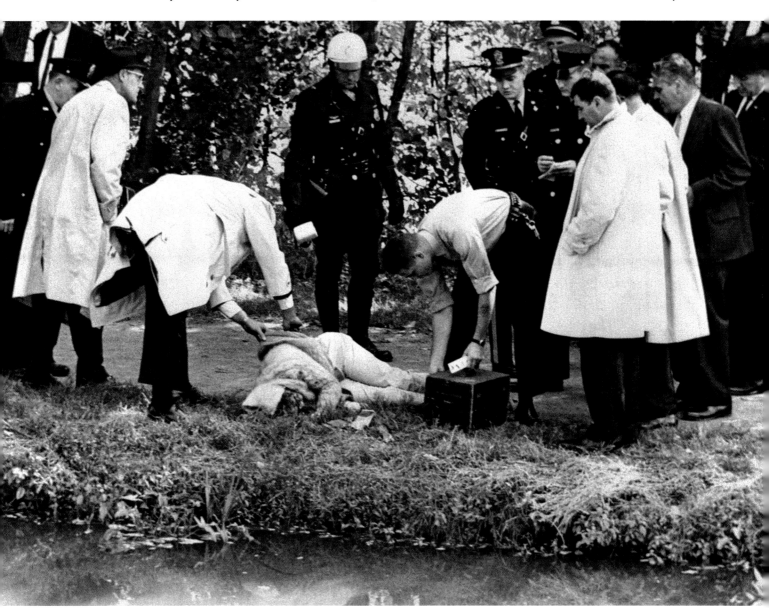

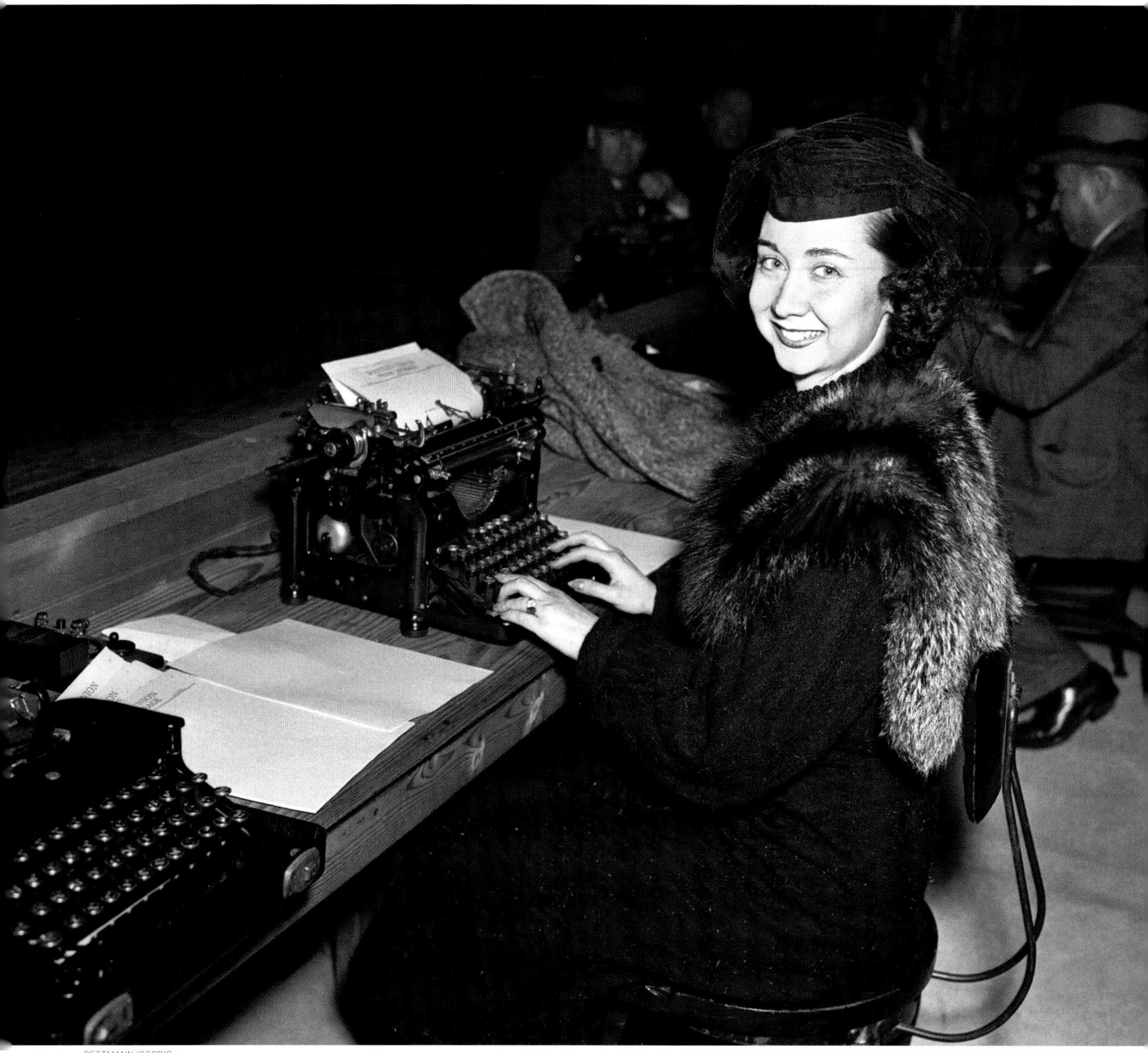

BETTMANN/CORBIS

How Did Dorothy Kilgallen Die?

So we have entered the Kennedy Era of Unsolved Mysteries, and perhaps not surprisingly, here is our second entry—without even touching on who killed JFK himself or whether the Kennedy brothers arranged to have Marilyn Monroe bumped off. Those spectacularly famous deaths will be deathlessly debated until all human breath is expended, but far more intriguing to us are these sideline cases. Why was Mary Pinchot Meyer killed? And did Dorothy Kilgallen die accidentally . . . or with prejudice?

She was, as a nationally syndicated columnist and television personality, much more famous than Meyer. And, we should note, she was far less directly connected to Kennedy himself. For instance, she never slept with him. But we'll get to all that.

She was born in Chicago in 1913 to the wife of a Hearst newspaperman and inherited her father's instincts. She quit college in her freshman year to join the *New York Journal-American* as a reporter. In 1938, she began her daily column "The Voice of Broadway," which when syndicated would deliver to her a national audience. The column included more than just showbiz gossip; there were items on politics and even organized crime. In 1945, Kilgallen began cohosting a radio talk show, *Breakfast with Dorothy and Dick*, with her husband, and in 1950, she joined the panel of the phenomenally popular TV game show *What's My Line?*

All this time, she continued to report. In her journalistic pursuits, she regularly failed—if she even tried—to separate opinion from fact. In a front page article in the *New York Journal-American* in 1954, she let it be known that she felt Dr. Sam Sheppard, who had been found guilty of murdering his wife in a sensational trial in Ohio, had been railroaded, saying the prosecutors "didn't prove he was guilty any more than they proved there are pin-headed men on Mars." And speaking of Mars, that same year she wrote in her column: "Flying saucers are regarded as of such vital importance that they will be the subject of a special hush-hush meeting of the world military heads next summer." In 1955, her dispatch from London read: "British

Returning to New York from Texas, Kilgallen told her friends that she planned to "bust the Kennedy assassination wide open."

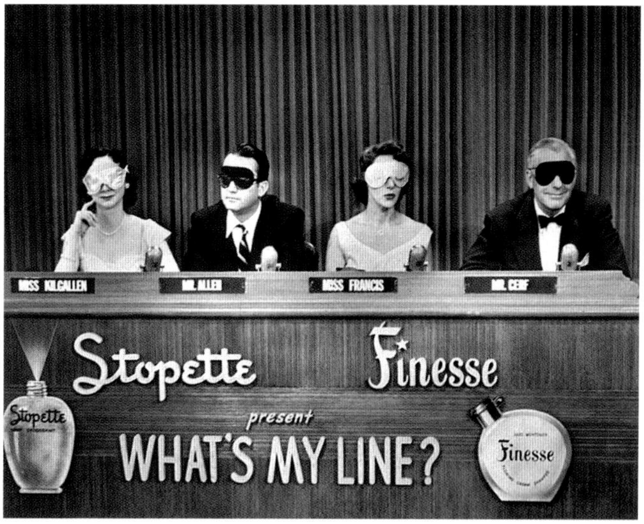
Stopette
Finesse
present
WHAT'S MY LINE?

Opposite: In 1936, Kilgallen, in her early twenties, is a bright-eyed cub reporter for the *New York Journal-American.* Above: By 1953, she is a nationally known multimedia celebrity with a regular gig on a popular TV quiz show.

scientists and airmen, after examining the wreckage of one mysterious flying ship, are convinced these strange aerial objects are not optical illusions or Soviet inventions, but are flying saucers which originate on another planet." These excerpts are offered here as examples of Kilgallen's hot style of reportage, and to show her willingness—her need, almost—to challenge common knowledge, orthodoxy, the standard view.

Which she did in spades with the Kennedy assassination and the subsequent Warren Commision Report's conclusion that assassin Lee Harvey Oswald had acted alone. Kilgallen, whose reporting on Kennedy was being monitored closely by FBI chief J. Edgar Hoover, smelled a conspiracy and a cover-up. "That story isn't going to die as long as there's a real reporter alive, and there are a lot of them alive," she wrote. During her limited remaining time as one of this fraternity, she stayed doggedly on the case, even landing a private interview in Dallas with the jailed killer of Oswald, nightclub owner Jack Ruby. Returning to New York, she told her friends that she planned to "bust the Kennedy assassination wide open."

She never got the chance. She was found dead at the age of 52 in bed in her town house on November 8, 1965. The coroner ruled that she had succumbed to acute alcohol and barbiturate poisoning but listed the cause of death as "undetermined" because there was no telling if it had been an accident or a suicide. In 1979, Kilgallen biographer Lee Israel added information concerning her mysterious death: that Kilgallen in fact never slept in the bed in which she was found; that no bottle of pills was ever discovered by investigators; that the book in her hands was one she had said she'd finished weeks earlier. In short, the implication is that the death scene had been orchestrated. By whom remains unclear.

Who Was the Zodiac?

"This is the Zodiac speaking" was the chosen salutation of the man who terrorized the San Francisco Bay Area in the late 1960s. Because of him, people avoided secluded places—his preferred killing grounds—and when he threatened to target school buses and "pick off the kiddies as they come bouncing out," units of armed police were installed on buses, and aircraft kept watch over hundreds of miles of bus routes. He communicated usually by letter to the newspapers, and each time one of his menacing missives was published, fear descended anew.

The first victims officially credited to the Zodiac were Betty Lou Jensen and David Faraday. On December 20, 1968, around 10 p.m., the teenage couple parked just off a desolate road in Vallejo, a waterfront town northwest of San Francisco. A stranger approached Faraday's car and fired two bullets at the vehicle, one into Faraday's skull and five into Jensen's back. Outside of several .22-caliber shell casings, a few shoe prints and a deep heel print, the crime scene yielded nothing that could help the police pinpoint a suspect. Seven months later on the Fourth of July, Darlene Ferrin and her friend Michael Mageau were riding in her '63 Corvair around midnight when they were chased by a light-colored car into the parking lot of Blue Rock Springs Golf Course. The pursuer pumped shot after shot into the Corvair, hitting Ferrin nine times and Mageau thrice. He would recover, but she was dead on arrival. That night, the killer made his first public confession in a phone call to the Vallejo police department's switchboard operator: "I want to report a double murder," he said. "They were shot with a 9-millimeter Luger. I also killed those kids last year."

The murder might have been dismissed as a random robbery-homicide, but the Zodiac required credit and sent a three-by-five-inch piece of the victim's bloody shirt to the *Chronicle.*

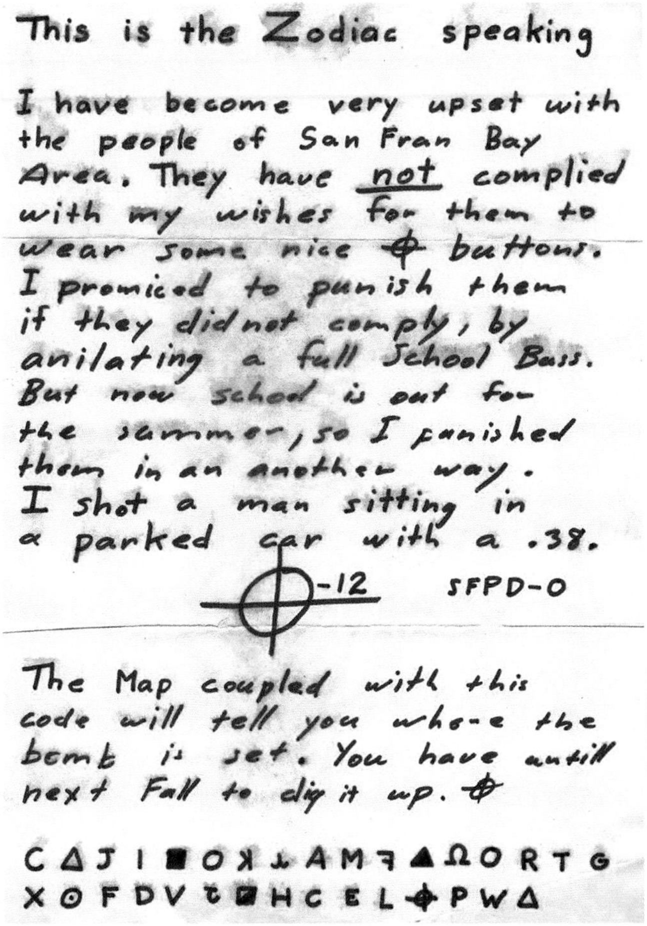
This is the Zodiac speaking

I have become very upset with the people of San Fran Bay Area. They have not complied with my wishes for them to wear some nice ⊕ buttons. I promiced to punish them if they did not comply, by anilating a full School Buss. But now school is out for the summer, so I punished them in an another way. I shot a man sitting in a parked car with a .38.

⊕-12 SFPD-0

The Map coupled with this code will tell you where the bomb is set. You have untill next Fall to dig it up. ⊕

CΔJI■OK⊥AM⅃▲ΩORTG
X⊙FDV⊺■HCEL⊕PWΔ

SAN JOSE MERCURY NEWS/MCT/LANDOV

As the police searched for leads, the killer crafted three letters, each of which was addressed to either the *San Francisco Chronicle*, the *San Francisco Examiner* or the *Vallejo Times-Herald* and included a third of a cipher that he claimed would reveal his identity. He demanded that each newspaper publish its portion of the cipher on its front page by August 1 or "I will go on a kill rampage." The papers complied, and a couple from Salinas was able to crack the cipher's code in a few days. Though it provided a motive, albeit an insane one, for the crimes—the killer said he was collecting slaves for the afterlife—alas it contained no name.

In the early autumn of 1969, Pacific Union College students Bryan Hartnell and Cecilia Shepard were enjoying a picnic near Lake Berryessa when the Zodiac, carrying a gun and wearing a black hood and a shirt emblazoned with a symbol consisting of a circle overlaid with a cross, hog-tied and stabbed them. He then scrawled on the door of Hartnell's car the circle-and-cross emblem followed with the note: "Vallejo, 12-20-68, 7-4-69, Sept 27-69-6:30, by knife." Again the male victim survived while the woman died. Two weeks later, police found cabdriver Paul Stine shot in the head. This case might have been dismissed as just another random robbery-homicide, but the Zodiac required credit. On October 14, the *Chronicle*'s letters editor received a gruesome delivery: a three-by-five-inch piece of Stine's blood-spattered shirt, plus the Zodiac's fifth letter. In it, he took responsibility for the cabbie's murder, chided the cops for failing to catch him (he had passed two officers who didn't try to stop him on his way from the crime scene) and threatened the schoolkids.

It appears that from this point on, the Zodiac attacked with a pen rather than a gun or a knife. We say "appears" because over a period of nine years, he issued 16 more letters but was officially linked to just one more crime: On March 22, 1970, he took Kathleen Johns and her 10-month-old daughter on the terror ride of their lives, from which they mercifully escaped. In one of his last letters, he boasted a body count of 37. In his book *Zodiac*, author Robert Graysmith lists a total of 49 possible victims—but we'll probably never know for sure.

In the 40-some-odd years since the Zodiac murders began, the police have investigated hundreds of suspects. In a recent development, on April 29, 2009, Deborah Perez claimed that her adoptive father, the late Guy Ward Hendrickson, had been the Zodiac, and that he even took her along on one of the murders when she was a girl. Most, including Graysmith, are skeptical, since the claims corresponded with the announcement of a documentary film on Hendrickson's life. So like the other real-life bogeymen in our book—Jack the Ripper, the Axman—the Zodiac remains a ghost.

UPI/CORBIS

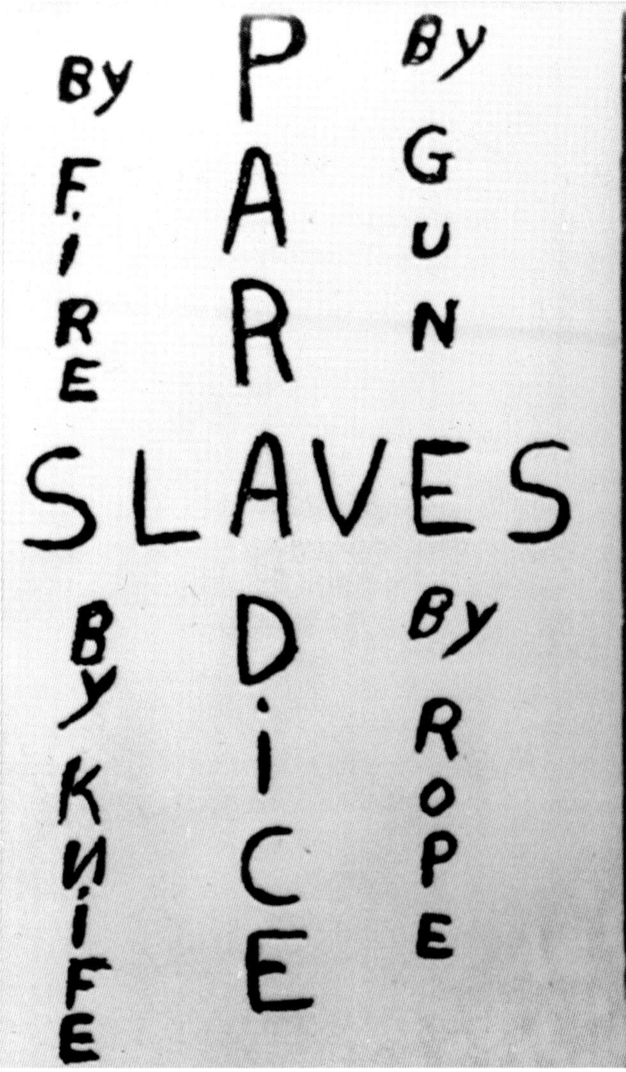

By Fire
Paradice
By Gun
Slaves
By Knife
By Rope

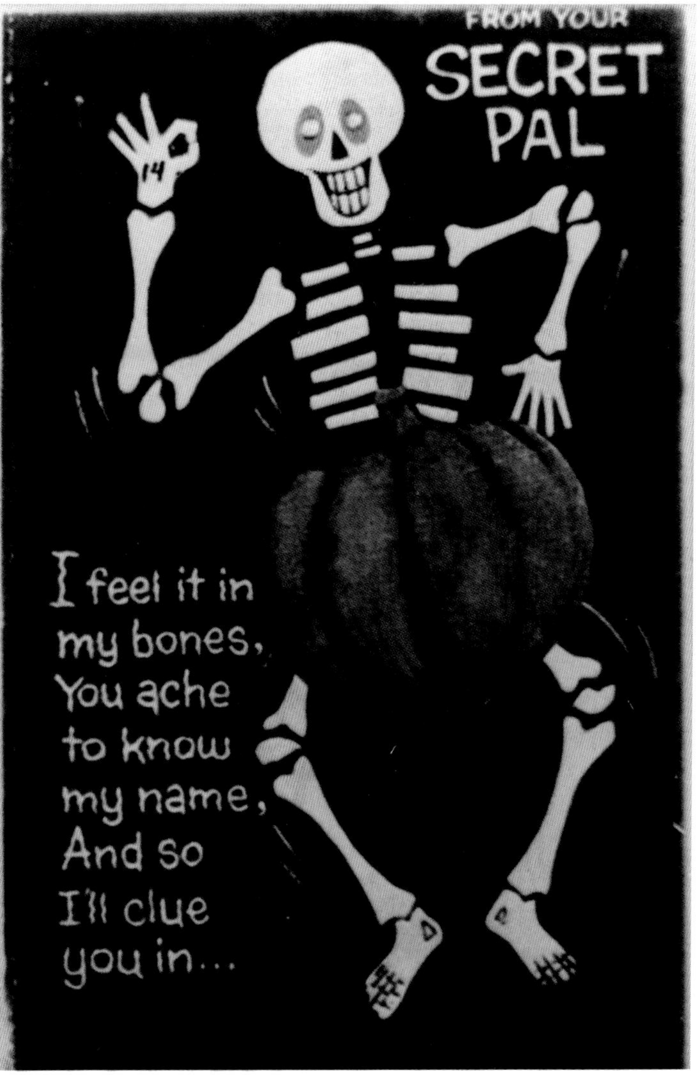

FROM YOUR
SECRET
PAL
14
I feel it in
my bones,
You ache
to know
my name,
And so
I'll clue
you in...

He kept the Bay Area on edge with letters and ciphers sent to the local newspapers, including these received by the *Chronicle*.

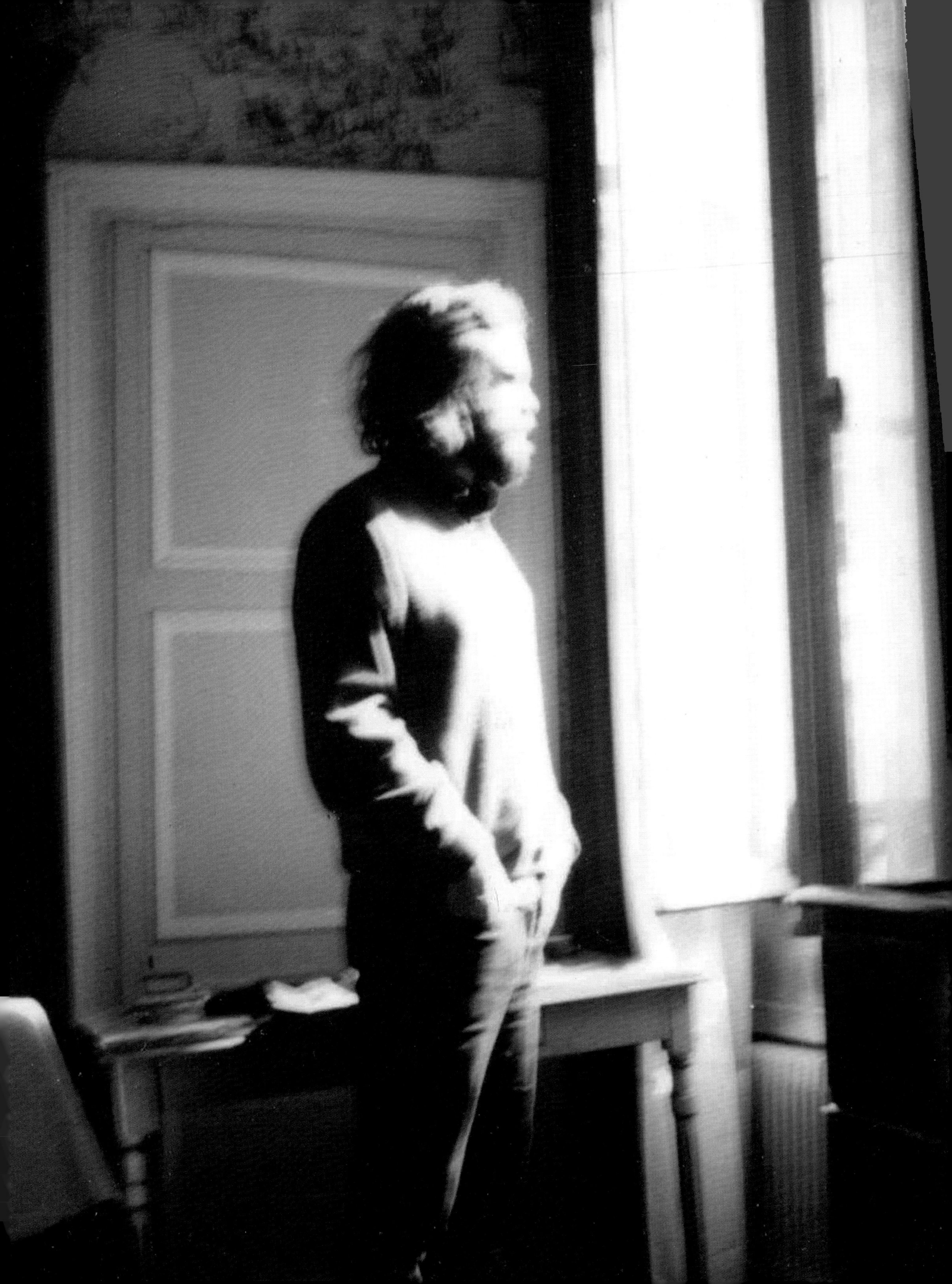

What Killed Jim Morrison?

The long-locked, leather-clad, strutting, sexy baritone who fronted the Doors, Jim Morrison—a.k.a. the Lizard King, Mr. Mojo Risin' and Dionysus—was the prototypical rock star. And his biographical sketch was by the book, too: graduates film school, joins a band, makes it big, performs on *Ed Sullivan*, has lots of sex, takes lots of drugs and dies young—in his case at 27 years old. But Morrison's cult has been sufficiently rabid and the circumstances of his death sufficiently obscured that there have always been questions concerning how he died. Or whether he died at all.

He was born in 1943 in Florida and had a nomadic boyhood as his father was a Navy man (eventually becoming an admiral). In 1965, having graduated from UCLA's College of Fine Arts, Jim was bumming around Venice Beach, California, when he more or less fell into the Doors. They hit it big in 1967 with the single "Light My Fire." Their sound was full of blues, hard rock, psychedelia—all glazed with a vague voodoo vibe—and this contributed to Morrison's image as a menacing but majestic mystic. The poetry helped as well: The guy was a pouting rock god and a poet to boot.

But he was in a bad way when he took time off from the band and moved to Paris in spring 1971. He was depressed for various reasons. One of these might have been his health: It has been reported that his asthma worsened in this period, and his colleagues in the Doors have said that he was coughing up blood for weeks while in Paris (although we should note that none of his bandmates were actually with him then). This supports the "natural causes" version of his death, which isn't the widely held one.

What is known for sure: He was found dead in the bathtub of a Paris apartment on July 3, 1971, and had indeed been coughing up blood. According to the account filed by French authorities, Morrison's body was discovered by his girlfriend, Pamela Courson. As there were no signs of foul play, no autopsy was performed—and no evidence was gathered as to what drugs might have been in his system; Courson apparently lied to police, saying that Morrison never took drugs, and they didn't bother to check. But according to at least one of her later scattered, "unofficial" accounts of what had happened, there would have been drugs aplenty to be found. She said that after a night of heavy drinking, Morrison had snorted heroin thinking it was cocaine. She, too, had taken the drug and nodded off as Morrison hemorrhaged and died in the tub. At one point, Courson told a writer she had killed Morrison, the implication being that she felt responsible. Of course, some fans took the words literally.

> And then there is the legend that he never died at all but wanted to disappear and thus staged the whole thing.

There has always been a strong rumor that Morrison died of his overdose at a Left Bank club, the Rock 'n' Roll Circus, and was hustled to the apartment to protect the club's owners. And then there is the legend that he never died at all but wanted to disappear and thus staged the whole thing. For years, fans have hounded surviving members of his family to see if there is any evidence that they might have seen Jim recently.

This story is a sad and sordid one. It's made sadder and more sordid still by the fact that Courson herself, who was named Morrison's common-law wife by the courts in the wake of his death, died of a heroin overdose in 1974. She, too, was 27 years old.

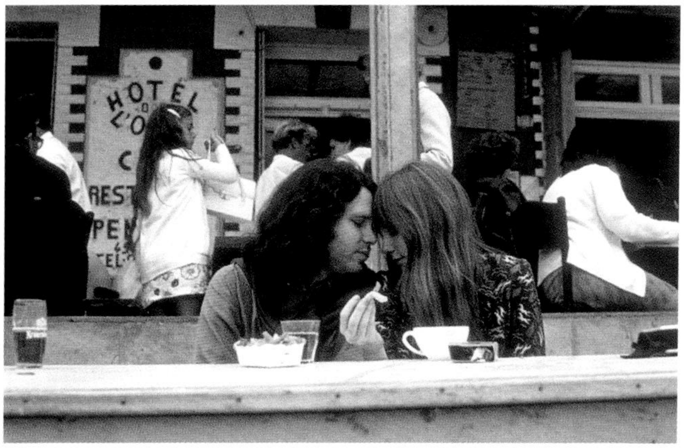

ALAN RONAY/OUTLINE/CORBIS

During his final weeks in Paris, when these photographs were taken, the rocker is often dissolute, sometimes desolate and, opposite, hirsute. Above: With Courson.

CAMERA PRESS/RETNA

Who Was Dan Cooper?

That was the alias used by a man in his mid-forties who boarded a Northwest-Orient Boeing 727 in Portland, Oregon, on the day before Thanksgiving in 1971. The flight was bound for Seattle: a short hop. Not long after take-off, the man handed a note to a flight attendant named Florence Schaffner. The note read, "I have a bomb in my brief-case. I will use it if necessary. I want you to sit next to me. You are being hijacked." So began the saga of a never-found and never-identified hijacker who, after a miscommunication to the press by the authorities, became known as D.B. Cooper.

He knew what he wanted, and this, too, was in the note: $200,000 in unmarked $20 bills and four parachutes, including two back chutes and two emergency chest chutes. These items were to be ready at Seattle-Tacoma International Airport before he would allow the plane to land. Cooper offered Schaffner a glimpse of the contents of his briefcase—red cylinders, a large battery and some wires—and convinced her that the bomb threat was real. Airline officials and law enforcement authorities on the ground decided to comply with Cooper's demands. As the plane was in a holding pattern and the ransom was being assembled below (and as the money was being

As the plane circled and the ransom was being assembled, Cooper smoked, drank whiskey and soda and was, according to one flight attendant, "rather nice." Such details later added to the legend of D.B. Cooper.

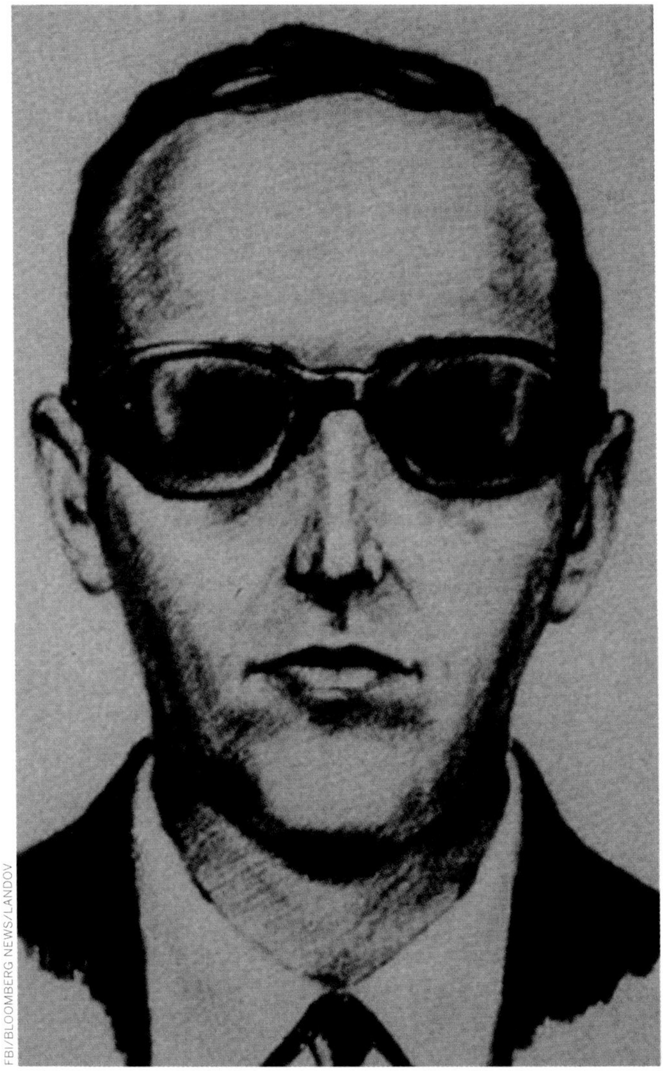

FBI/BLOOMBERG NEWS/LANDOV

Artists' renderings of Cooper (above) led nowhere. Opposite: The hijacked 727 waits to be refueled in Seattle before taking off again for Reno; flight attendant Flo Schaffner tells reporters she thought that Cooper was trying to "hustle" her when he handed her the bomb note; some of the money has been found—but the man, never.

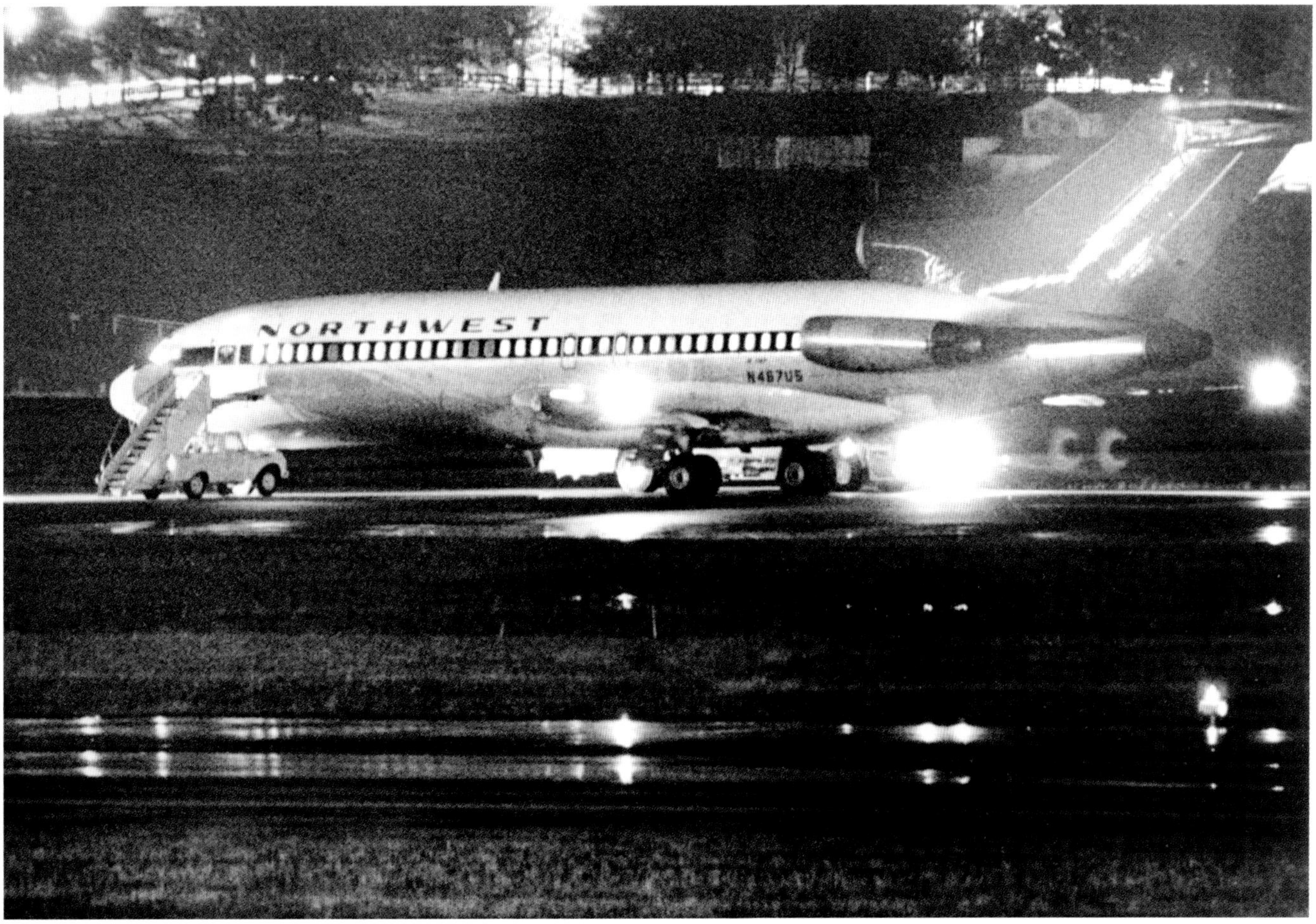
NORTHWEST
N467US

BRUCE MCKIM/SEATTLE TIMES/CORBIS

quickly scanned to record the serial numbers), Cooper smoked, drank whiskey and soda and was, according to one flight attendant, "rather nice." All of this would later add to his legend, and to the reason—in addition to the fact that no one (except possibly the perp) got hurt—that D.B. Cooper is still celebrated today throughout the Pacific Northwest as a kind of antihero.

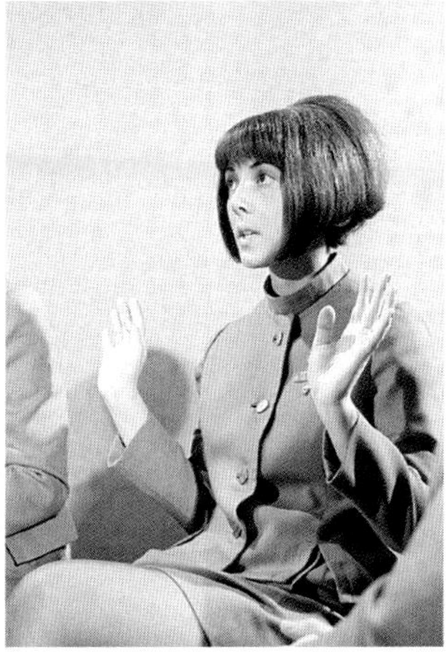

BETTMANN/CORBIS

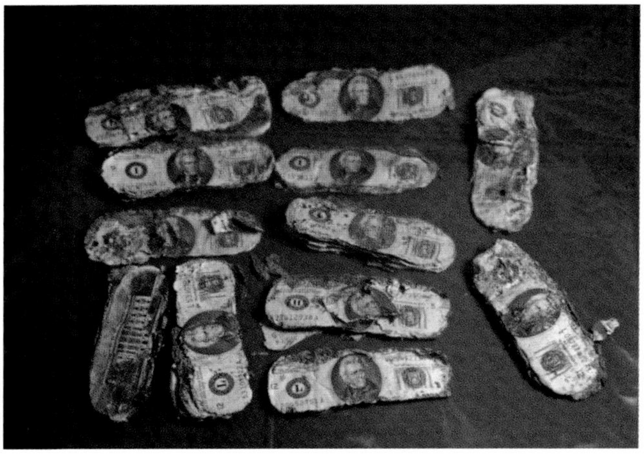

BRIAN LANKER

The plane landed, the money and parachutes were handed over, the passengers were released, and after a refueling that took a bit long and made Cooper jumpy, the jetliner was ordered back into the air. After consultations between Cooper and the cockpit, a flight plan to Reno, Nevada, at a low altitude of 10,000 feet was devised. At Cooper's insistence, the cabin was depressurized.

And then, from the aft doors, he jumped. The crew in the cockpit felt a bump at 8:13 p.m., and this was later assumed to be the effect of Cooper leaping from the stairs. He plunged into a dark and driving rainstorm, and if he landed safely—an eventuality seen as highly unlikely by the FBI—he did so somewhere near Ariel, Washington, about 30 miles north of Portland. Today, Ariel stages its annual Cooper Day on November 24.

There have been several suspects over the years—a man who committed a copycat crime and was caught, a mass murderer who was on the lam at the time, a fellow who told his wife on his deathbed, "I'm Dan Cooper"—but nothing has stuck. Some of the money was found, but neither the man nor the parachutes ever turned up.

The legend of D.B. Cooper lives.

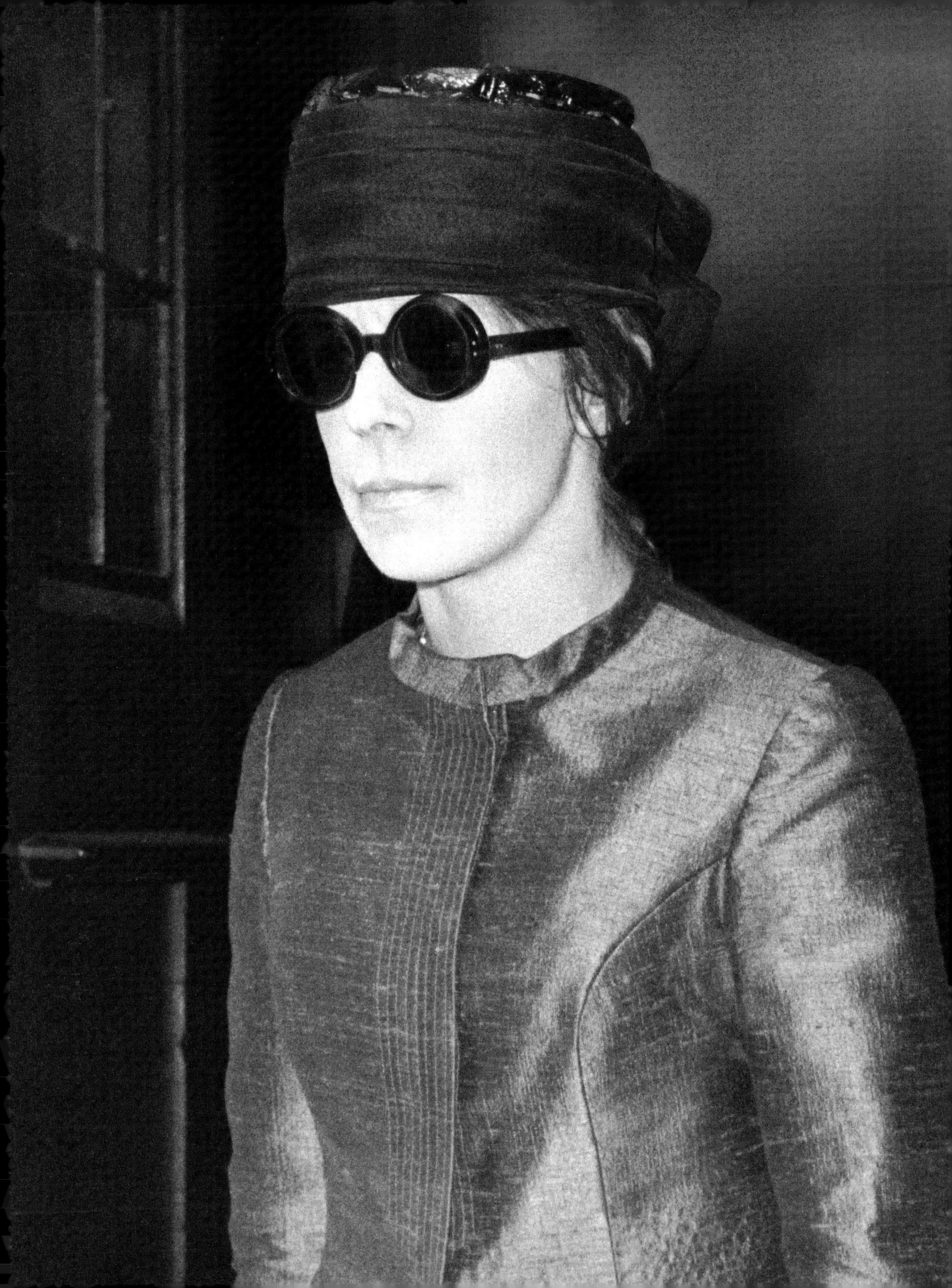

Did Lucky Lucan Live?

Below: In 1969, Lord Lucan takes dead aim at . . . a target in the yard of his friend Baron Gustav von Fürstenberg during pistol practice. But it just so happens that the woman in his sights on the opposite page is indeed Lady Lucan.

Richard John Bingham, the seventh Earl of Lucan, who was born in 1934, was called Lord Bingham or Lord Lucan or (by the tabloids after he seemingly got away with murder) Lucky Lucan. Whether he was indeed lucky, and whether he is today living out his eighth decade somewhere in this wide, wide world, is a point refuted by the British courts, which declared him legally dead in 1999, and also by Lady Lucan, who sometimes uses the word *dowager* before countess in her formal title.

She has reason to want Richard deceased since the outlines of this case indicate that that is how he very much wanted her. Deceased, that is. He didn't get his way—he killed another woman by mistake, it seems—but it's pretty certain that he had Lady Lucan in his sights.

His was a good life that went bad. The eldest son of Charles Patrick Bingham, Lucky Lucan had everything going for him: Eton College education; an earldom and a fortune to inherit; a posting

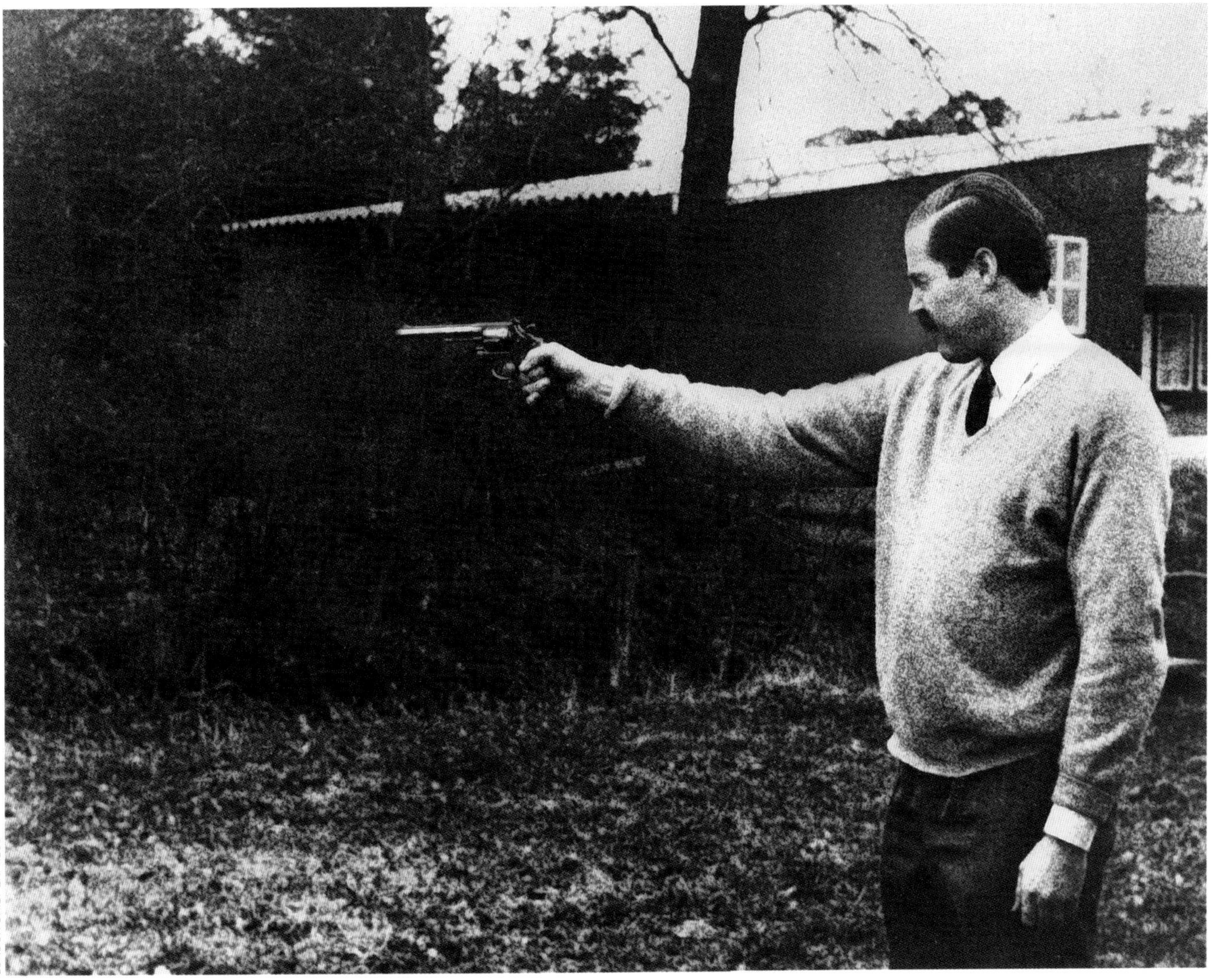

LONDON DAILY EXPRESS

PA PHOTOS

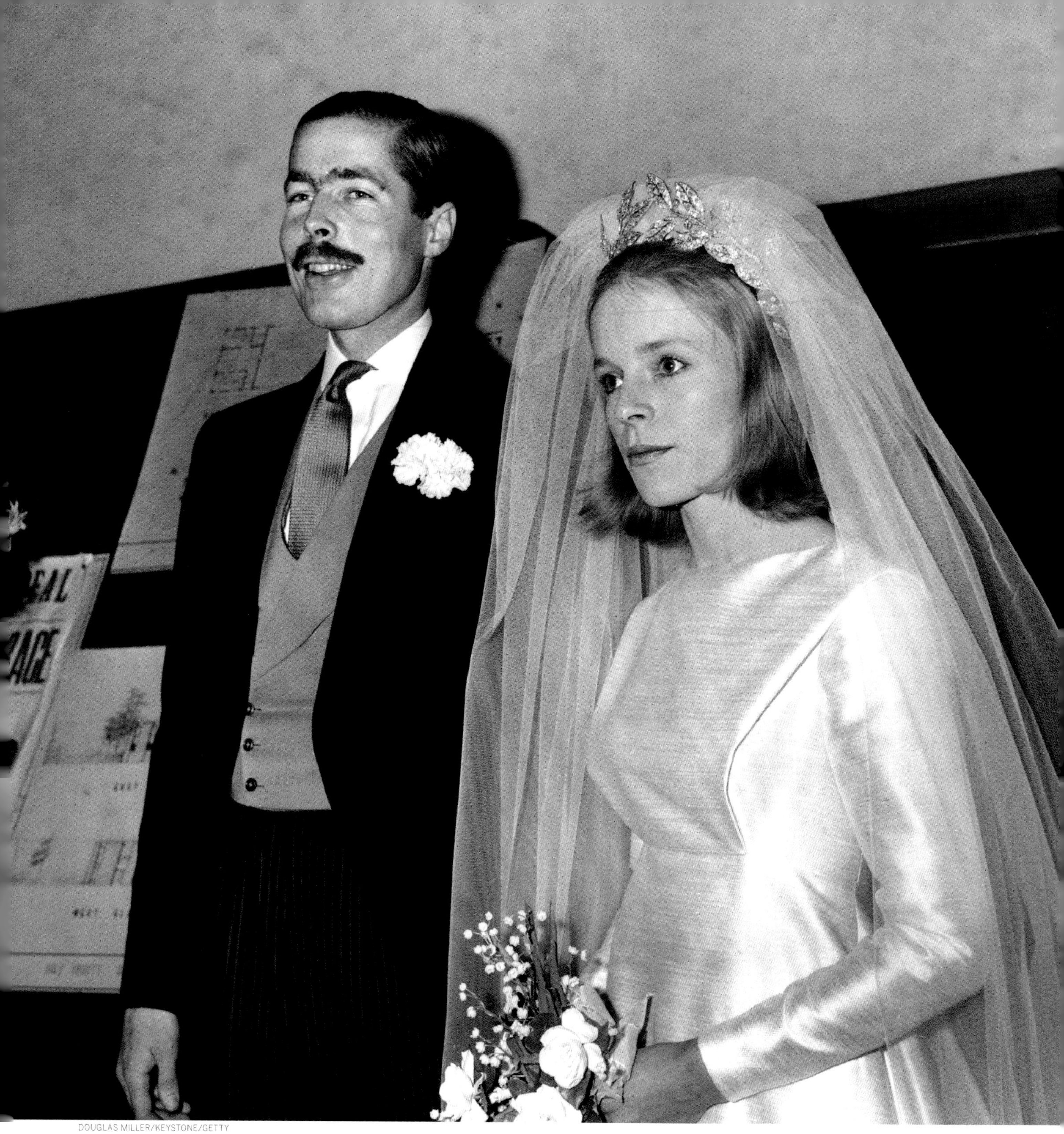

DOUGLAS MILLER/KEYSTONE/GETTY

in the Coldstream Guards, in which he would reach the rank of lieutenant. But he didn't have the disposition to be a quiet, esteemed, stiff-upper-lip British aristocrat. At gambling, for which he had a disturbing propensity, he was anything but lucky. His finances became a disaster. And in love, well . . .

He married Veronica Mary Duncan in 1963, and they had three children in the next decade before separating. Lady Lucan stayed on the estate with the kids and hired a nanny, Sandra Rivett. Richard moved out.

But apparently he returned on the Thursday evening of November 7, 1974. It is probable that his wife was his quarry, but the nanny Rivett, who was unfortunate enough to be approximately the same size and shape as Lady Lucan, was also unfortunate enough to be downstairs, in the dark, when Richard entered just before nine p.m. with murder on his mind. She was killed with the business end of a lead pipe. The murderer did not immediately flee; perhaps he knew he hadn't yet dispatched his intended victim. Eventually, Lady Lucan went looking for Rivett. Suddenly, the assailant stepped from a cloakroom and started wielding the pipe again. Lady Lucan recognized her husband and fled from the house. She startled the patrons at a nearby pub, the Plumber's Arms, by screaming, "Murder, murder! I think my neck has been broken. He tried to kill me!"

Lord Lucan hastened to the comfort of a friend's house, where he wrote letters implying that there had been another assailant,

Opposite: The lord and lady are wed on November 28, 1963; their marriage is one of the major London social events of the year. Later, Lady Lucan (below, left) shows off an unfinished portrait of her husband—"painted," she says, "in the full bloom of love." Below: The victim, Sandra Rivett, was stuffed into a canvas mail sack after being killed. In the photograph at bottom, coppers use copters to hunt his lordship.

LONDON DAILY EXPRESS

ANGELA DEANE-DRUMMOND/EVENING STANDARD/GETTY

PA PHOTOS

Suddenly the patrons of the Plumber's Arms pub were met with a bloodied woman, who shouted, "Murder, murder! I think my neck has been broken. He tried to kill me!"

and that, in fact, he, passing by, had sought to intervene. He also suggested, pretty accurately, that his wife would try to blame him. The court and most of the public sided with the lady, and on June 19, 1975, Lord Lucan was the last Englishman found guilty of murder by an inquest jury—a hitherto in absentia procedure that has since been ruled unlawful.

He has been sighted in New Zealand, South Africa, India and elsewhere. These people who were identified were probably not him, however. Most of his friends and associates assume he committed suicide shortly after the night in question, possibly by sinking his boat in a nearby lake.

Was that, indeed, Lucky Lucan's last roll of the dice?

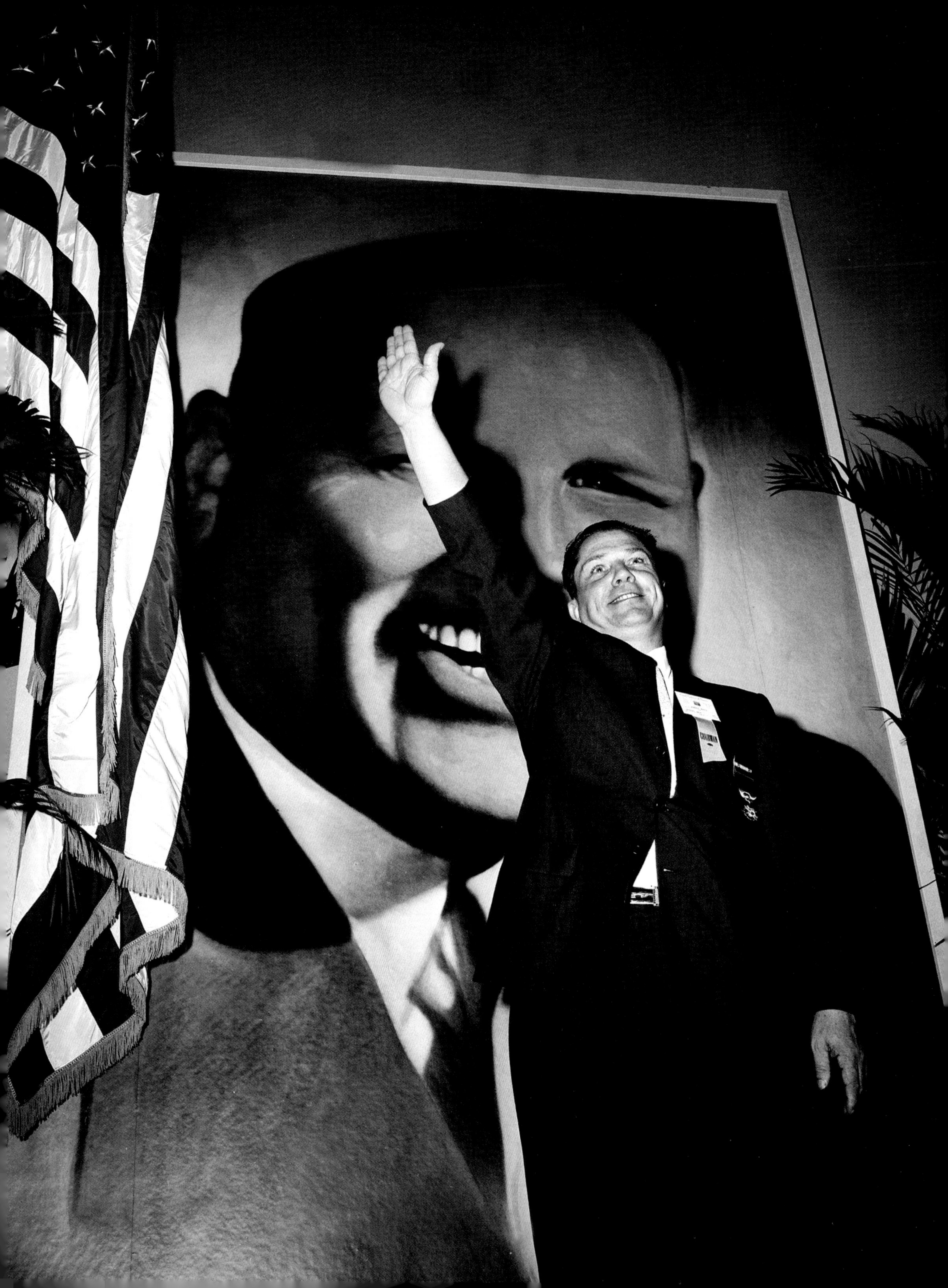

Where's Jimmy Hoffa?

All too perfect for a book titled *Unsolved Mysteries:* Jimmy Hoffa's middle name was Riddle. Or should we say his middle name *is* Riddle? Could he possibly still be alive?

The U.S. government thinks not: It declared the former leader of the International Brotherhood of Teamsters legally dead on July 30, 1982. Others believe he was already deceased seven summers earlier, eliminated by one of the thugs with whom he had had a long association. The Mafia was always alongside Hoffa during his rise and fall as the kingpin of organized labor in the U.S. Was the Mob there at the bitter end?

It remains a question—a riddle, if you will.

Though we don't know precisely when (or if) Hoffa may have left this world, we do know when he entered it: on February 14, 1913, in Brazil, Indiana. Hoffa dropped out of school after ninth grade, and by 19, he had moved with his family to Detroit, where he got his first taste of hard-nosed labor relations while unloading boxcars for 32 cents an hour in a grocery warehouse. Leaving a shipment of perishable fruit on the loading dock, he organized a fight for higher wages—and won. As leader of Teamsters Local 299 a few years later, he battled, often literally, for his union. "I was hit so many times with nightsticks, clubs and brass knuckles, I can't even remember where the bruises were," he said. "But I can hit back. Guys who tried to break me up got broken up."

Hoffa clawed his way up the Teamsters national leadership ladder. His strong-arm tactics found him regularly in the company of organized-crime figures, who helped him solidify power. He seized the national presidency of the union in 1957. Then he tirelessly (and ruthlessly, critics charged) grew its membership to 2.2 million.

But his hobnobbing with criminals did not escape notice. U.S. Attorney General Robert F. Kennedy went after Hoffa and won: The Teamsters czar began a 13-year sentence in 1967 for jury tampering, fraud and conspiracy. In 1971, President Richard Nixon commuted Hoffa's sentence—a release that carried the stipulation that he refrain from union activities until 1980.

But he just couldn't. The still-tough, five-foot, five-inch, 58-year-old bulldog started angling for a return to power. The problem: While Hoffa had been in the slammer, his successor, Frank Fitzsimmons, had consolidated his own base—not just among the rank and file but with some mobsters close to the organization.

On July 30, 1975, Hoffa reportedly drove to the Machus Red Fox Restaurant in Bloomfield Township, northwest of Detroit. Some have speculated that a midday sit-down had been arranged with local mafioso Anthony "Tony Jack" Giacalone and New Jersey racketeer Anthony "Tony Pro" Provenzano to quell a feud and discuss Hoffa's future with the Teamsters. If so, it seems that the mobsters knew exactly what Hoffa's future looked like.

When he still hadn't returned home the next morning, his wife, Josephine, called the police, who found his unlocked car in the restaurant parking lot. Given Hoffa's connections, foul play has always been presumed. Among the theories as to what happened to him:

- His body, in the trunk of a car, visited a giant compactor near Detroit.
- He was whacked in Michigan and unceremoniously interred at Giants Stadium in New Jersey, which was under construction at the time.
- He was buried somewhere in Michigan—in a gravel pit in Highland, under a swimming pool in Bloomfield Hills, beneath a garage in Cadillac.
- And a sunny one: He split for Brazil with a go-go dancer.

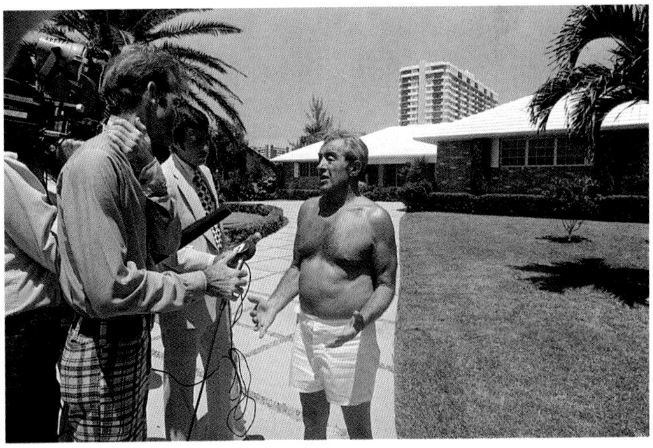

BETTMANN/CORBIS

Opposite: During his campaign to become Teamsters president in 1957, Hoffa waves to delegates at the union's convention in Miami Beach. Above: On August 5, 1975, newsmen catch up with Provenzano, also in Florida, less than a week after Hoffa was thought to be meeting him for lunch. Tony Pro says he knows nothing—*nothing.*

In May 2006, the FBI searched Hidden Dreams Farm in Milford Township, Michigan, where a drug dealer said he had seen "suspicious activity" some years earlier. The feds came up empty.

So Jimmy Hoffa's fate, which was probably an ill fate, technically remains a riddle—even as he remains legally dead.

AP

Was Pope John Paul I Murdered?

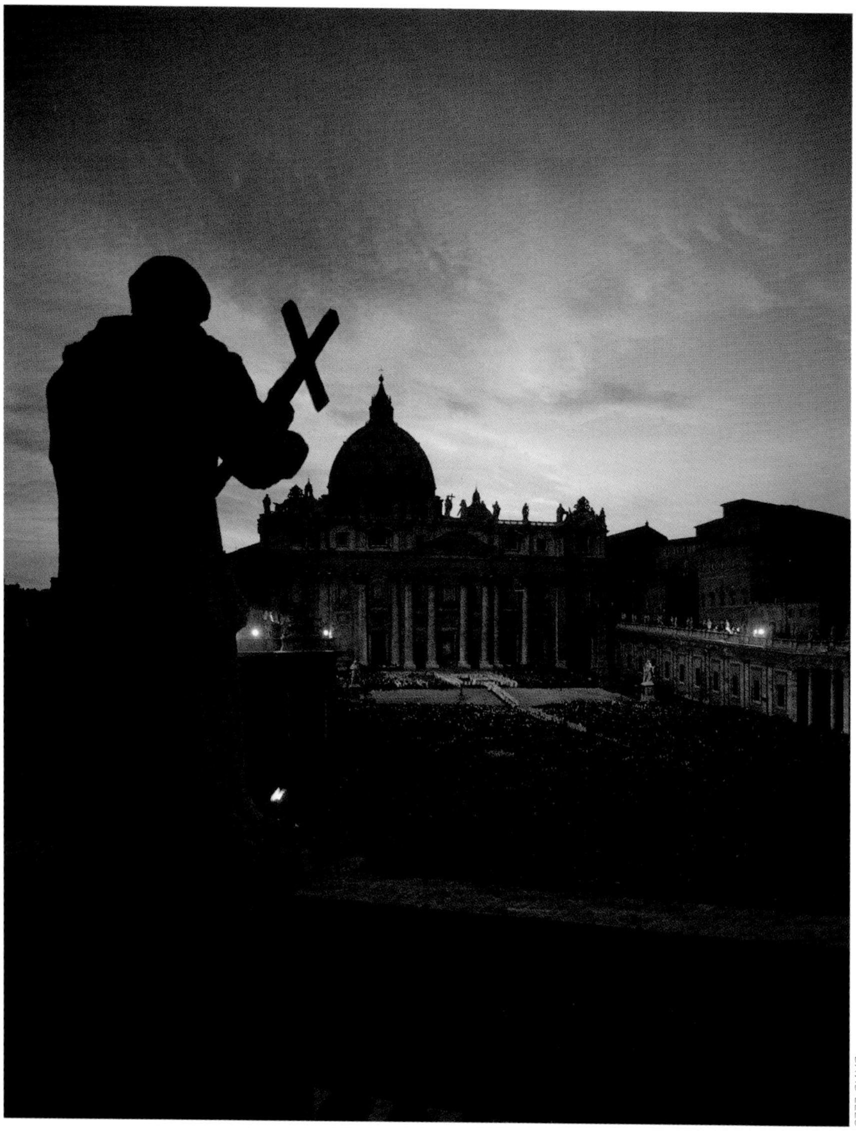

DAVID LEES

This isn't a wild and crazy theory from a Dan Brown novel, although it may be the equivalent of one: that the "smiling pope," who died barely a month after ascending to Saint Peter's throne, was poisoned.

Papal history is actually chockablock with intrigues about poisoned pontiffs, and the Vatican brings a lot of this misery upon itself with its culture of nondisclosure and reconditeness. The Vatican chooses not to elucidate, and therein lies the problem when such news hits.

Sometime in the night of September 28, 1978, only 33 days after being elected, Pope John Paul I, the former Albino Luciani, archbishop of Venice, died at age 65. The Vatican, taken unawares and scrambling, announced that he had been discovered by his secretary, an Irish priest named John Magee. In fact, the pope had been found dead in his bed, in an attitude of reading, by his housekeeper, Sister Vincenza (although at least one theory has Magee and a second secretary, Don Diego Lorenzi, finding the pope dead on the floor and rearranging him in bed to

Left: On September 3, a High Mass is said on the steps of Saint Peter's Basilica following the investiture of John Paul I; not a month later, he would be dead. Opposite, clockwise from left: John Paul I (left) greets the man who will become John Paul II, Cardinal Karol Wojtyla from Poland; the gold chalice into which the College of Cardinals placed its votes while electing both men; and Boris Georgievich Rotov Nikodim, Metropolitan of Leningrad, who collapsed and died during an audience with John Paul I on September 5, a fact later seized upon by assassination theorists.

make the death look more natural since they were both aware that the pope had health problems but had not intervened). Then, too, the Vatican said that the last thing John Paul I was reading was *The Imitation of Christ,* by Thomas à Kempis. This lovely touch was pure PR; he had been reading a report on the church's Jesuit order. Also: The time of death, the time the body was found, the time the undertakers were called—all were uncertain or, in various reports, conflicting. It is a rule that autopsies are never performed

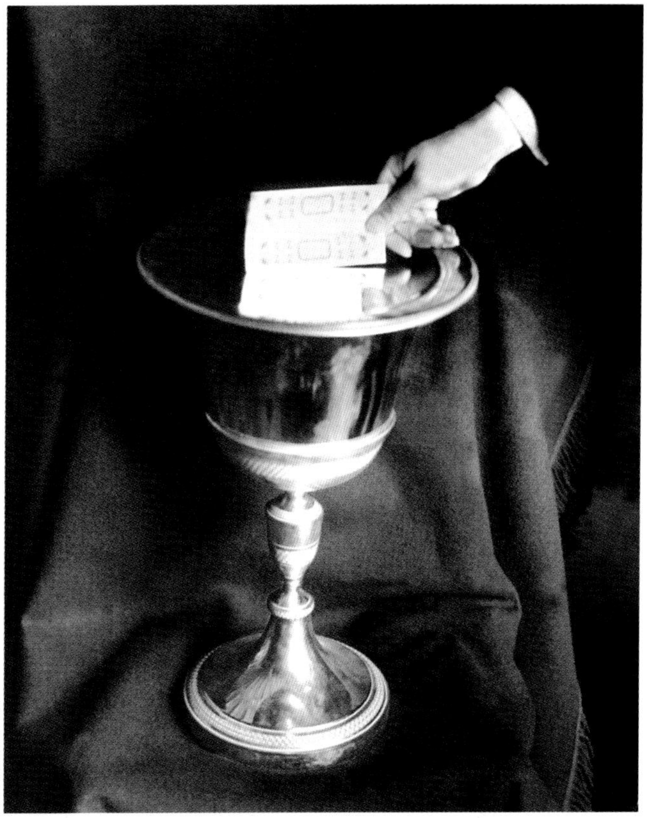

KEYSTONE/EYEDEA

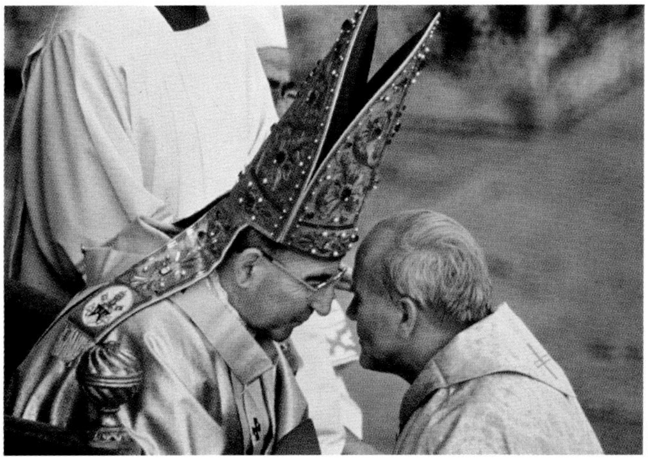

TEAM

on popes, and one was not ordered in this case. Not even a death certificate was issued—just the news that a heart attack had claimed the life of the pope. Clearly the Vatican had opened its pearly gates to conspiracy theorists everywhere and most cordially said, "Please, do come in!"

Papal history is chockablock with intrigues about poisoned pontiffs, and the Vatican brings a lot of this misery upon itself with its culture of nondisclosure and proprietary information. Still . . . where there's smoke, there's often fire.

Any pope's philosophy will find dissenters within the Catholic community—dissenters or even (cue the dark, ominous music) enemies. John Paul I was considered too liberal on the matter of contraception by some colleague prelates; he was about to blow open the (very real) corruption at the Vatican Bank; he was going to purge the clandestine and illegal Masonic lodge Propaganda Due (P2), which was said to include Vatican insiders in its membership

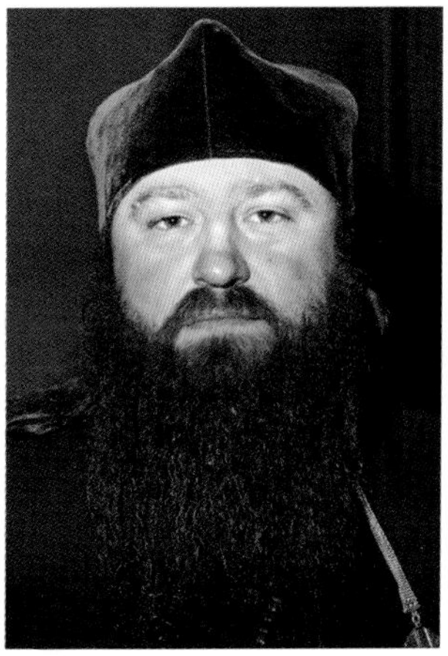

KEYSTONE/GETTY

(this last fact has never been proved). Once it was decided by some that the pope had probably been poisoned, it was revealed that shortly beforehand a monk had died after having had tea at the Vatican. Surely the pope had been the target of that "lethal" brew.

The scenario that has gotten the most traction, one laid out breathlessly in a 1984 bestseller by the British journalist David Yallop, is that the pontiff was ordered killed by one or more of a half-dozen suspects who had "a great deal to fear if the papacy of John Paul I continued." The suspects included a cardinal who was the Vatican secretary of state and another who was archbishop of Chicago; yet another archbishop who headed the Vatican Bank; a bank president who had been manipulating Vatican funds (and who was found hanging from a bridge in London in 1982 wearing, by unconfirmed reports, Masonic garb); a second banker who knew about the Vatican Bank's laundering of Mafia money (and who was later sentenced to 25 years in a New York prison for fraud); and, finally, the grand master of P2.

There you go, David Yallop (and Dan Brown) fans.

Or maybe the pope just had a heart attack.

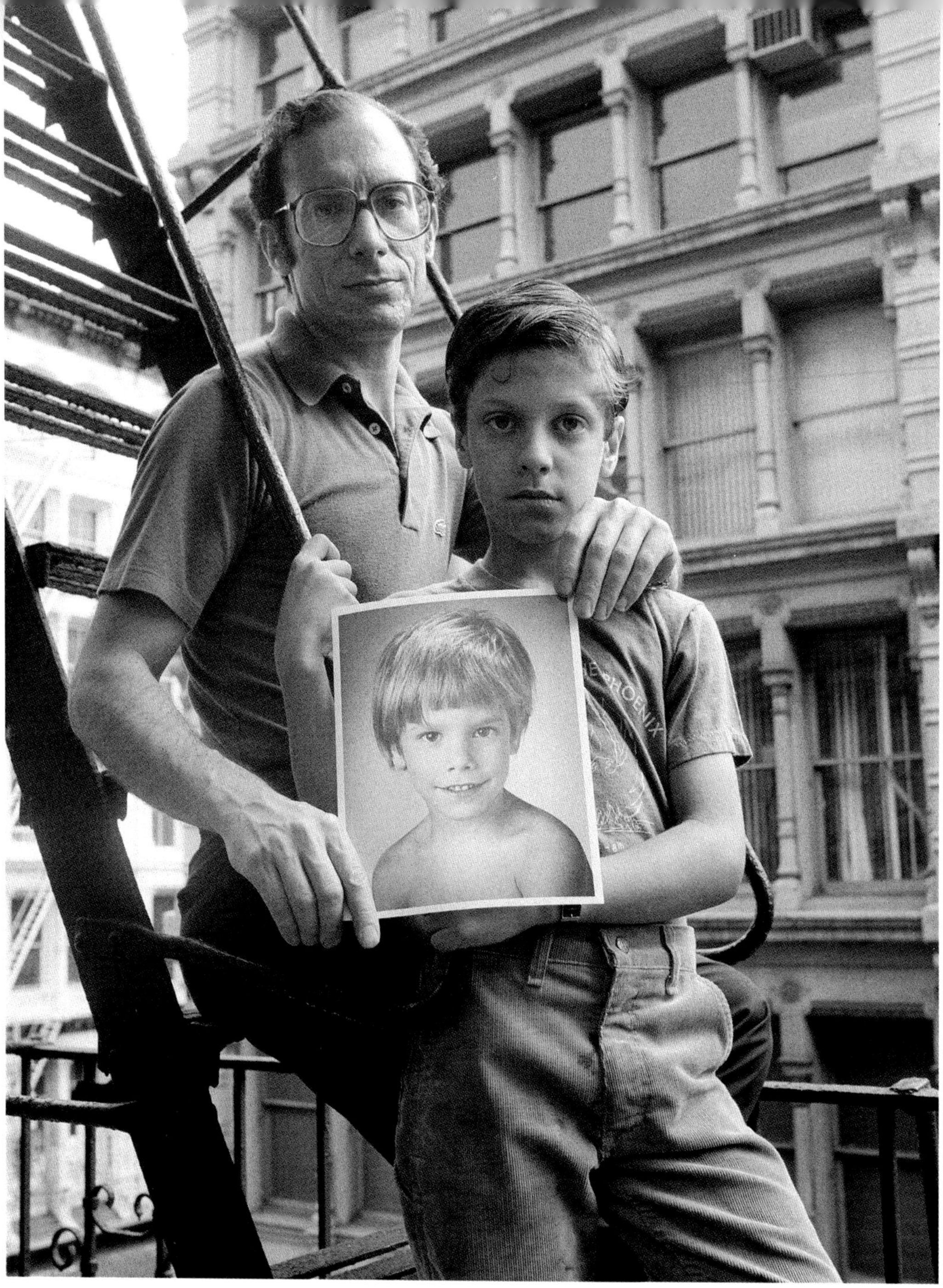
PHOENIX

RON FREHM/AP

On this page, we see Stanley Patz and his son Ari in a photograph taken outside their Manhattan apartment on May 18, 1985, holding a picture of Ari's older brother, Etan, that was taken about the time he went missing six years earlier. Opposite: Madeleine McCann rides her bicycle outside her home in Rothley, Leicestershire, in England in the spring of 2007.

What Happened to the Abducted Children?

This chapter, which is unquestionably one of the saddest in our book, concerns the modern-day phenomenon of children and adolescents suddenly disappearing, apparent victims of kidnappers and, most probably, murderers. Several of these crimes have attracted national and even global attention. Among the first of such cases to gain widespread notoriety was the May 25, 1979, presumed abduction of a six-and-a-half-year-old New York City schoolboy Etan Patz. He had begged his parents to allow him to walk the two blocks to the school bus stop by himself, and the first time they acceded, Etan went missing. His father was a photographer and spread copies of black-and-white portraits of Etan wherever he could; one photograph of the boy became the first of hundreds of missing-kid pictures to appear on the side of a milk carton, and the story spread across the land—in 1983, President Ronald Reagan named May 25 National Missing Children's Day, and the fact of child abduction became a declared issue. Etan has never been found, and no one has ever been charged, but there has long been a prime suspect. Jose A. Ramos is a convicted child molester currently in prison in Pennsylvania who was known to be interested in Etan and had knowledge of the Patz family's living situation. He has fairly taunted authorities and the Patz family through the years and even posted a message on a Web page that read in part, "As to what actually happened to Etan Patz, if any freedom-loving American wants the true story, I kindly ask that you send $2 to my snail-mail address." Ramos's 20-year sentence for an unrelated attack on a child is due to expire in 2012.

It is estimated that, in an average year, up to 2,000 children are reported missing in the U.S., with 100 of them eventually murdered by their abductors. Not all of these horrendous cases become as well known as Etan's—or as that of Jacob Wetterling. The 11-year-old was biking with his brother and a friend in St. Joseph, Minnesota, when the boys were accosted by a masked gunman, who abducted Jacob. He hasn't been seen since. In 1994, the Jacob Wetterling Crimes Against Children and Sexually Violent Offender Registration Act was passed in response.

Other children have been taken and killed, and their stories do

Etan had begged his parents to allow him to walk the two blocks to the school bus stop by himself. The first time they acceded, in the spring of 1979, the boy went missing and hasn't been seen since.

not represent unsolved mysteries: In 1993, 12-year-old Polly Klaas was abducted during a slumber party in Petaluma, California, by a man with a knife, spurring a two-month search by thousands of people; Richard Allen Davis was eventually arrested and convicted of her murder. In 1994, seven-year-old Megan Kanka was lured by repeat sex offender Jesse Timmendequas into a house across the street from her family home in Hamilton Township, New Jersey. She was raped and strangled, and Timmendequas is now incarcerated for life. In 1994, her home state passed the first of many so-called Megan's Laws, calling for authorities to publicize information concerning the whereabouts of sex offenders registered under the Jacob Wetterling Act. In 1996, nine-year-old Amber Hagerman was snatched from her bike in Arlington, Texas, and her corpse was found four days later—so we do know her fate, even if no one has ever been convicted of the crime. The AMBER Alert system, meant to get the word out quickly when a child is abducted, was made a federal law in her memory in 2003.

These cases are not confined to the United States. On May 3, 2007, days before her fourth birthday, Madeleine McCann, vacationing in Portugal with her parents and twin siblings, disappeared from the resort apartment where she and her family

PA PHOTOS/LANDOV

were staying, having been left unsupervised. There have been suspects, including her own parents, but Madeleine remains missing, and the crime remains unsolved.

These are unspeakably sad cases, the child abductions.

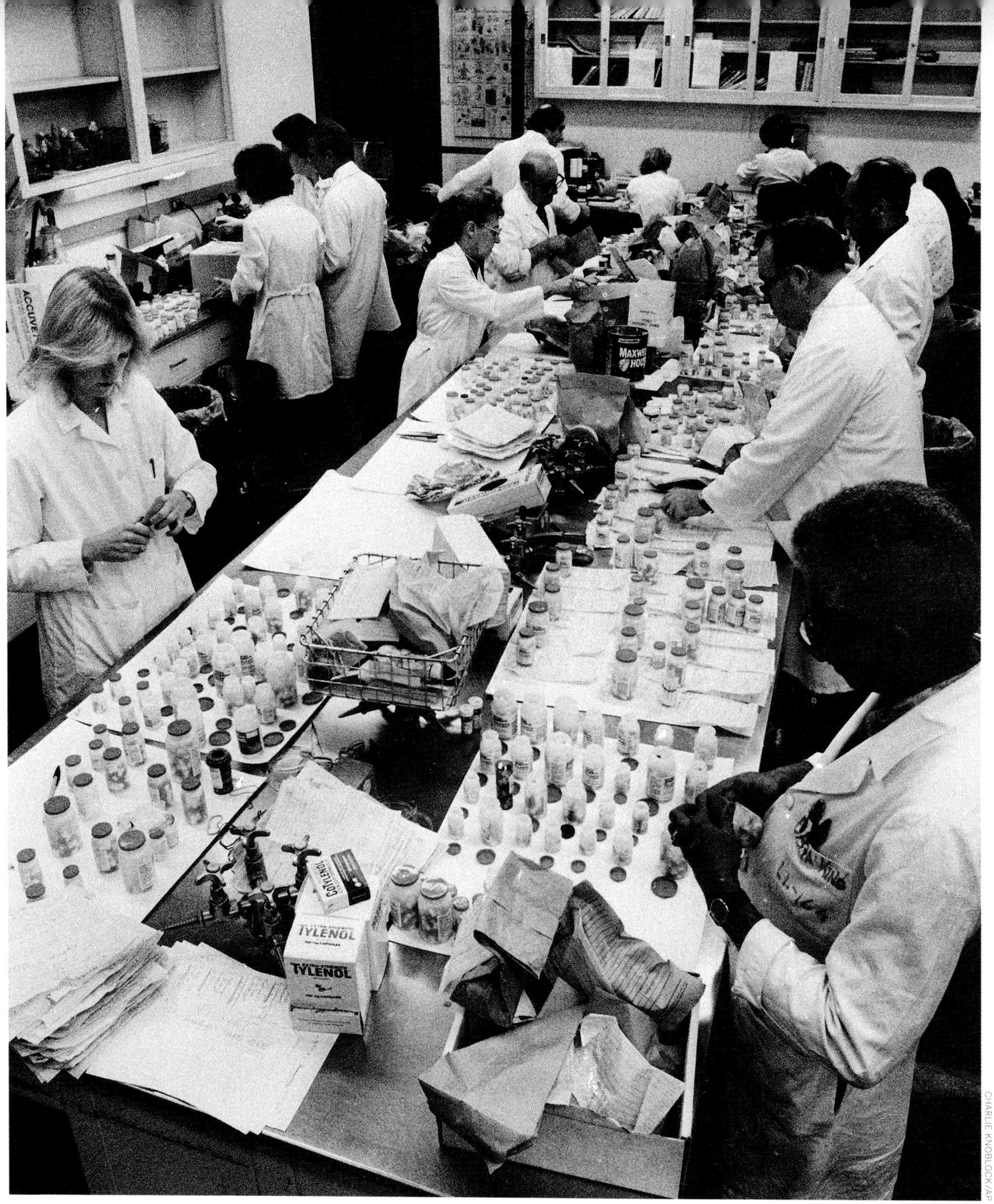
TYLENOL
TYLENOL

CHARLIE KNOBLOCK/AP

Will the Case of the Tylenol Poisonings Ever Be Solved?

A report in *Time* depicted a scene out of a Batman movie: "Police cruisers, rolling through Chicago streets Thursday afternoon and evening, blared warnings over loudspeakers."

The phrase *murder most foul* applies to few other crimes as aptly as it does to this one, in which an anonymous murderer tampered with a pain-relief product and indiscriminately sentenced Chicago-area users to death. The poisonings in September and early October of 1982 have represented a very cold case for years, although there are renewed efforts to find out who doctored the Tylenol.

The beginning of it all: Adam Janus, 27, who lived in the suburb of Arlington Heights, was experiencing chest pains and reached for his Extra Strength Tylenol. He took a few, then collapsed and died within an hour. Of course, his younger brother, Stanley, 25, and Stanley's bride, Theresa, 19, who were freshly back from their honeymoon, were struck by sorrow. They ingested Tylenol from Adam's supply and also died. Meantime, in Elk Grove Village, 12-year-old Mary Kellerman had a cold. She took Tylenol and died.

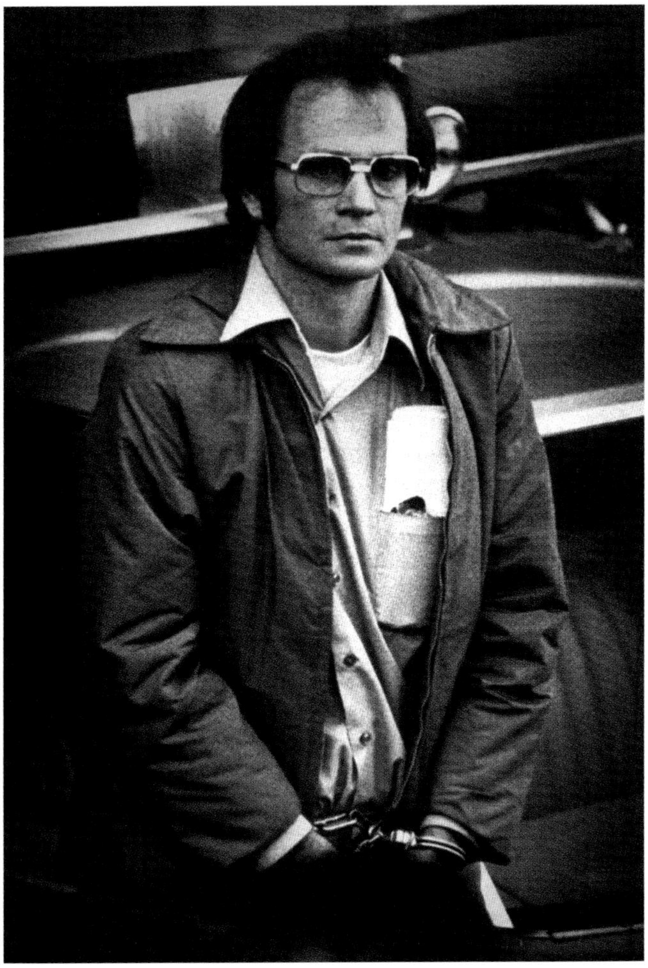

AP

As did Mary Reiner, 27, in Winfield; Mary McFarland, 35, of Elmhurst; and Paula Prince, also 35, who lived in the city itself. When the public learned that Tylenol laced with cyanide was out there, panic was general. A report in *Time* magazine depicted a scene out of a Batman movie: "Police cruisers, rolling through Chicago streets Thursday afternoon and evening, blared warnings over loudspeakers." Tylenol was withdrawn from the shelves in Chicago and elsewhere, and since the scare happened during the Halloween season, communities in Illinois cancelled trick-or-treating.

Johnson & Johnson, the makers of Tylenol, received an extortion demand: $1 million would "stop the killing." This was eventually traced to James W. Lewis, who, after a nationwide manhunt, was arrested in December at a New York City library. Lewis gave investigators a detailed description of how cyanide might have been added to the pills, though he denied doing it himself. He later told the Associated Press that the perpetrator was "a heinous, cold-blooded killer, a cruel monster." He served more than 12 years for extortion and tax fraud but was never charged with murder.

In 2007, responding to the quarter-century anniversary of the spree that claimed seven lives and to, it is believed, new information, the FBI searched Lewis's home in Massachusetts. "All I can tell you is we have conducted a search on Gore Street in Cambridge, and it's connected to an ongoing criminal investigation," said an agency spokesperson. Lewis responded defiantly about "the curse of being labeled the Tylenol Man." Where this recent activity will lead, if anywhere, is uncertain.

It is worth noting that although very few of the cases in this book have a silver lining, this one does: The Tylenol poisonings led to regulations regarding tamper-proof seals and other protections concerning the manner in which food and medicines are packaged. If it is a commentary on our times that these initiatives are necessary, it is also a fact that the lives of more innocent victims may have been spared since 1982 precisely because the Tylenol murders created such a sensation.

Opposite: On October 7, 1982, employees of the Chicago Department of Public Health test Tylenol for the presence of deadly cyanide, which has terrified the city for a week. Left: James W. Lewis, who gave investigators a detailed description of how cyanide might have been added to the pills, in federal court in Kansas City in January 1983—on unrelated charges.

Where Did the Boston Paintings Go?

This was a big-time caper. Even the FBI thinks so: Its Top Ten Art Crimes list places the Isabella Stewart Gardner Museum theft "second only to Iraqi Looted and Stolen Artifacts." The feds' description of the events of March 18, 1990, hints at frustration: "The [museum] was robbed by two unknown white males dressed in police uniforms and identifying themselves as Boston police officers . . . All logical leads have been followed . . . with no positive investigative results." In other words, no arrests made, no art recovered.

Which is not to say this story lacks characters. Myles Connor, for example, is an intriguing subject. The five-foot, seven-inch native of Milton, Massachusetts, became a person of interest soon after the heist at the Venetian-style palace, which opened in Boston in 1903 to house paintings, sculptures and artifacts accumulated by heiress and arts patron Isabella Gardner.

The intruders handcuffed the museum's two guards, then went straight to the Dutch Room. They swiped three Rembrandts and a Vermeer. From the Short Gallery, they took five Degas drawings. Finally, they raided the Blue Room and took a Manet. When the police arrived, they were perplexed that the museum's most valuable piece, Titian's "The Rape of Europa," had been left behind.

The thieves handcuffed the two guards, then went straight to the Dutch Room, where they swiped three Rembrandts and a Vermeer. They weren't done.

Connor, a connoisseur of fine art as well as an illegal trafficker in it, said this oversight proved he wasn't involved; that painting would have been the first one he would have seized. Besides, there was no way he could have been at the Gardner that night. His airtight alibi: He was serving time for fencing stolen art.

Though the police suspected that Connor might have masterminded the most lucrative art theft in U.S. history from his prison cell, they followed other leads. With such a potentially huge economic upside—the black-market price tag for the otherwise priceless booty was estimated at $300 million—perhaps Boston's powerful Irish mob (please see page 118) was involved. Or maybe

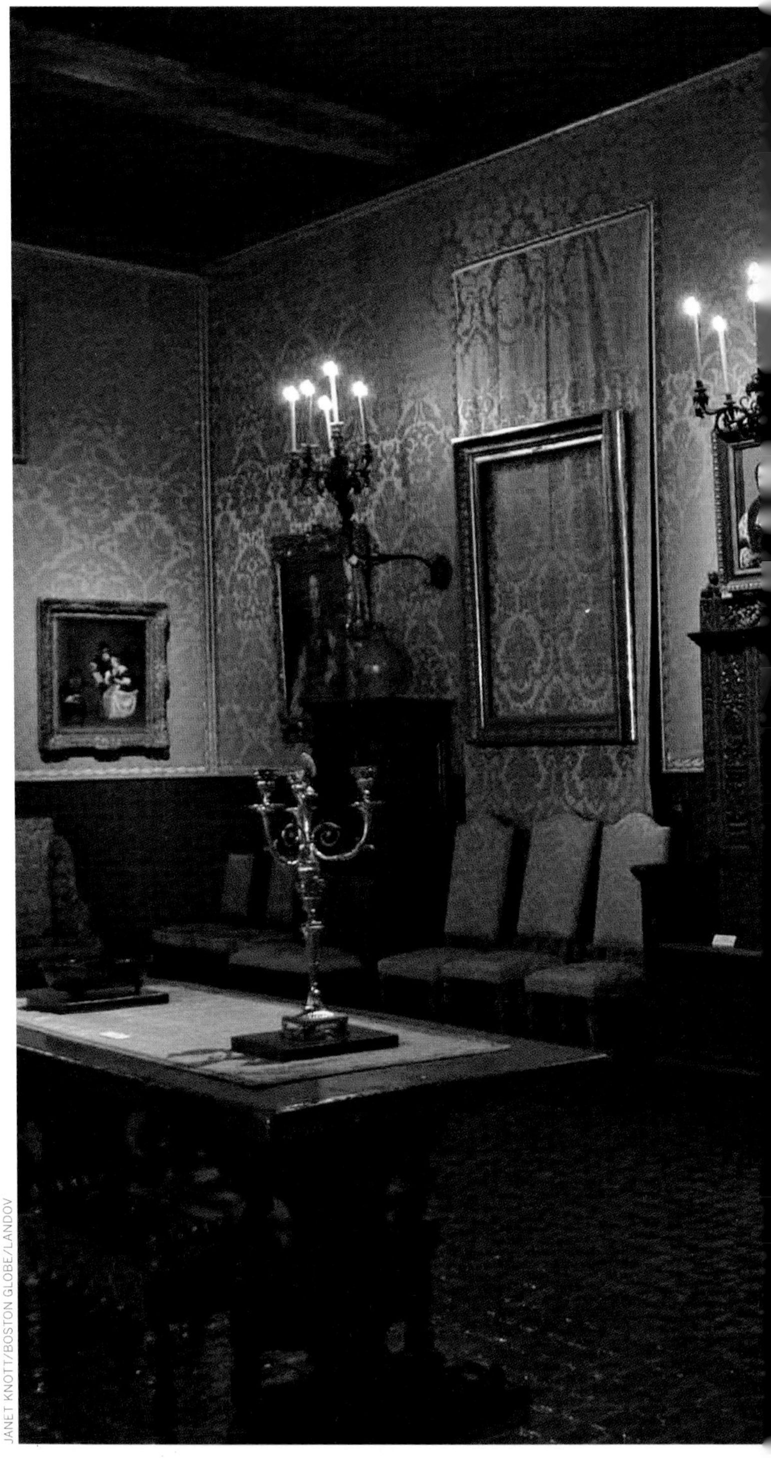

JANET KNOTT/BOSTON GLOBE/LANDOV

Below: Ever since the night of the heist, empty frames on the walls of the Gardner Museum have testified to what occurred there.

the job was simply the handiwork of local burglars.

Six years later, when the statute of limitations ran out, new information surfaced. From behind bars in 1997, Connor told *Time* magazine that he and reputed gangster Bobby Donati had cased the Gardner in the mid-1970s. Connor claimed he'd had no hand in the eventual caper and pointed to Donati and an accomplice, David Houghton, as the culprits. The accused's response? Well, dead men tell no tales: Donati had been the target of a probable Mob hit in 1991; Houghton had died of natural causes in 1992.

The FBI was wondering if Connor was publicly angling for a deal when Billy Youngworth, an associate of Connor's, told authorities that he knew where the paintings were. He said if they would drop the auto-theft charges against him, grant him immunity and give him the $5 million reward—plus spring his pal Connor from prison—he would help solve the case. No deal.

Connor and Youngworth were released from prison in 2000, and since then news reports have regularly suggested that either or both men might ultimately help to recover the elusive treasure. Until that day, the Isabella Stewart Gardner Museum goes forward—with a hole in its heart.

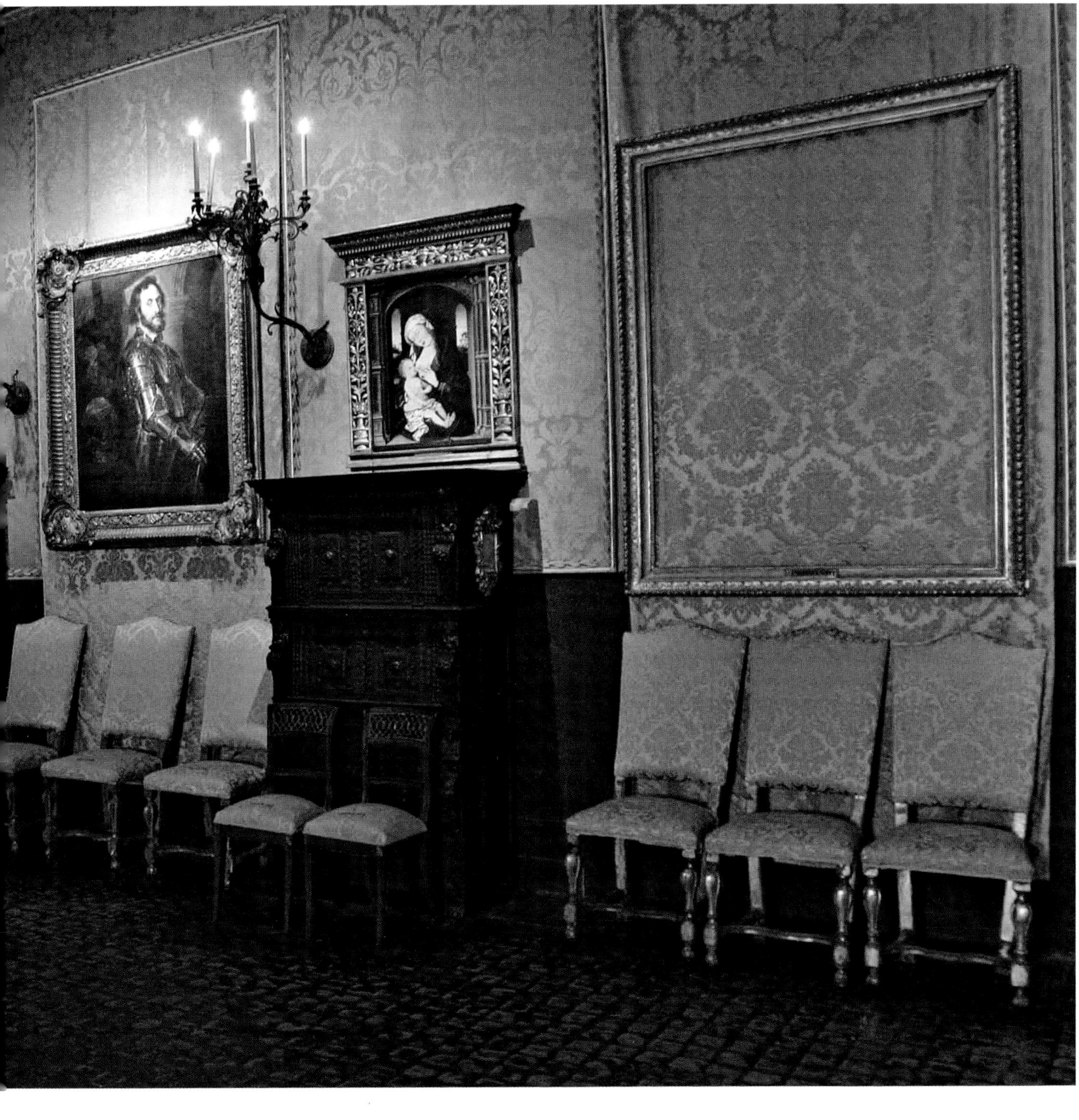

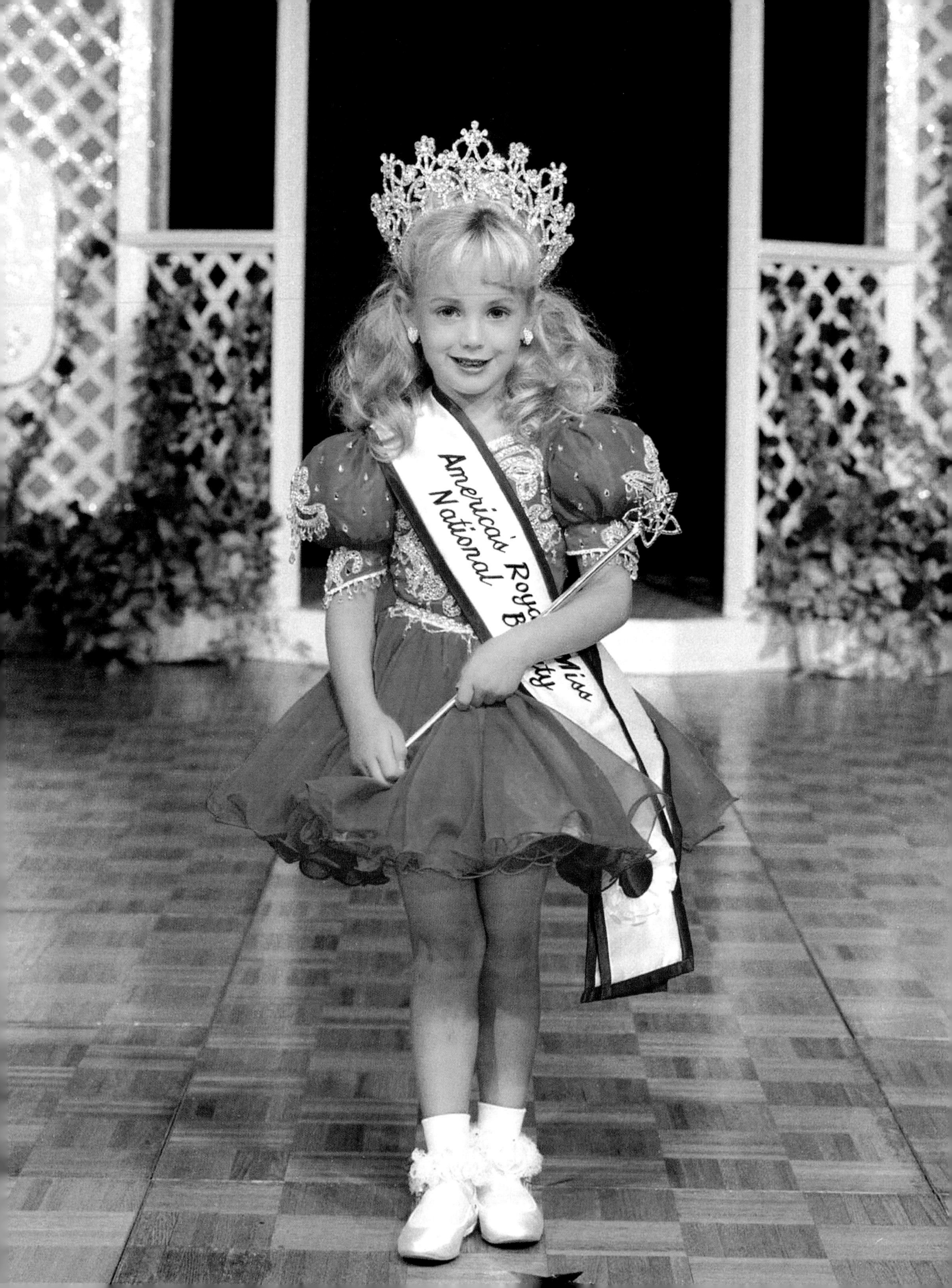
America's
National
Miss

Who Killed JonBenét Ramsey?

For months and even years, no American could go past a magazine rack or through the checkout counter of a supermarket without seeing her lovely young face and shining eyes, her blonde curls and sweet smile. There were a select few photographs of the six-year-old child-beauty-pageant winner that gained the widest circulation—used over and over and over again—and they haunted our collective consciousness in late 1996, throughout 1997 and to this very day: Who could have killed this little girl, and why?

Her body was found on the day after Christmas '96 in the basement of her family home in Boulder, Colorado. Her mother, Patsy Ramsey, had earlier found a ransom letter demanding $118,000 on the staircase, she told investigators, and called the police, family and friends. The first official search of the house turned up nothing, but during a second search, nearly eight hours after the child was discovered missing, JonBenét's father, John, and two friends found the corpse under a white blanket. The skull had been fractured and the child strangled with a makeshift garrote made of cord and the broken handle of one of Patsy's paintbrushes.

In hindsight, it is clear that the investigation did not proceed cleanly. The crime scene wasn't sealed. Suspicions that one or both of the Ramseys—or their son, nine-year-old Burke—had done the deed turned attention away from other possibilities. Much later it was revealed that there had been more than 100 burglaries in the Ramseys' neighborhood in the months leading up to the attack on JonBenét, and that there were dozens of registered sex offenders living within a two-mile radius of the home. But whether the theory that an intruder killed JonBenét was thoroughly plumbed in the earliest stages of the investigation continues to be a strong point of criticism.

> In the year of her death, JonBenét was crowned Little Miss Colorado. She had also been named America's Royale Little Miss (opposite), National Tiny Miss Beauty and Colorado State All-Star Kids Cover Girl.

> Sometimes, in the furor over beauty pageants, it got lost that a six-year-old girl had been brutally murdered.

In any event, the case turned into a huge media play, and sentiment turned largely against the Ramseys for two reasons: leaks by authorities concerning their own suspicions and this business of children's beauty pageants, which much of the American public viewed as an unpleasant revelation. The idea that Patsy Ramsey, a former beauty queen herself, was dolling up her child with makeup and sophisticated hairdos, parading her about in various fashion and even bathing suit competitions, was seen by some as unsavory. They expressed revulsion at the whole JonBenét story, even as they were fascinated by it and scooped up the tabloids covering it. Sometimes, in the furor over beauty pageants, it got lost that a six-year-old girl had been brutally murdered.

A grand jury, presented over the months and years with mountains of information, failed to indict anyone. Defamation lawsuits flew left and right—filed against media companies, authors, suspects, law enforcement officials. As time went on, various investigatory techniques improved, and in 2003 a DNA profile based upon evidence from the crime scene cleared those many registered sex offenders in Boulder and established the assailant as an unknown male. In 2006, a man named John Mark Karr, a former schoolteacher who was being held on child pornography charges in California, claimed that he had been with JonBenét on the night she died, but the DNA evidence indicated that he wasn't the murderer either. By 2008, the Boulder district attorney's office announced that DNA sampling had officially cleared the Ramseys of involvement in JonBenét's death. In 2009, the Boulder police department took back the case from the DA and said it was reopening the investigation.

Earlier, in 2006, Patsy Ramsey, who had once been most wanted in the minds of many of her countrymen, died of cancer, and was buried next to JonBenét.

Who Wasted the Rappers?

Tupac Shakur and the Notorious B.I.G. were enormously popular hip-hop stars in the mid-1990s when they were assassinated within months of each other. No one has ever been charged in the crimes, nor in the execution-style murder of Yafeu "Kadafi" Fula, who was a backup singer for Shakur and reportedly had information he was willing to share with the authorities. Theories involve rival record labels ordering the hits on the opposition and even industry bigwigs killing their own clients for economic reasons. But one thing seems clear: The murders emanated from inside the rap community. Think of it as gangland action, with bullets flying within a closed society, and thank goodness no bystanders were caught in the cross fire.

Shakur was a hard-core hip-hop artist, poet and actor who was born in New York City in 1971 to a mother active in the radical Black Panther movement. Guns were a part of his life from the time he was young, and he was involved in shootings himself—on both sides of the weapon—as an adult. On December 1, 1994, for instance, he entered a New York courthouse in a wheelchair after having been shot five times in the lobby of a recording studio. He was in court that day to face the music in a sexual-abuse charge for which he was found guilty and served time in prison. It is interesting to note that he remains the only recording artist to have the No. 1 album in the country while in stir. Such was the world of Tupac Amaru Shakur.

Rumors quickly circulated that Smalls was involved in Shakur's murder, and only six months later, out in L.A., he got his.

In the aftermath of that first shooting, Shakur had become convinced that a former friend of his, Christopher Wallace, also known as the Notorious B.I.G. or Biggie Smalls, had somehow been involved in the attack. Wallace denied this but also recorded "Who Shot Ya?," a song that seemed to be a taunt. After being released from prison, Shakur replied with "Hit 'Em Up," a frontal attack on Smalls and his entourage. These two rappers quickly became the poster boys for what was seen as an East-West civil war within the rap community, as Shakur's greatest success came while recording for the Southern California–based Death Row Records, run by Suge Knight, and Smalls was affiliated with the

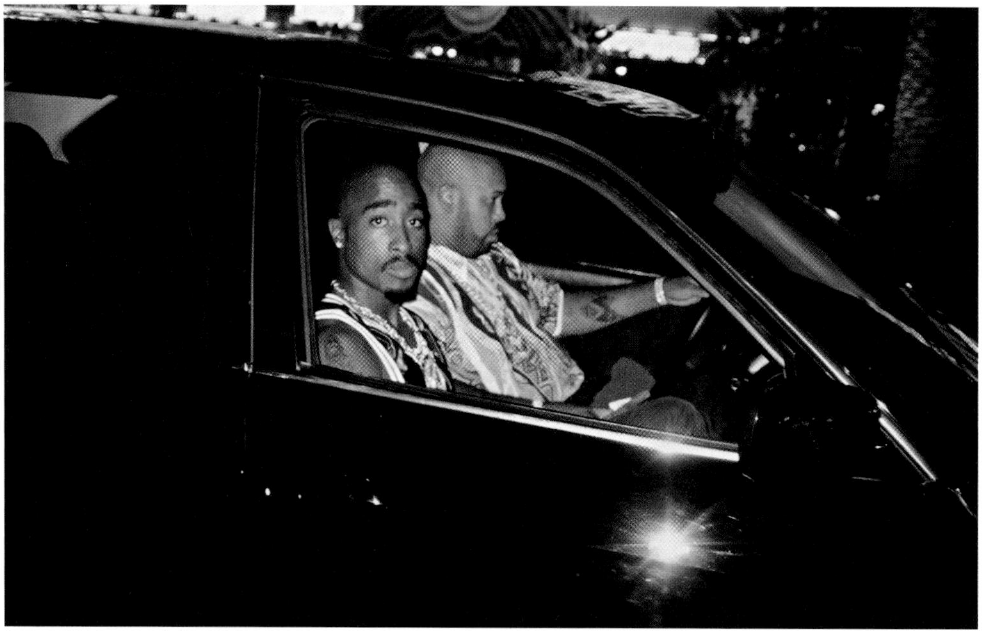

CORJUNI/OUTLINE/CORBIS

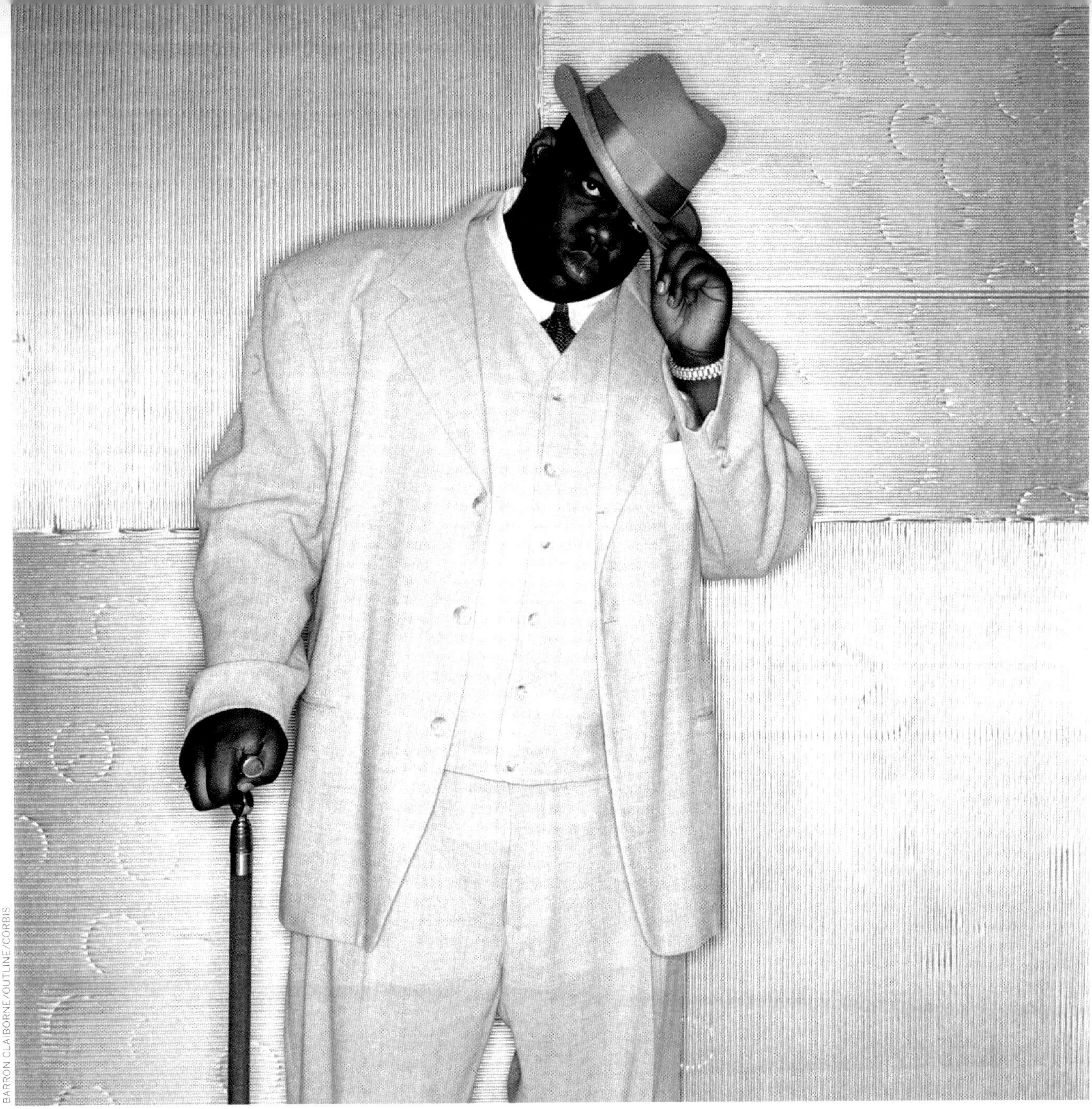

BARRON CLAIBORNE/OUTLINE/CORBIS

Opposite: In Sin City in September 1996, Shakur gazes from the passenger seat while Suge Knight keeps his eyes on the road; within minutes, Shakur will be shot. Above: The very big B.I.G.

rival Bad Boy Entertainment, headquartered in New York City and run by Sean Combs (a.k.a. at various times Puffy, Puff Daddy, P. Diddy, etc.).

On September 7, 1996, Shakur was in Las Vegas for the Mike Tyson–Bruce Seldon boxing match when he got into a scuffle in the lobby of a hotel with Orlando "Baby Lane" Anderson, a reputed member of the Southside Crips gang in L.A. It was believed that Baby Lane had earlier beaten up one of Shakur's bodyguards. Later that night, Shakur was in the passenger seat of a car driven by Knight that was stopped at a traffic light at the corner of East Flamingo and Koval. In a drive-by shooting, 13 bullets pierced the car and four hit Shakur, who died six days later. Rumors quickly circulated that Smalls was involved in the killing. Six months after Shakur was killed, a Chevy Impala pulled up next to a green Suburban that was stopped at a light in L.A. and a gunman with a 9-millimeter automatic pistol—a dapper black man in a suit and bow tie—pumped several shots into Biggie's chest. He was DOA. The back-up singer Fula was killed in New Jersey months later, and Baby Lane Anderson has also since been murdered.

Who ordered the killings may be straightforward (rival factions) or complicated; one of the many books on the subject alleges that each record company wasted its own talent, as they could make more money selling albums of a dead artist who is not constantly haggling for a larger share. (Indeed, both rappers have continued to have enormous careers in death.) Whatever the case, in the mid-1990s the violence that routinely permeated the tracks of these men's records burst into life, claiming them both.

Where's Whitey?

When relating the tale of James "Whitey" Bulger, a longtime member of the FBI's Ten Most Wanted list, Ed MacKenzie wrote in his book *Street Fighter*, "It's a story that could have played itself out only in the movies or a novel." Indeed, Hollywood has borrowed pages from the life of Whitey Bulger: The Showtime series *Brotherhood* about two siblings—one involved in crime, the other in politics—was inspired by Bulger and his brother Billy, once the president of the Massachusetts state senate. And the character Frank Costello, played by Jack Nicholson in the film *The Departed*, was loosely based on the crime boss.

Born on the cusp of the Great Depression, one of six children, Whitey Bulger cut his teeth on the hardscrabble streets of South Boston. He took to a felonious life early, hanging out with a gang called the Shamrocks. He was arrested for the first time at 14 for larceny and spent a few years in reform school. A subsequent stint in the Air Force did little to dissuade Bulger from his law-breaking ways, and soon after his discharge, he hooked up with a group of bank robbers. When they were busted, he tried to hide in plain sight, dyeing his platinum blond hair, which had earned him the nickname Whitey, black—but to no avail. He was nabbed at a bar in Revere, Massachusetts, and for the bank robberies he was sentenced to 25 years.

That could have been the end of the road, but Bulger was able to shorten his sentence to nine years by agreeing to participate in a CIA program that was testing the effects of LSD. When he returned to Boston in 1965, his brother was able to get him a janitorial job at the Suffolk County Courthouse. Bulger was careful not to violate his parole, but he just couldn't keep his nose clean. By decade's end, he was the muscle for the Killeen brothers. When Donnie Killeen was killed (a murder some law enforcement officials suspect Bulger of carrying out) in May 1972, Bulger moved to the Winter Hill gang and met his soon-to-be partner-in-crime,

MASSACHUSETTS STATE POLICE
VIOLENT FUGITIVE APPREHENSION SECTION

MOST WANTED

JAMES JOSEPH BULGER Jr.

1994 Photos

WANTED FOR:
19 Counts of MURDER,
Numerous Weapons Offenses
& Violation of the RICO Statute

DOB:	9/03/29
Height:	5'-8"
Weight:	165lbs.
Hair:	White / Silver
Eyes:	Blue
Complexion:	Fair
Race:	White
Social Security:	018-22-4149
F.B.I.#:	169486A
Peculiarities:	Glasses / Balding

AKA's:...Thomas F. Baxter, Tom Harris, Mark Shapeton, Thomas Marshall Jimmy Bulger, Whitey

Stevie Flemmi. Seven years later, the gang's leader, Howie Winter, was convicted of fixing horse races and left the Boston rackets that weren't controlled by the Mafia to Flemmi and Bulger. Soon Bulger was thought to be the most powerful mobster in Boston.

Bulger had cultivated a reputation for extreme brutality if crossed, but he could also be charming and thoughtful, handing out Thanksgiving turkeys to the poor, keeping heroin off the streets of South Boston. According to *The Boston Globe*, an FBI agent once remarked, "Isn't he a great guy?" In fact, it was Bulger's cozy relationship with the FBI, which began in 1971, that kept him out of reach of the law for years. His downfall wouldn't come until the early '90s, when the Massachusetts State Police put the squeeze on bookies who were paying him "rent." In January 1995, indictments against Bulger and Flemmi were handed down. The cops were able to nab Flemmi, but Bulger was nowhere to be found.

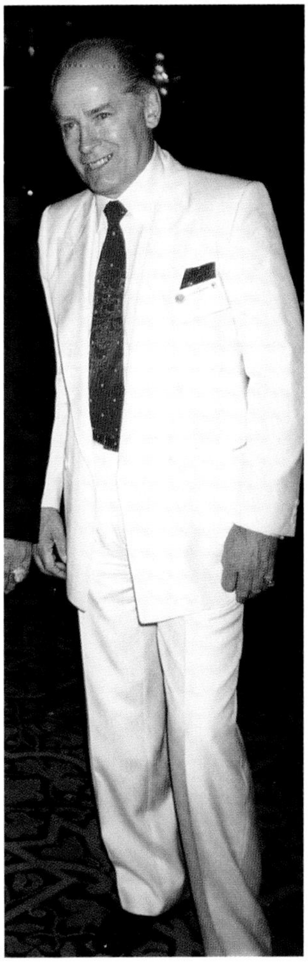

AP

Whitey, dapper in white (right) in a photograph taken just before he disappeared in 1995, has been on the FBI's Ten Most Wanted list (opposite) for more than a decade. Below: His younger brother Billy, then-president of the University of Massachusetts, is sworn in before the House Government Reform Committee on June 19, 2003, in Washington, D.C. The committee is hearing testimony regarding the use of informants by the Justice Department.

It's Shakespearean: One Bulger brother stays clean and rises in politics and the halls of academe; the other goes dirty and is a mobster on the lam. Billy swears that he doesn't know where Whitey is and that he hasn't been in touch.

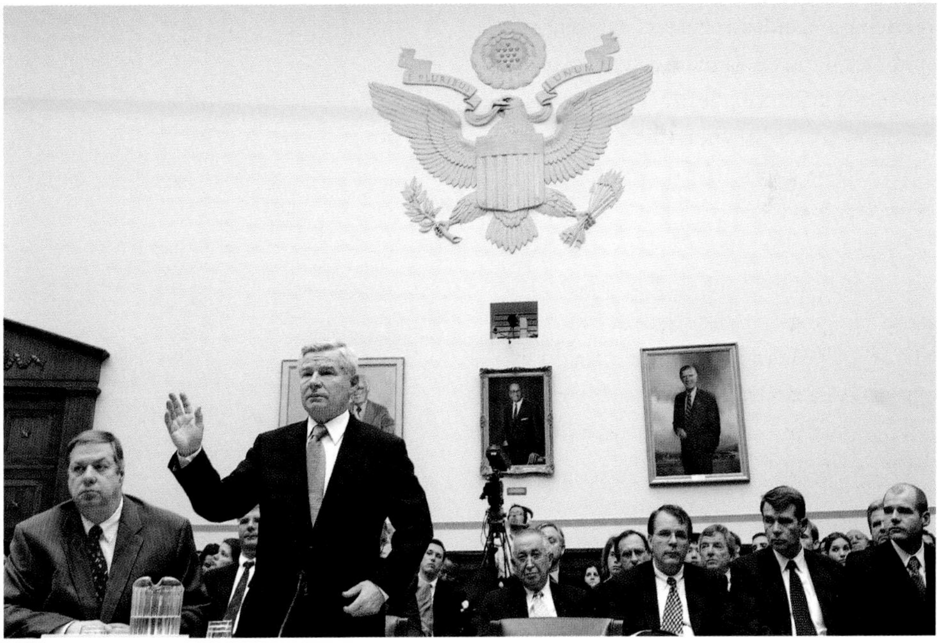

STEFAN ZAKLIN/GETTY

The gangster had celebrated the New Year in New Orleans with his common-law wife, Theresa Stanley. As they were driving back to Boston, Bulger found out there was a warrant for his arrest. He laid low for a few weeks, then returned to Boston to drop off Stanley, who didn't want to live on the lam, and picked up his mistress Catherine Greig. From there, the couple hopped around the country under aliases. They were spotted in Wyoming and Mississippi and in Chicago, and they even made friends in Grand Isle, Louisiana. Bulger was last spotted for sure in London in 2002. Even though there is a $2 million reward for his capture and he has been featured on the TV show *America's Most Wanted* 14 times, Bulger continues to evade the long arm of the law. And seeing that he has reached the twilight of his years—he turned 80 on September 3, 2009—it seems the question "Where's Whitey?" is one that may never be answered, perhaps to the relief of a fair few as-yet-unindicted FBI agents who worked with Bulger during his reign over the Boston underworld.

Where Is Natalee Holloway?

This story was bound to be a media sensation: A smart, pretty, blonde American high school student on an unofficial graduation trip to Aruba, the exotic swaying-palms island in the Caribbean, packs her bags for the trip home, leaves them in her hotel room and is never seen again. If we might only imagine that she *chose* to disappear, there might be some relief. *Perhaps she's still out there, living her new life.* But the details of the case point to a sad denouement, and whatever happened to Natalee Holloway, whether by her own hand or that of someone else, is probably not something that will make anyone rest easier.

She was a 18-year-old graduate of Mountain Brook High School in Alabama, a National Honor Society member headed for college, when she boarded the plane for five days in Aruba. There were 125 recent grads on the junket from Mountain Brook, an upper-class suburb of Birmingham, plus seven adults. Jodi Bearman, the chaperone who organized the trip, later said, "The chaperones were not supposed to keep up with their every move." This sounds reasonable but in hindsight is perhaps regrettable, for there was, according the local police commissioner, commenting after Holloway's disappearance, "wild partying, a lot of drinking, lots of room switching every night. We know the Holiday Inn told them they weren't welcome next year. Natalee, we know,

COURTESY BETH TWITTY/ZUMA

she drank all day every day. We have statements she started every morning with cocktails—so much drinking that Natalee didn't show up for breakfast two mornings." Classmates of Holloway's said they "agreed that the drinking was kind of excessive."

Ponds and lakes and the ocean itself have been searched, as have most of the square inches of land on Aruba, but the girl has not been found.

On Monday, May 30, the evening before their return home, at a bar called Carlos 'n Charlie's, schoolmates saw Holloway at around 1:30 a.m. They later said she left with Joran van der Sloot, a 17-year-old Dutch student living in Aruba (which is part of the Kingdom of the Netherlands), and two friends of his from Surinam, the Kalpoe brothers Deepak, 21, and Satish, 18. These three young men have been arrested and rearrested a cumulative eight times in this case but have never been charged. Holloway's parents and her supporters still look at these three hard and feel their liberty is a product of favoritism extended by local authorities.

Without knowing what really happened, it can still be said that the accounts of van der Sloot and the Kalpoes have been vague at times and contradictory at others. After such personalities as Dr. Phil, Nancy Grace and Greta Van Susteren went to town with this story, leaked videos and formal interviews became de rigueur. Van der Sloot said at one point that he had dropped Holloway back

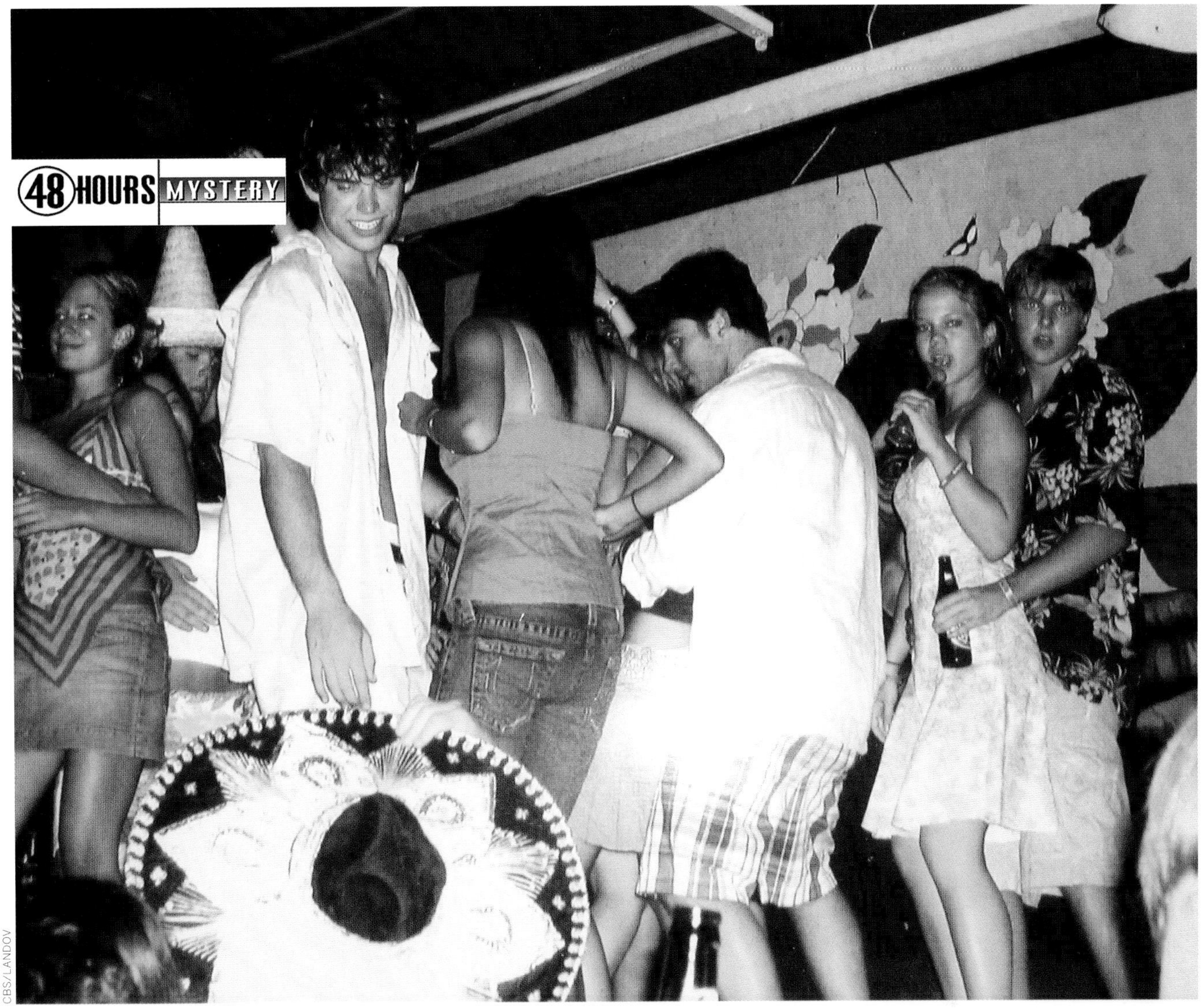
48 HOURS MYSTERY

CBS/LANDOV

at her hotel; another time, apparently under the influence of marijuana, he claimed he had disposed of the body; on a third occasion, he said he had sold Holloway into slavery, and she had been spirited out of the country (he later recanted both the second and third unofficial statements). He also claimed that the Kalpoe brothers had driven off with her, which they denied. In a video of Deepak Kalpoe shown on American TV, it seems he is alleging that Holloway had sex with all three men. In another version of the video, however, Kalpoe indicates, in slightly different testimony, that there had been no sex. Was one tape doctored?

Opposite: Holloway with her mother, Beth Twitty, at their home in Alabama on May 24, 2005—graduation day at Mountain Brook High School. Above: Holloway is at far left in a photograph taken at Carlos 'n Charlie's on the night she disappeared; the picture was obtained by CBS News's *48 Hours Mystery* TV show. Right: A prayer vigil at the lighthouse, another place that Holloway reportedly visited on the fateful night.

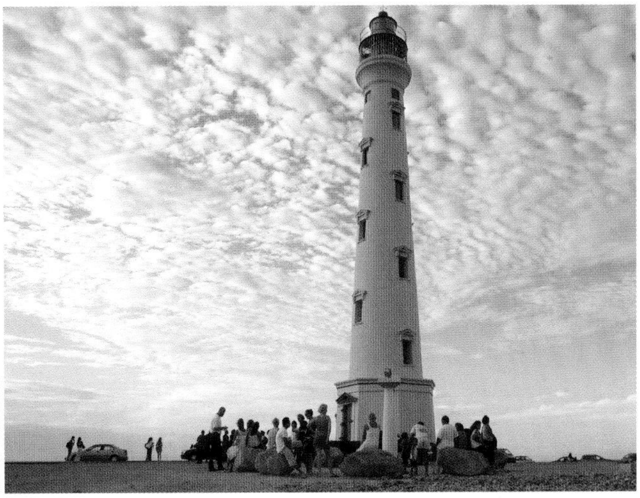

LESLIE MAZOCH/AP

Ponds, lakes and the ocean itself have been searched, as have most square inches of land on Aruba. Natalee Holloway has not been found. A local police officer says she might have died of alcohol or drug poisoning, her corpse removed by someone else. Her dearest ones don't accept that and are active in lobbying for further investigation. This case may be cold, but it is far from closed.

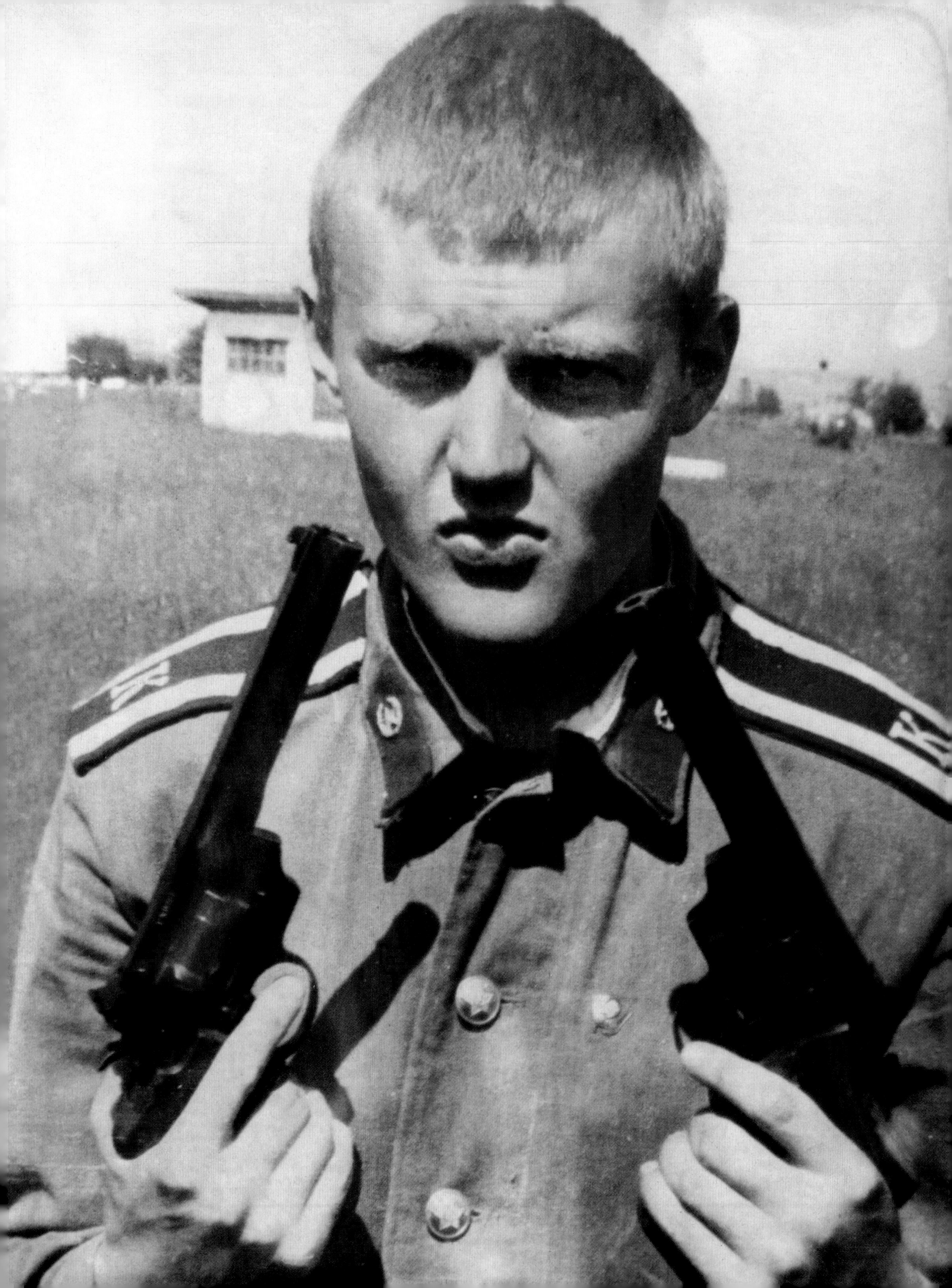

Did the Russians Poison Alexander Litvinenko?

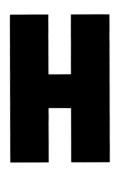

He probably was assassinated, since the poison that killed him was so rare. And therefore he was probably killed by his former comrades, since they would have had the best and perhaps the only motive for wanting him dead. If all that is so, and if the trail of suspicion is followed to the top, then one has to wonder if the most powerful man in all of Russia—one of the world's most prominent statesmen—ordered the hit. Alexander Litvinenko's greatest enemy at the time of his death was Russian President Vladimir Putin, who is now the country's prime minister but continues to control the state. And Putin was an inconvenient enemy to have.

Born in 1962, Litvinenko was drafted into the Internal Troops of the Ministry of Internal Affairs as soon as he graduated from secondary school. He had various positions in security and counterintelligence throughout the 1980s, and in 1991 he was promoted to the Central Staff of the Federal Counterintelligence Service. He was involved in military operations and with the infiltration of organized crime in Moscow. In the former Soviet Union during this period, the idea of who were the criminals and who were the authorities was hopelessly gray; according to his widow, Marina, while Litvinenko was working for the Federal Security Service (FSB), the successor of the KGB, he became aware of all sorts of associations between higher-ups in law enforcement and the Russian mob. She says he wrote a memo about this to then-president Boris Yeltsin and, in 1998, told FSB head Putin of corruption in the agency. Putin was unmoved. Late that year, Litvinenko started to go public with what he knew, and his troubles in his homeland began. He said that he and others in the agency had been ordered at times to frame, kidnap or even murder Russian politicians and businessmen (Litvinenko claimed that he had been ordered in December 1997 to assassinate Russian tycoon Boris Berezovsky, for whom he was moonlighting as a

In a statement released posthumously, Litvinenko pointed his finger squarely at the man he felt had ordered his death: Vladimir Putin.

Opposite: Litvinenko, when he was a cadet at Military High School in Vladikavkaz, Osettiya. Right: On November 17, 1998, Litvinenko is more open than his undercover colleague at a news conference in Moscow that will land him in very hot water after he accuses his bosses of ordering kidnappings, extortion and contract murders, including a plot to kill the controversial business mogul Boris Berezovsky.

ИНТЕРФАКС
RMF

VASILY DYACHKOV/AP

REX USA

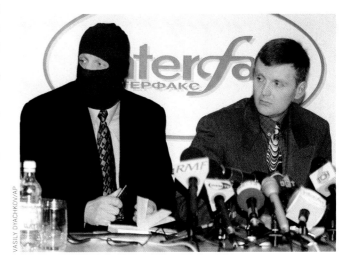

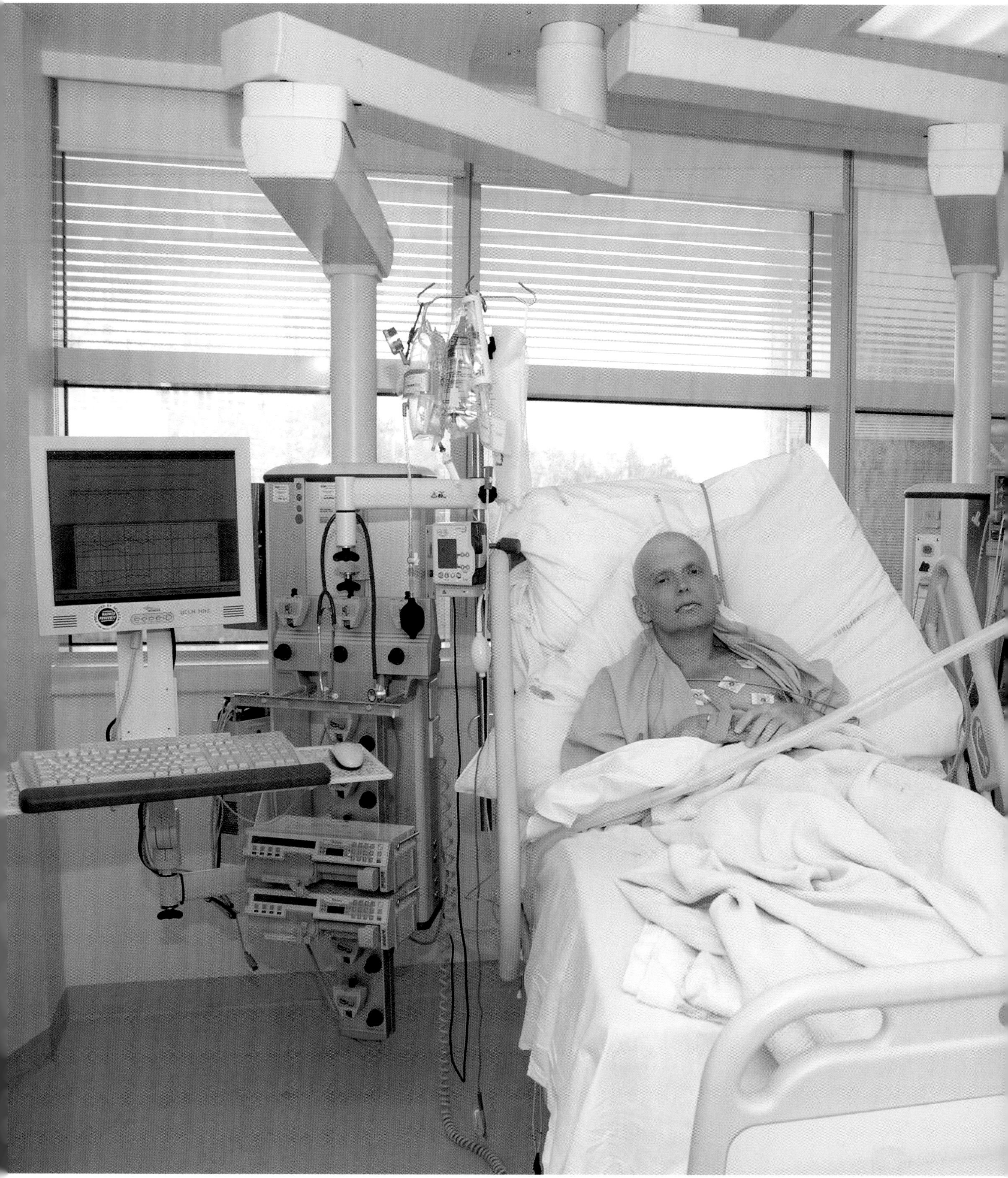
UCLH NHS

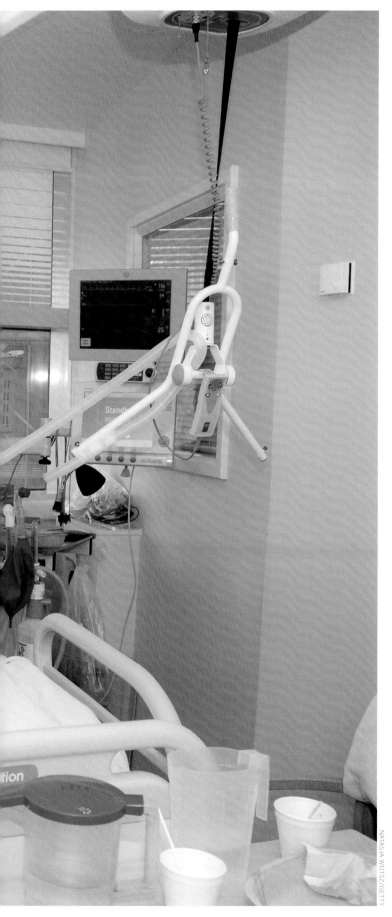

REX USA

security agent). Putin canned Litvinenko from the FSB and was later candid about it: "I fired Litvinenko and disbanded his unit…because FSB officers should not stage press conferences. This is not their job. And they should not make internal scandals public."

Litvinenko was arrested twice on charges that included abuse of duties—he felt Putin was behind the arrests—and released from prison only after signing an agreement that he would not leave the country. But he did flee, in October 2000, with his family, first to Turkey, thence to England, where he was granted political

Left: Litvinenko, on November 20, 2006, on his London death-bed. He had at the time only three more days to live, and it was in this period that he wrote the note implicating Putin. Above: The former spy Lugovoi, Great Britain's prime suspect in the case. Thus far, Russia has rebuffed all entreaties to extradite the man.

asylum on May 14, 2001. In London he became a journalist and author, detailing in books such as *Blowing Up Russia* what he knew from his days inside while laying out conspiracy theories linking Russian authorities to various nefarious deeds. He was also during this time, according to reports published after his death, on a retainer from the British intelligence agency MI6.

On November 1, 2006, Litvinenko met with two former KGB agents who were in London, Dmitry Kovtun and Andrei Lugovoi. Later that day, Litvinenko became extremely ill, and soon he was in decline at University College Hospital. On November 23, he died, and the next day a posthumous statement was released in which Litvinenko accused Putin of poisoning him. The British certainly believe someone did: Toxic amounts of the radionuclide polonium-210 were found in his body; and on January 26, 2007, police found "a 'hot' teapot" at London's Millennium Hotel with an off-the-charts reading for polonium, the radioactive material used, they said, in the killing. A senior official said what they had was "a 'state-sponsored' assassination orchestrated by Russian security services." British authorities suspected the former spy Lugovoi, and they asked Moscow for his extradition so that he could stand trial in London. Moscow, of course, refused.

NATASJA WEITSZ/GETTY

Who Is Setting the Coatesville Fires—and Why?

Whether the end is in sight for one of the most bizarre and destructive crime sprees in modern American history is unclear. For more than a year, beginning in early 2008, Coatesville, Pennsylvania, a hard-bitten suburban satellite of Philadelphia, has been burning, with arsons big and small set at an alarming rate by at least several

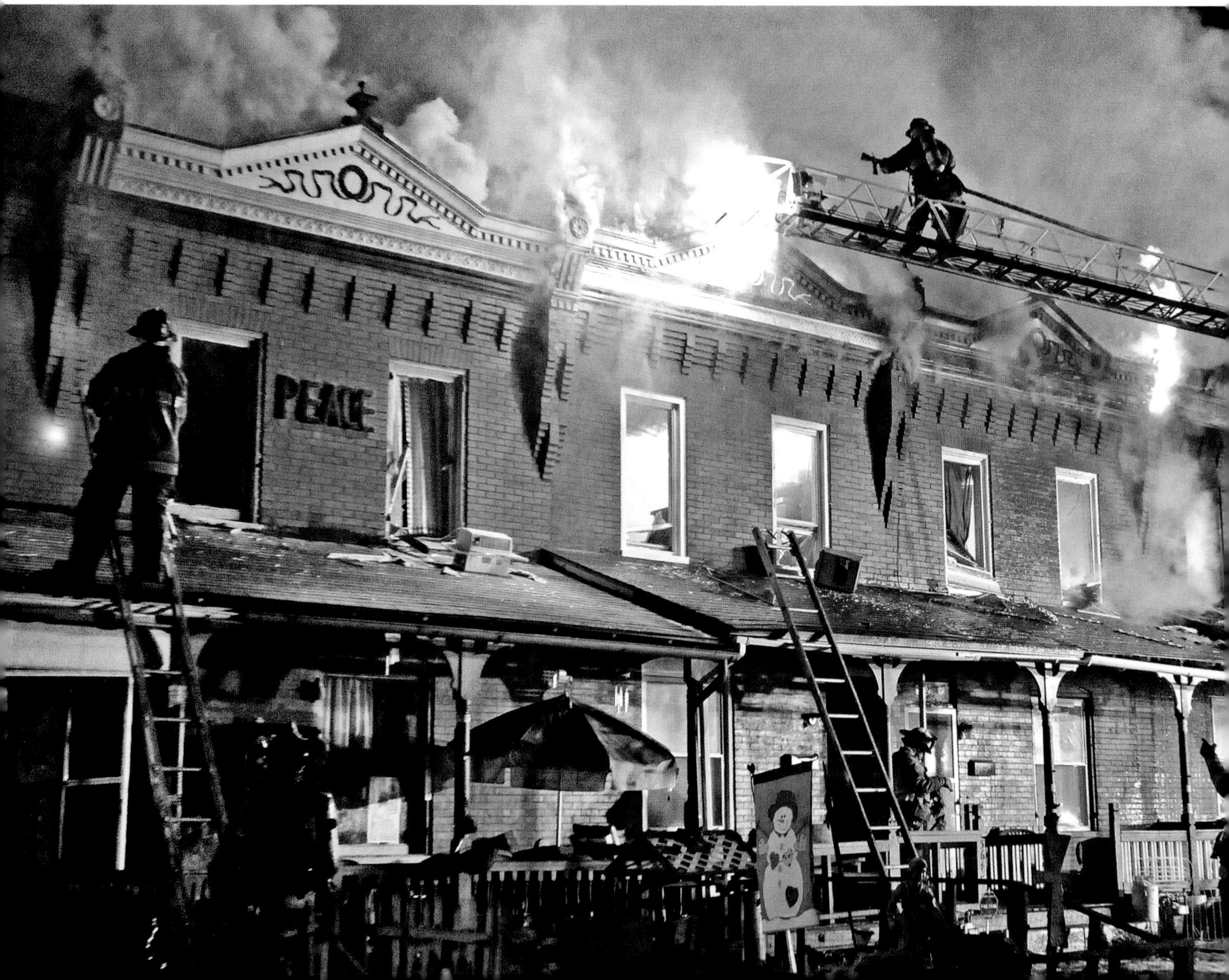

PEACE

individuals. Any statistic that we establish here runs the risk of being obsolete by the time you read this, but there were, by all estimates, scores of fires set in greater Coatesville between February '08 and the advent of spring '09—at a rate of several arsons a month for more than a full year. This plague of fire is without rhyme or reason, and for Coatesville's 10,000 citizens, it has come to represent a constant terror.

Suspects, some of whom have confessed to certain of the crimes, have been arrested, and as a set they do not represent any kind of unified effort. The first six to be nabbed included, according to press accounts, a homeless man, a volunteer firefighter who responded to blazes that he caused, a wayward teenager and another with developmental issues, an alcoholic, a man who heard voices that told him to "set fires and kill people." They are all young, ranging in age from 18 to 25. But if there is any kind of

Firefighters spray water on burning row houses in Coatesville late on Saturday, January 24, 2009. This is the largest—but not the last—in the string of arsons that have shaken the Pennsylvanian city.

TOM KELLY IV/AP

There have been scores of arsons in greater Coatesville during a period of more than a year. This plague by fire has come to represent a constant, almost daily terror.

vague profile in that group of outcasts, it was shattered in March 2009 with the arrest of Robert Tracey Jr., 37, a 25-year veteran firefighter and former member of the West End Fire Company No. 3, who had only a month earlier joined the City of Coatesville Fire Deparment. Tracey was a married father of five when he was accused of setting two small fires—one on Charles Street and the other on Hope—on March 20. Said Chester County District Attorney Joseph Carroll at the time: "I would love to say that this is the end, but it's not. There are a number of unsolved arsons that likely cannot be tied to the suspects who have already been arrested."

Clearly some group-psychology factors have been at play during the spree. Newspapers clips regarding earlier Coatesville fires have reportedly been found in the possession of suspects, and any fires after the first blazes might have been copycat crimes. Also, the chief of police hinted that some fires might have been gang related while refusing to elaborate. A "don't snitch" campaign has been active on the Coatesville streets, and how much information is being withheld for fear of reprisal will never be known.

Many of the fires have been small: porch fires, fires in back alleys. But some have been large and consequential. A mobile home has been torched and so have idle school buses. In February of 2009, Roger Leon Barlow, 19, a student at an automotive school in nearby Exton, confessed to involvement in nine of the Coatesville fires, according to court documents, including a January 24 blaze that gutted 15 row houses on Fleetwood Street, leaving more than 50 residents homeless. Police described Barlow as a "classic pyromaniac" and said he had told them that he and a friend "were responsible for numerous additional Coatesville fires." Barlow later recanted that statement.

Only one person has been killed, and while that fact is no doubt fortunate, it is still tragic—and, in its particulars, poignant. On December 7, 2008, Irene Kempest's home on Strode Avenue was set ablaze. Emergency responders found the 83-year-old woman unconscious upstairs from smoke inhalation and rushed her to the hospital, where she died the next day. The widow Kempest, her life taken by one of the fires of Coatesville, had been a survivor of the Nazi death camps.

JUST ONE MORE

Are We Alone?

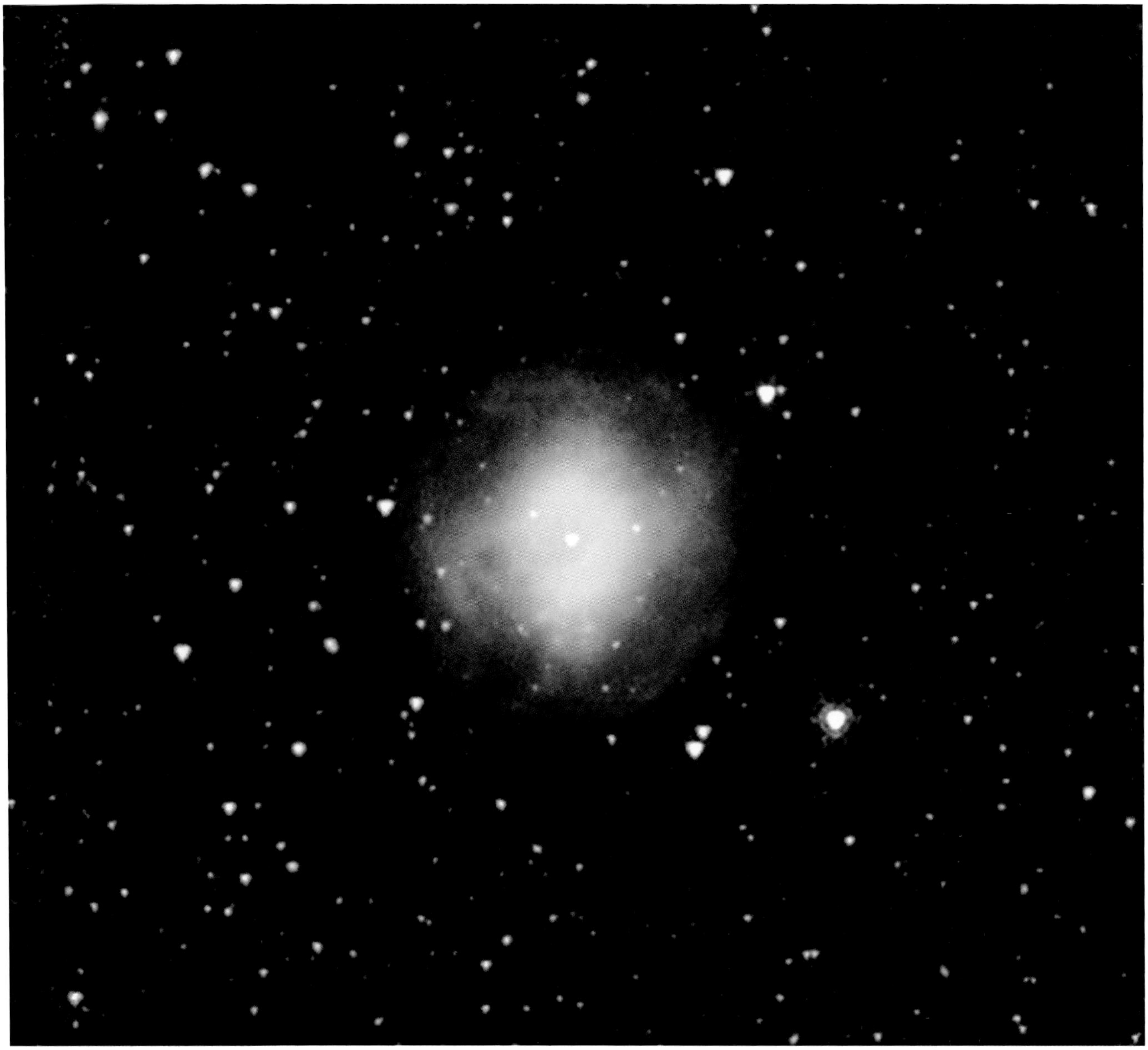

NASA/JPL-CALTECH

Ever since Adam asked Eve the question, this has been the biggest unsolved mystery. Still today, it is posed regularly by schoolkids and scientists alike. With apologies to the denizens of Roswell, New Mexico, there is no certain evidence that we are anything but alone. Still . . . There are so many stars . . . so many planets . . . so many galaxies . . . so *many* . . .

What you see in this picture, taken by the Spitzer Space Telescope on July 18, 2009, is a dying star with the decidedly unpoetic name NGC 4361. It was once, according to scientists, quite like our sun. It may have had planets in its orbit. To try to get closer to the romance of this big question—are we alone?—let's not even get into how many light-years away it might be. Let's just say it is way far away. Was it ever the focal point of a solar system like ours? Did it have an Earth? Did it warm beings when it rose in the morning? Is there another NGC 4361 blazing bright in this universe?

Are we alone?

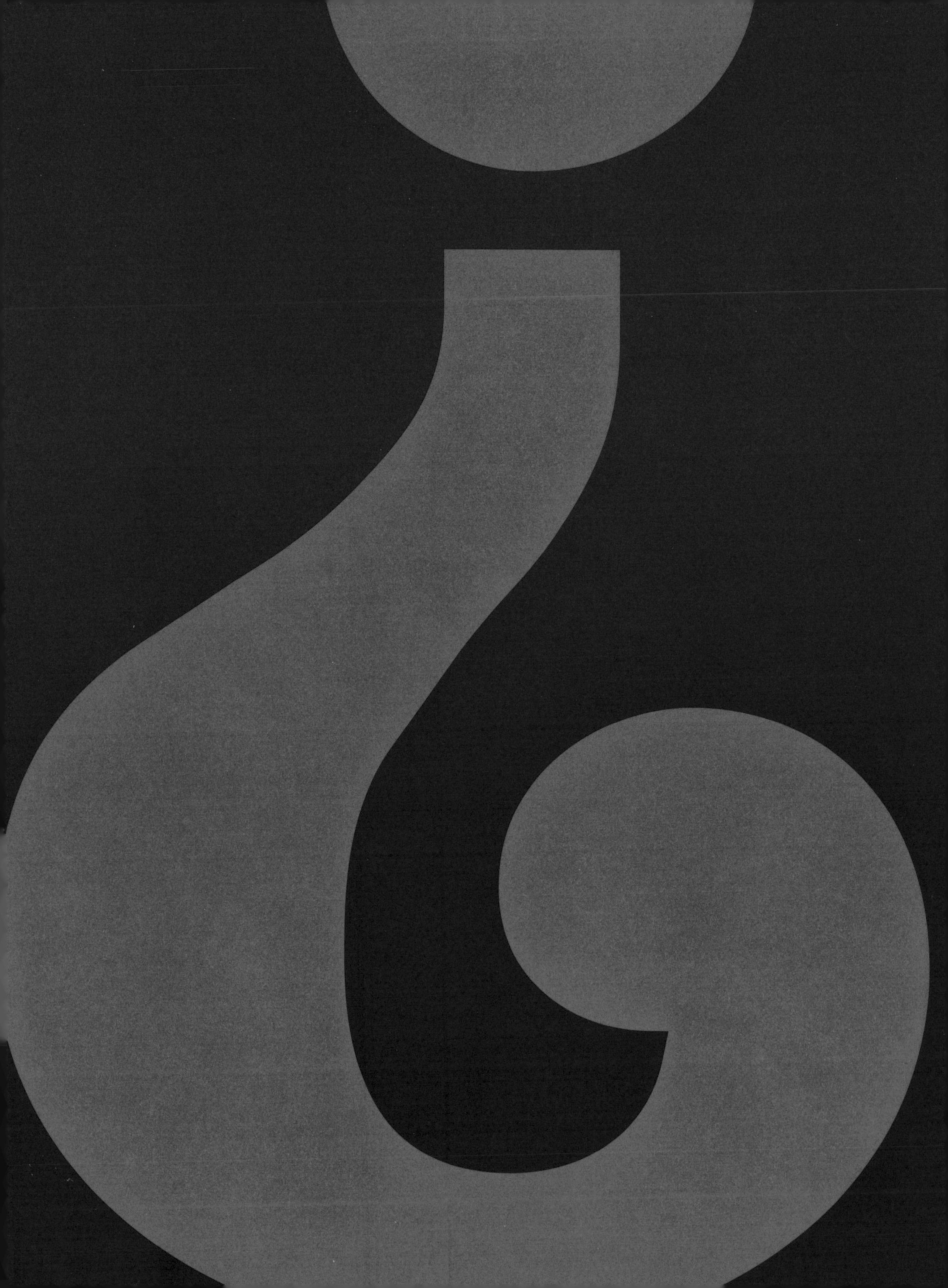